the CUTTING

EDGE

Social Movements and Social Change in America

the CUTTING
EDGE

John R. Howard

State University of New York
College at Purchase

J. B. LIPPINCOTT COMPANY
Philadelphia , New York , Toronto

ISBN 0-397-47310-9
Library of Congress Catalog Card Number 74-2453
Printed in the United States of America

1 3 5 7 9 8 6 4 2

Library of Congress Cataloging in Publication Data

Howard, John R   1933–
    The cutting edge.

    Includes bibliographical references.
    1. United States—Social conditions—1945. 2. Social movements. 3. Social change. I. Title. II. Title: Social movements and social change in America.

HN65.H597   301.24′2′0973   74-2453
ISBN 0-397-47310-9

American society has undergone enormous cultural and social transformation since the beginning of the Kennedy years. These changes have been brought about, in part, by social movements representing various dissident groups. Unique to the time is the fact that movements representing a number of disadvantaged groups—blacks and other non-white minorities, homosexuals, women, and youth have sought simultaneously to effect massive changes in the distribution of power, privileges, and opportunities. It is unlikely that any society could accommodate such major shifts in status and power without great conflict. Inevitably, relatively privileged groups come to feel threatened by the demands from below.

This book focuses on both the movements of dissident minorities and on the responses and counter movements of marginally more advantaged segments of the population—the white working class and the supporters of the radical right. Attention is given to the social base of support for each movement, to the structure and ideology of the organizations which spearhead a movement's drive, and to the political strategies developed by movements in the pursuit of their goals.

The movements dealt with in this book may be spoken of as having careers. Although it would be difficult to speak of a successful career in that none of them have in any ultimate sense realized their goals, it is possible to speak of unsuccessful careers in the sense that some have collapsed. The analysis undertaken here identifies the crucial junctures in the careers of these movements, specifying the conditions which determined their fate.

Many of the organizations discussed in the book are relatively inhospitable to direct study by social scientists (the Black Muslims, the John Birch Society, and the Black Panthers, for example.) Much of the data, however, was gathered via interviews and participant and non-participant observation.

This data provided insight into the personality configurations of supporters of a movement. It also provided a grasp of the processes whereby a movement met or failed to meet the psycho-social needs of its supporters.

The analysis also places the movements in an historical context. Contemporary movements differ greatly from each other with regard to historical background. The Gay Liberation Movement, for example, is historically unique—homosexuals in the United States having never before engaged in open and massive protest. Youth protest, on the other hand, has been a recurrent phenomenon in American history, although the contemporary youth movement differs in striking ways from the youth movement of the 1930's or the movements of earlier generations of bohemians.

The Women's Movement presents yet another historical pattern. In the United States it had one major antecedent, the feminist movement of the period 1848 to 1920. It is significant that similar sociopolitical circumstances attended the rise of each and that the social characteristics of participants of each had marked similarities.

As regards blacks, protest has been an historical constant, but the dominant contemporary themes of black power and community control represent in their present strength a major departure from previous emphases on civil rights and integration.

The historical data provide a framework within which to better understand the data gathered via interviews and participant observation.

In reading this book students should absorb a considerable amount of information on social movements. They should also come to grasp the various analytic frameworks for interpreting and integrating this information. Most important, however, the book should help to nurture a better understanding of the world in which they live, to heighten their sensitivity to the political and moral questions posed by social movements, and thus to improve their facility for arriving at informed and rationally conceived positions on these questions.

ACKNOWLEDGMENTS

I would like to acknowledge the contribution made by a number of people to the completion of this book. Mary D. Howard, Mary S. Strong and Hank Lopez read and criticized earlier versions of the manuscript. Shirley Lee Lewis, Ellen Grasso, and Joyce Gapco provided invaluable assistance in the preparation of the manuscript.

The research on which some of the discussion of the youth movement is based was made possible by a grant from the Office of Education. The positions advanced are my own and in no way necessarily reflect their thinking.

I am grateful in addition, to the following publishers for permission to use material brought out under their auspices:

Chapters Seven and Eight in this book contain material initially appearing in my article "The Flowering of the Hippie Movement," *Protest in the Sixties*, Robert Rosenstone and Joseph Boskin, eds., *Annals of the American Academy of Political and Social Science*, March, 1969.

Chapter Eleven is a rewritten and updated version of my paper "The Radical Right as a Minority Group," *The Other Minorities*, Edward Sagarin, editor, Blaisdell Press, Inc., 1971.

CONTENTS

Introduction 1

The Minority Revolt

1 VIOLENCE AND SOCIAL CHANGE: *from Integration
to Black Power* 11
2 BLACK PANTHERS AND BLACK MUSLIMS 41
3 SOUL POLITICS: *The Political Meaning of Black Power* ... 67
4 THE OTHER MINORITIES: *Mexicans, Indians, and
Puerto Ricans* 89

Movements for Sexual Liberation

5 THE TRANSFORMATION OF STIGMA: *An Analysis of
the Gay Liberation Movement* 121
6 THE WOMEN'S LIBERATION MOVEMENT 139

The Youth Movement

7 OF YOUTH AND YOUTH MOVEMENTS 163
8 THE LIFE AND DEATH OF
THE HIPPIE MOVEMENT 181
9 AFTER THE FALL: *Communes, New Religions, Vocations
for Social Change* 199

The Revolt of the Masses

10 PUBLIC POLICY *and the White
Working Class* 221
11 THE RADICAL RIGHT AS A
MINORITY GROUP 237

Conclusions

12 GETTING IT ALL TOGETHER AGAIN 255
Index 269

INTRODUCTION

In recent years, movements of blacks, women, homosexuals, and youth have become prominent on the American scene, demanding equality and participation. This volume examines these movements as well as those of the white working class and the radical right, two groups often in opposition to protesting minorities.

Attention is given both to social movements and to the organizations which seek to achieve a movement's objectives.[1] Social movements find expression through organizations. Organizations contain the most active and involved members of a movement but may represent only a fraction of the movement's supporters. Thus, the National Organization for Women, the largest women's liberation group, had chapters in 30 cities in 1970 with a national membership of 3,000. Support for the movement was much broader, however, with more than 50,000 women marching on August 26 of that year, a national day of protest.

Below, the central questions to which this book addresses itself are listed and briefly discussed.

1. *The approach taken here is socio-historical.* This approach answers a number of questions about each movement. Is the movement recurrent or unique? If it is historically recurrent, does it always arise out of similar social conditions? If it is recurrent, can inferences be made from its earlier fate to its contemporary prospects?

The socio-historical discussion provides background for the examination of contemporary movements.

2. *The identification of the social base of support of each movement is a major concern.* Although movements purport to speak for broad categories, such as "women," "youth," "gays," and "blacks," they draw support selectively from their putative constituencies. Some women are involved in the women's movement; most are not. Some youth supported the youth movement; many did not. Attention is given to those social characteristics (age, level of education, occupational status, etc.) which differentiate supporters of a movement from those among its constituency who remain indifferent or even hostile.

3. *The social-psychological basis of personal involvement in movement organizations is also discussed.* In other words, what personal needs of an individual are met by joining an organization? These needs may

or may not be consonant with the goals and purposes of an organization. Some members of the Black Muslims joined because they received organizational support for their careers or businesses. In the chapter on the Muslims, persons with these motives are referred to as "Protestant-ethic Muslims." In that circumstance, organizational purposes happened to coincide with personal motives.

On the other hand, the student homophile organization, discussed in the chapter on the gay liberation movement, had been formed for the purpose of educating the public about homosexuality and thereby, it was hoped, lessening prejudice against homosexuals. But the campus homosexuals who joined the group were motivated primarily by the desire for membership in a pleasant social club. In that circumstance, personal motives and initial organizational purposes differed, and eventually the organization changed.

4. *The structure and ideology of the organizations which carry a movement's message are described and their functions analyzed.* Many organizations find themselves in a hostile environment. They are made objects of public scorn and ridicule. In order to survive, they must devise structural mechanisms which insulate supporters against outside pressures.

Some organizations—Krishna Consciousness and the Black Muslims, for example—develop womb-like structures which significantly reduce sustained contact between members and nonmembers. Also, both organizations have elaborate and complex ideologies. Members who have mastered the ideology acquire intellectual defenses against the ridicule and hostile criticism to which they are exposed.

On the other hand, some recent communes have repudiated the notion of structure entirely.

The relationship between structure, ideology, and survival, is examined for several movements.

5. *The social sources of organizational diversity within movements are also analyzed.* Within a movement, some organizations may be reformist in character, others revolutionary; some may be rigid and authoritarian in structure, others more open and fluid. These differences of organizational structure have a social base.

The constituency of any social movement is heterogeneous. Within the black movement, for example, the profile of members of the Black Muslims is different from that of the black members of the National Association for the Advancement of Colored People, as the membership of the former is largely lower class and that of the latter largely middle class.

As is indicated in the section on the black movement, the different existential circumstances of middle-class and lower-class blacks draw them to different types of organizations.

The supporters of the gay movement, the women's movement, and the youth movement are also heterogeneous, and this fact partly accounts for the structural and ideological diversity within these movements.

6. *Conflicts among organizations within a movement are discussed.* Inevitably, there is a tendency on the part of some organizations in any movement to define their own goals as the only legitimate ones for the movement. This tendency provokes severe criticism from other organizations. Radical organizations accuse more moderate organizations of "selling out the movement," while moderate organizations accuse the radicals of creating a bad image for the movement and its supporters, thereby arousing public hostility and bringing on repression.

Insofar as different types of organizations in a movement tend to have supporters with different social profiles, these debates do not spring solely from intellectual disagreements. They reflect different life experiences and therefore different conceptions of what the world is like, of what accounts for a group's problems, and of what the possibilities are for change.

All women have problems as women, but the precise definition and character of these problems vary depending on whether they are middle-aged and married or young and single. Their views of the women's movement and their conceptions of its legitimate ends are likely to vary accordingly, leading them to join different and possibly antagonistic groups.

The causes and consequences of conflict within a movement are given close scrutiny in this book, particularly in connection with the women's movement and the gay movement.

7. *Conflict between protesting minorities and more privileged groups in the society are also examined.* Blacks, women, homosexuals, and youth seek a redistribution of rewards, privileges, and esteem. Of necessity, they come into conflict with other groups in society which feel threatened by their demands. The white working class and the radical right fall into this category, and these two groups will be considered.

Rewards, privileges, and esteem are unequally distributed in society, and the movement of disadvantaged groups to effect their redistribution has inspired counter movements among more privileged sections of the population. The result has been a period of intense conflict. This conflict occurs on four fronts: substantive, symbolic, ideological, and cultural.

Substantive conflict revolves around the distribution of highly valued and scarce resources, such as good jobs, good housing, and good schools. Insofar as these resources are limited, attempts by protesting minorities to increase their share pose the threat of loss to more privileged groups. For example, since there are a limited number of college teaching positions in the United States, an end to discrimination in the hiring of women and minorities will necessarily make it more difficult for the white male to find academic employment.

Conflict over *symbolic* issues is much less intense. Symbolic issues include such demands as having Martin Luther King, Jr.'s birthday declared a holiday. Gains of this character confer greater prestige on minority groups at little tangible cost to more privileged groups.

Systems of inequality seldom rest solely on force. They are legitimated by *ideological* systems that rationalize and justify the differences between haves and have-nots. Thus, racism and sexism are ideologies as well as sets of practices that systematically deny opportunities to racial minorities and women. Every elite group—whether it is men in relation to women, whites in relation to blacks, "straights" in relation to homosexuals, adults in relation to youth, or nobility in relation to commoners—develops an ideology that rationalizes its own advantaged position. These ideologies, with greater or lesser degrees of sophistication, account for the position of lower-status groups by reference to their presumed inadequacies; thus blacks are "culturally deprived" or "too lazy to work and prefer to live on welfare," homosexuals are "sick," women "too emotional," and so on. There are simplified, barroom versions of these ideologies of domination, and there are more complicated textbook versions.

As minorities attempt to break what they believe are the ideological ties that bind, they come into conflict, then, not only with those who have a stake in their subordination, but also with people who simply take for granted the legitimacy of traditional ideas.

Finally, *cultural* conflict arises from a difference of life-style between protesting minorities and other groups in the population. These minorities often advocate new life-styles in addition to the redistribution of power and privilege. While many elements of life-style are essentially trivial (a preference for bowling rather than tennis, for example), others touch on deeply-held conceptions of what is moral or immoral. Thus, drug use as a style in the counter culture is seen by more conservatively oriented segments of the population as not only dangerous but immoral. The repudiation of a middle-class life-style by many youths was seen as perverse. Life-style was made an issue, particularly by the youth movement, and became a source of severe conflict.

Substantive, symbolic, ideological, and cultural conflict between protesting minorities and other groups will be examined in the pages that follow. In this examination, particular attention will be given to the role and perspective of the white working class in relation to those minorities.

Not all of the issues, questions, and concerns reviewed above are equally relevant for all the social movements examined in this volume. Indeed, in the discussion of certain movements, attention is given to only one or two of these issues. They comprise, however, the range of relevant concerns in a broad discussion of social movements and social change in American.

The book deals, then, with contemporary social movements. It places them in historical context, analyzes their structure and ideology, and examines conflict among movements over the distribution of rewards and privileges in the society.

HOW THE DATA WERE GATHERED

A major portion of the data on contemporary movements was gathered by interviews and by participant observation. Black Muslims, members of the John Birch Society, homosexuals, and hippies were interviewed. Muslim temple meetings, meetings of the John Birch Society, and meetings of homophile groups were attended. Communes were visited.

The research was not done specifically for this volume but was carried out over a number of years, for different purposes. While all of this research focused on social movements, the specific concerns varied from study to study. The work on the Black Muslims, a deviant organization even by the standards of the black community, focused on the processes whereby the organization develops and sustains the commitment of members.[2] A study of the Black Panthers was done in the context of research on cities in which race riots had occurred.[3] The research on hippies, done in Haight-Ashbury, focused on the impact of the counter culture on higher education.[4] Participant observation data on the John Birch Society were gathered in the course of a comparative study of authoritarian political organizations.[5] Campus homophiles were interviewed in a study of the process by which homosexuals decide to "come out of the closet."[6]

Interviewing and participant observation as data-gathering techniques are very useful in providing insight into the perspective of supporters of a movement. They allow a movement's members to speak for themselves, to present their own "definition of the situation." They also provide an understanding of the structure and ideology of the organizations which carry a movement's message.

The limitations of interviewing and participant observation lie in their failure to provide an understanding of the historical dimension of social movements. They yield a clear picture of the present but a dim picture of the past. Consequently, for this volume, the historical dimension was added. In addition, the passage of time and greater reflection necessitated a great many revisions in most of the original pieces.

Some of the more important contemporary social movements are not given attention. Among these is the peace movement. The peace movement differs in a very fundamental way from the movements examined in this volume. It was directed at a specific event, the Vietnam War, and with the termination of that event, the movement evaporated. By contrast, the movements discussed here represent basic social categories in the population—women, blacks, youth, the white working class, the middle and lower class, and homosexuals. The peace movement comprised people who shared certain sentiments whereas the supporters of each of the movements discussed here share a basic condition. The problems confronted by these movements are historically of much longer standing, more deeply rooted in the social structure, and more intractable than those faced by the peace movement. This comparison is not intended to devalue the peace movement and the struggle against the war; its purpose is merely to clarify that this movement was a different type of phenomenon.

Within the movements discussed, certain organizations and certain orientations receive more attention than others. Thus, in discussing the youth movement, I have devoted much more attention to the hippie phenomenon than to the new left. This emphasis is a result of the initial research I did on the youth movement, which dealt much more with the affective-expressive aspect of the new youth culture (the hippie movement) than with its instrumental-political aspect (the new left).

FORMAT

Section One, "The Minority Revolt," deals primarily with the black movement. An initial historical chapter provides a context for a discussion in subsequent chapters of the Black Muslims, the Black Panthers, and various manifestations of urban black electoral politics. These chapters discuss the transition from integration and civil rights as the dominant themes of the black movement to black power and "community control." Three manifestations of the new orientation are examined: separatism, black radicalism, and urban black politics.

A chapter on American Indians, Mexican Americans, and Puerto Ricans is included in this section for comparative purposes.

Section Two, "Movements for Sexual Liberation," contains chapters on the gay liberation movement and on the women's movement.

The gay liberation movement is discussed in the context of understanding the processes by which homosexuals decide to "come out of the closet." The analysis of the women's movement is primarily comparative and historical. Certain similarities between the 19th and 20th century women's movements are examined, and the social organization of the contemporary movement is analyzed.

Section Three, "The Youth Movement," contains a chapter on the cultural and social roots of the counter culture. There is also a chapter on the life and death of the hippie movement and one on the communes, new religions, and "vocations for social change" that have replaced the hippie movement. It is suggested that the hippie movement collapsed primarily because of internal contradictions in its social organization. Communes and new religions represent "safe deviance," deviance that does not evoke public wrath. "Vocations for social change" represents a new form of social involvement for left and radical youth.

Section Four, "The Revolt of the Masses," focuses on the white working class and the radical right. It is suggested that the white working class, although somewhat more privileged than protesting minority groups, can itself be analyzed as a minority group. Various reasons are advanced to explain why the white working class does not identify with other nonelite groups. The chapter entitled "The Radical Right As a Minority group" presents the perspective of a group that feels itself victimized. The persistence of a radical right is traced to basic pressures inherent in the American social system.

In the last chapter, "Getting It All Together Again," alternative futures for the United States are discussed. Minority group movements and movements in opposition to them present radically different visions of the American future. The relative strength of these opposing interests is examined, and projections are made about the future of the country.

REFERENCES

1. Sociologists disagree on the definition of social movements. Herbert Blumer defined them as "collective enterprises to establish a new order of life," in *College Outline Series: Principles of Sociology* (Alfred McLung Lee, ed., New York: Barnes and Noble, Inc., 1951), pp. 199–220. Ralph Turner and Lewis Killian in *Collective Behavior* (Englewood Cliffs, New Jersey: Prentice-Hall, 1972), p. 246, offer an enlarged definition: "A movement is a collectivity acting with some continuity to promote change in the society or the group of which it is a part. As a collectivity, a movement is a group with indefinite and shifting membership."

2. John R. Howard, "The Making of a Black Muslim," *Transaction* (December, 1966), pp. 15–21.

3. Very preliminary conclusions on the Panthers, differing from the analysis undertaken in this volume, appeared in *Life Styles in the Black Ghetto*, by William

McCord, John R. Howard, Bernard Friedberg, and Edwin Harwood (New York: W. W. Norton, 1969).

4. What finally amounted to a series of articles chronicled the rise and fall of the hippie movement: "The Flowering of the Hippie Movement," which appeared in *Protest in the Sixties* (Robert Rosenstone and Joseph Boskin, eds.; *Annals of the American Academy of Political and Social Science*, March 1969), pp. 43–55, dealt with the movement while the bloom was still on the rose; a rewritten version in *Seasons of Rebellion* (Robert Rosenstone and Joseph Boskin, eds., New York: Holt, Rinehart and Winston, Inc., 1972), pp. 260–285, caught the movement as the flower began to wither; and "Youth and the Counter Culture," Copyright© 1972 by John R. Howard (with Mary D. Howard), in *Outsiders USA* (Patricia Keith-Spiegel and Donald Spiegel, eds., San Francisco: Rinehart Press, 1973) pp. 326–342, deals with the movement after the snows had come.

5. John R. Howard, "The Social Basis of Political Extremism: A Comparison of the Black Muslims, the John Birch Society and the American Communist Party," presented at the meetings of the Western Political Science Association, Victoria, British Columbia, March, 1965.

6. John R. Howard, "The Transformation of Stigma: An Analysis of the Gay Liberation Movement," presented at the meetings of the Pacific Sociological Association, April, 1970.

THE
MINORITY
REVOLT

1

VIOLENCE AND SOCIAL CHANGE:
from Integration to Black Power

The urban riots of the late 1960's were pivotal in the history of race relations in the United States. Before the riots, everyone knew that blacks wanted something called "civil rights," and indeed the surge of black and white protest immediately prior to the riots seemed to result in substantial progress toward realizing such rights. But the riots and the events which followed in their wake made the old vocabulary of the civil rights struggle obsolete, and to this day there is little consensus on an alternative vocabulary.

The character of race conflict in the United States is more complex than the vocabulary popularly used to discuss it would suggest. In the popular mind, for example, the term "black militant" covers everything from the separatist Black Muslims to the quasi-Marxist Black Panthers. White racism exists, but to explain the circumstance of blacks in the United States one must get beyond the issue of white racism.

Indeed, the times do not lend themselves to easy characterization. The proportion of black families in middle-income categories has expanded rapidly,[1] but, at the same time, the number of black children in impoverished households headed by a female has risen sharply[2]. The proportion of the white population believing that blacks are innately inferior has declined steadily,[3] yet many whites continue to think that black poverty can be accounted for by lack of energy and initiative on the part of blacks.[4] The number of blacks holding elective office in the eleven southern states rose from 72 prior to the Voting Rights Act of 1965 to 388 in 1969,[5] but the avowed segregationist George Wallace ran stronger in 1972 in all the state primaries he entered than he had four years earlier. School integration came to Mississippi in 1970, sixteen years after the *Brown* vs. *Board of Education* decision, yet that same year the busing of school children to achieve racial balance became a passionate political issue throughout the country.

The purpose of this chapter is to develop a framework within which to discuss contemporary black protest movements. This framework is socio-historical and identifies significant differences in the protest movement between the period before the riots of the 1960's and the period since.

In differentiating between pre- and postriot conflict, I have borrowed two elementary concepts from game theory. Game theory provides some useful concepts for the analysis of conflict processes and also offers a relatively "clean" language. Phrases such as "power structures," "black militant," and "white racism" are less and less useful analytically, given the tendency of each writer, acting as a kind of verbal entrepreneur, to invent whatever meanings suit the convenience of the moment or the imperatives of his ideology. In the heat of battle, language as well as logic suffers, and it can become more and more difficult to relate words to reality.

Among the many types of conflict situations discussed in game theory are those designated "variable sum games" and those referred to as "zero sum games." A variable sum game is one in which gains by one party do not necessarily entail losses by the other. The desegregation of lunch counters, for example, gives blacks access to such counters without denying access to whites. Blacks collectively gain something while whites collectively lose nothing.

A "zero sum game," on the other hand, is one in which gains by one party entail losses by another. If, for example, there are a limited number of openings available nationally in law schools, a commitment to admit racial minorities and women will necessarily make it more difficult for white males to secure admission.

For purposes of clarity, the position developed in this chapter is briefly outlined below.

1. Prior to the riots of the late 1960's, the central issue in race conflict in the United States was the caste-like status of blacks. The thrust of such black organizations as the National Association for the Advancement of Colored People, the Southern Christian Leadership Conference, the Congress of Racial Equality, the Urban League, and the Student Non-Violent Coordinating Committee was to overcome these barriers.

2. The caste-like status of blacks was reflected in every facet of the relationship between blacks and whites; therefore, inevitably, black protest groups sought both those changes in which black melioration carried no real costs for whites (desegregation of drinking fountains) and those in which it might (equal opportunity for trade union membership). In the variable sum category can be placed the struggle to acquire elementary civil liberties, liberties which whites simply took for granted; these ranged from safety against arbitrary physical attack to the right to use parks, libraries, and other public facilities. In the zero sum category can be placed the struggle to achieve equal opportunities in employment, education, and housing.

3. The civil rights movement, particularly in its activist phase of 1960 to 1965, brought about the erosion of the explicitly legal supports

for caste. It also established stronger protection for the elementary civil liberties of blacks. These were variable sum gains and symbolic confirmations of status, and in that area the movement was successful. It was much less successful in achieving zero sum gains and the substance, as opposed to the mere symbols, of status.

The movement was aided immensely during the 1960-65 period[6] (what might be referred to as the "classical civil rights period") in being able to invoke those elements of the national ideology which emphasize "treating all people alike." In a sense, Southerners, the antagonists in the drama, were morally on the defensive. They were never able to articulate a case which conformed to the major moral imperatives of the national ideology. Once "sit-ins" and freedom-rides began, they were not able to deny that gross racial segregation and discrimination existed and they were not able nationally to make a convincing case that these practices were "right."

4. With the onset of the urban riots of 1965-1968, the axis of the movement shifted from the symbolic confirmation of status to the actual redistribution of wealth and services. It shifted to issues of "black community welfare" and "black power." In a rhetorical question, Bayard Rustin indicated the connection between the two phases of the movement. "What is the value of winning access to public accommodations for those who lack money to use them?"[7] New black organizations arose, not because the civil rights movement had failed, but because its successes had created an awareness of a new set of issues. Once melioration had been realized on matters of ordinary civil liberties, once affronts to the basic humanity of blacks had decreased, a new set of issues, more fundamental and more subtle, came to the fore.

Postriot thinking shifted the emphasis to the needs of the black community *qua* community. It was recognized that opportunities theoretically available to blacks as individuals were meaningless as long as the great mass of blacks were restricted to ghetto conditions which prevented them from exploiting these possibilities.

It came to be more clearly recognized that the "rules of the game," in terms of access to employment, admission to college, and so on, might not be racist in intent but were racist in consequence. For example, to become a New York City building inspector requires three years of experience in the building trades, but since blacks and Puerto Ricans have trouble getting into building trade unions, they cannot acquire the necessary experience. This is a "rule of the game" not specifically aimed at minorities, but, it has the consequence nevertheless of promoting their exclusion.

5. Once it began to critize the rules of the game, however, the postriot movement entered an area of moral ambiguity in which the old

civil rights movement had not been required to operate. The locus of debate with regard to the rules of the game came to be the question of "quotas" by race or sex for highly desired but limited opportunities (union cards, academic employment, etc.). In a sense, it is beside the point whether those groups which feel threatened by attempts to change the expressed rules of the game actually did "work their way up"; even if they are simply rationalizing their self-interest, they are able, rhetorically, to seize the moral advantage by attacking blacks and other minorities with the very vocabulary which the classical civil rights movement had used: "every person should be judged as an individual, not as a member of a group."

The historic claims of American blacks to justice are posed in the postriot era, then, against the seemingly moral claims of various white interest groups. For that reason, the postriot movement is a more subtle and complex phenomenon than the preriot movement, and this complexity is reflected in the types of black movements which have come to prominence in the postriot era.

Issues of black community welfare contain some of the attributes of zero sum games. In a sense, with the passage of the Civil Rights Acts of the mid-1960's, the larger society said, "We will not discriminate against the 'qualified' black." Were there a single voice for the movement, it might have responded, "Yes, that is fine, it represents progress— but the number of what you call 'qualified' blacks is kept small by housing, bad schools, and bad health care. Moreover, it may be the case that a number of whites, *even without personal hostility*, have a genuine stake in institutional arrangements which work to the harm of blacks collectively."

Conflicts over "the rules of the games" relate to the other major postriot issues—community control and black power. The preriot movement broadened the opportunities of "qualified" blacks to obtain white collar and professional employment, and disputes over the "rules of the game" sought to broaden these opportunities even further.

The successes of the preriot movement, the movement for integration, revealed the limits of integration as a meliorative strategy. The problems of blacks could be defined, not only in terms of blocked opportunities for individuals, but also in terms of the policies of institutions—school systems, the police, city hall, welfare bureaucracies, and the like.

That more blacks were hired as policemen or teachers or social workers, that more institutions became integrated, was important, but did not necessarily lead to changes in the policies of those institutions. Police departments, in which the representation of blacks rose from 3.5 to 6 percent, still pursued a "stop and frisk" policy more vigorously in black neighborhoods than in white. School systems, despite recruiting more black teachers, still, virtually automatically, assigned black children to lower, nonacademic tracks.

Thus, the limits of preriot successes lay in the fact that the policies of many institutions, policies which worked to the detriment of blacks, were unaffected, even where increased integration was achieved.

Writing in the wake of the riots, Harold Baron commented:

Negroes realize that one reason the status quo in housing, jobs, and education continues is that the black community lacks control over decision-making. Negroes remain second class citizens partly because of the discrimination of individual whites, but mainly because of the way whites control the major institutions of our society.[8]

In the postriot era, demands for "community control" of institutions affecting the ghetto arose. Black power, as advocated by black radicals, reformers, or separatists, in one way or another came back to this demand.

Of necessity, this demand posed a threat to various white interest groups, groups which were able to accept a measure of integration. They saw their vital interests threatened by demands for black power in the form of community control and by pressure for changes in the rules of the game.

It is much more difficult to accomplish changes in these areas because the substance of privilege is at stake rather than mere symbols of privilege. There is also the possibility that, in defense of their substantive privileges, whites will seek to revitalize the symbols of racism and caste.

This process raises questions about the potential of American society for melioration. Does that society compel the black protest movement to go round and round in a vicious circle? Specifically, does the erosion of caste stigma and a serious address by blacks to collective problems of institutional opportunity pose such a threat to the material interests of whites that a revitalization of the ideological supports for caste becomes inevitable? As that happens, does black status come once again to be characterized by an ever greater set of caste restrictions? Does black protest then come, of necessity, to focus on the elementary assaults on black humanity involved in caste distinctions? Do these assaults gradually recede again because they run counter to certain broadly held national norms regarding freedom and equality and because they touch on the symbols rather than the substance of white privilege? Once the symbols become less important and blacks gain somewhat more freedom to contest the substance of privilege, does this revive white support for the ideology of caste as a mechanism for protecting material advantages? As that happens, does black status then come once again to be defined by an ever greater . . . ?

In other words, is the American experience melodrama or tragedy?

In the following pages, these propositions are developed.

CASTE AND COLOR

The caste-like status of blacks evolved in the period following the Civil War and began to change in significant ways only in the period following World War II.

Caste imposes an inherited and permanent limit on one's opportunities. Skin color, sex, age, or any of a number of other characteristics can serve as the axis along which caste differences are drawn. To occupy a lower caste position is to serve a lifetime sentence. Class, on the other hand, is inherited but not necessarily permanent. American mythology makes heroes of men who have improved their class position through their own efforts. William Lloyd Warner, the anthropologist, has enlarged on the difference between caste and class.

> *Caste as here used describes a theoretical arrangement of the people of a given group in order that privileges, duties, obligations, opportunities, etc., are unequally distributed between the groups which are considered to be higher and lower. There are social sanctions which tend to maintain this unequal distribution; such a definition also describes class.*

> *A caste organization, however, can further be defined as one where there is no opportunity for members of the lower groups to rise into the higher groups or of the members of the upper group to fall into the lower ones. In class, on the other hand, there is a certain proportion of inter-class marriage between lower and higher groups, and there are, in the very nature of the class organization, mechanisms established by which people move up and down the vertical extensions of the society.[9]*

To be kept out of a Miami Beach hotel because of skin color is a matter of caste stigma; to be unable to register due to lack of money involves class disadvantage. A civil rights bill affecting public accommodations will get a middle-class Negro into Miami Beach's finest hotel, but it does not help the man who lacks the price of a bus ride downtown.

The position of blacks in the United States was in some ways analogous to that of "outcasts" in India. In both countries, widely held ideologies supported caste differentiation. It is conceivable that racism as an ideology in the United States commands more allegiance than does Hinduism in India. It has been the single most persistent element in American thought, predating the Revolutionary War, the Declaration of Independence, and notions of "the rights of man."

The United States and India differ principally in that in the United States there has been a powerful counter ideology. This ideology, deriving from the Enlightenment Era of the 18th century and resting on the assumption of "inalienable rights," runs counter to racism. The United States has never resolved the conflict and has generally settled for efforts to accommodate the reality of quasi-caste for blacks to the ethic of "human rights." Enlightenment ideas with regard to "rights" arose in post-Renaissance Europe in defense of the individual against the usurpations of the state. Intellectually, the American attempt to resolve the conflict between racism and the concept of human rights was consistent with the historical origins of the Enlightenment. That is, from the end of the Civil War through the post-World War II period, the American reconciliation of racism and human rights rested on the doctrine that the state, meaning the federal government, could not legislate segregation or discrimination. This solution, however, left the separate states and private individuals free to translate racism into a quasi-caste position for blacks.

CASTE AS AN INSTITUTION

Caste as an institution manifested itself in rigid segregation and in an elaborate set of "rituals of deference." Segregation was found in every phase of institutional life. Schools, parks, hospitals, libraries, restaurants, etc., were segregated, and where separate facilities did not exist, access was still denied, particularly in the south, where most of the black population was concentrated.

In education, there were separate and unequal schools or, in some instances, no schools at all. In Atlanta, Georgia, for example, into the 1920's there were no high schools for black students. Black parents who wished their children to go beyond the seventh grade and who had the money had to pay tuition at Atlanta University, a black school which maintained high school departments, despite the existence of publicly supported high schools for whites.[10] Throughout the South, black public school teachers received less pay than white teachers even when their qualifications were equal.[11]

In law enforcement, lynching was a common occurrence. Between 1886 and 1914, 3,380 persons were lynched in the United States, the overwhelming number black.[12] These acts occurred principally in the South and often with a degree of horror that is numbing. *The New York Times* recounted a Mississippi lynching in 1937, the first year of the second Roosevelt administration:

> *Two Negroes were tortured and lynched by a mob of more than 100 white men near Duck Hill this afternoon within two hours after they had pleaded innocent in Montgomery County Circuit Court to a charge of murdering a white man.*
> *A third Negro, suspected by the mob of complicity in the slaying of George Windham, a country storekeeper, was severely whipped and run out of the county after narrowly escaping the fate of the other two Negroes.*
> *Roosevelt Townes, who had confessed, Sheriff E. E. Wright said, that he shot Windham, was tied to a tree near his victim's store and tortured slowly to death with flames from a blowtorch.*
> *A Negro identified only as "Bootjack" McDaniels, indicted with Townes in the Windham slaying, was shot by members of the mob and his body burned.*
> *Townes and McDaniels were taken from Sheriff Wright and two deputies early this afternoon as they were being led from the court house to be returned to the jail to await trial Thursday.*
> *The Negroes were handcuffed and placed in a waiting school bus. Members of the mob piled into the bus and others into automobiles. The caravan sped northward toward Duck Hill as the Negroes screamed for mercy. The bus stopped near the small country store where Windham was fatally shot through a window one night last December. The Negroes were tied to a tree and tortured.*
> *Towne's eyes were gouged out with an ice pick and a blowtorch was applied to parts of his body before he died.*
> *McDaniels was flogged by members of the mob who took turns with a chain and a horsewhip. Still alive, he was riddled with buckshot.[13]*

The phenomenon continued into the immediate post-World War II era.

> *Two young Negroes, one a veteran just returned from the war, and their wives were lined up last night near a secluded road and shot dead by an unmasked band of twenty white men.*
> *The ghastly details of the multiple lynching were told today by*

Roy Harrison, a well-to-do white farmer who had just hired the Negroes to work on his farm. Harrison was bringing the Negroes to his farm when his car was waylaid by the mob eight miles from Monroe. Questioning of one of the Negroes by the mob indicated, Harrison said, that he was suspected of having stabbed his former employer, a white man. The Negroes, Roger Malcolm and George Dorsey, both 27, were removed from the car and led down a side road.

The women, who were sisters and who had just recently married Malcolm and Dorsey, began to scream. Then a mob member said that one of the women had recognized him.

"Get those damned women too," the mob leader shouted. Several of the men came back and dragged the shrieking women from the automobile. A few moments later Mr. Harrison heard the shots— many of them—and the mob dispersed.

The grotesquely sprawled bodies were found in a clump of bushes beside a little-used sideroad, the upper parts of the bodies scarcely recognizable from the mass of bullet holes.

Dorsey's mother, Monia Williams, said that her son had just been discharged after five years in the Army and that she had received his discharge button in the mail just this week.

The lynching was the first in the nation in nearly a year and was the first multiple lynching since two 14-year-old Negro boys were hanged by a Mississippi mob in October, 1942. For Georgia it was the first lynching of more than one person since 1918 when ten Negroes were lynched in Brooks County.[14]

Employment of blacks was largely restricted to low-paying, un-skilled jobs irrespective of their level of education. The armed services were segregated, and blacks in the Navy were restricted to being mess corpsmen. Hospital facilities were either segregated or nonexistent for blacks.

In every phase of institutional life, segregation was the rule. This was most common in the South, but also characterized the North. Not until 1948 did the Board of Education in Freehold, New Jersey, abolish rules mandating segregated schools.[15]

In the same year, New Jersey desegregated its national guard and the governor of Connecticut announced renewed efforts to desegregate that state's national guard.

The quasi-caste position of blacks was reinforced by an elaborate set of rituals of deference. These rituals regulated the manner in which blacks and whites interacted and were intended to reinforce the superior status of whites.

Blacks were constrained to address whites as "Mr.," "Mrs.," or "Miss." Where there was a degree of intimacy, the first name might also be used, as with "Mr. William" and "Miss Ann." On the other hand, blacks were addressed by their first names regardless of age or other attributes. Thus, the 50-year-old black addressed a ten-year-old white as "Mr. John" but was in turn addressed as "Jim."

A story, perhaps apocryphal, circulated before Warld War II bearing on the rituals of deference required in black-white interaction. A black walked into a store in the South and asked for a can of "Prince Albert smoking tobacco." The white storekeeper shouted, "What did you ask for?" "Prince Albert," replied the black. "Nigger," said the storekeeper, taking a pistol from under the counter with one hand and pointing to the picture of Prince Albert on the tobacco can with the other, "What did you want?" "*Mr.* Prince Albert," replied the black, suddenly aware of his transgression.

Blacks doffed their hats when talking to whites and entered the homes of whites by the back door. They waited for service in stores until whites had been served.

There were, then, a number of tangible, institutional manifestations of the black's inferior position. Some of these had instrumental, utilitarian meaning; restricting blacks to undesirable jobs, for example, increased the opportunity for white men to get desirable jobs. Rituals of deference, however, had no meaning that could be measured in dollars and cents. Their only function was to symbolize the status difference between the races. They continually dramatized the black's separate and subordinate position.

Buttressing and justifying the caste-like system was an elaborate ideology. In the context of this ideology, blacks were seen as bearing a kind of tribal stain. The ideology reinforced the caste system by projecting two contradictory but nevertheless powerful themes: the black as a child and the black as a beast. The black-as-child theme suggested that blacks were immature, impulsive, and irresponsible, but nevertheless lovable "in their place." They needed the strong hand of the white to keep them in line as a child needs the authority of the parent. The black-as-beast theme suggested that blacks were brutish, insolent, and lust-ridden and needed the billy club of the sheriff to keep them from continual bouts of drunken violence and the lyncher's rope to keep them from being a threat to whites.

From a conjoining of social structure and ideology came the anti-black pogrom as an habitual mode of racial violence in that era. Pogroms were numerous. For example, in Whiteboro, Texas, on August 12, 1903, a black was lynched, the black quarter was attacked, its residents were ordered to leave town, and many fled. "As a result, outgoing trains on all roads were filled with Negroes." On August 4, 1910, blacks fled Dady,

Florida, in the wake of a white mob which was aroused over the murder of a school girl. On January 3, 1916, the black quarter of Blakely, Georgia, was burned after six blacks had been killed following the death of a white man allegedly killed by blacks.[16] In 1917, 2,500 blacks were driven by force from Dawson and Forsyth counties in Georgia.

Ray Stannard Baker, the journalist, writing just after the pogrom which began in Atlanta in September of 1905 and swept into black communities outside the city, caught the tone and feeling of a society in which caste was an obsession. He recounted the observations of a perceptive young white woman:

> *I had a terrible experience one evening a few days ago. I was walking along—street when I saw a rather good looking young Negro come out of a hallway to the sidewalk. He was in a great hurry, and, in turning suddenly as a person sometimes will do, he accidentally brushed my shoulder with his arm. He had not seen me before. When he turned and found it was a white woman he had touched, such a look of abject terror and fear came into his face as I hope never again to see on a human countenance. He knew what it meant if I was frightened and called for help and accused him of insulting or attacking me. He stood still a moment then turned and ran down the street, dodging into the first alley he came to. It shows, doesn't it, how little it might take to bring punishment upon an innocent man.[17]*

The Atlanta pogrom had been inspired, in part, by inflammatory newspaper stories about "crime in the streets." A real or alleged assault would bring out three or four "extra" newspaper editions with headlines such as one carried by the *Atlanta Journal*, "Angry Citizens in Pursuit of Black Brute Who Attempted Assault—Mrs. Chapin Rescued from Fiend by Passing Neighbor."[18] Widespread concern over "safe streets" fueled the passions which culminated in the Atlanta pogrom.

A slackening of the frequency of pogroms coincided with changes in social structure. These changes in social structure fostered the development of the "civil rights" movement and also produced a range of other forms of black protest, including the urban "race riot" and mass-based separatist groups.

The first major indication of a significant change came in Chicago in 1919 when a major race riot swept the city. The race riot differed from the pogrom in that significant numbers of blacks battled whites. The riot was characterized by clashes of blacks and whites rather than black flight.

Arthur Waskow, the historian, has commented on the importance of the year 1919:

> . . . *the propensity of Negroes in 1919 to challenge the assumption of their own subordination startled America and constitutes one major reason to study the explosion of race riots that characterized 1919. For the 1919 riots gave birth to "the New Negro"—the first generation of Negroes to win that appellation—and signalled the first new departure since the Emancipation in the history of the Negroes' efforts to end their subordination.[19]*

The conditions preceding the Chicago riot were typical of those in other cities that were engulfed by race rioting during what came to be called "Red Summer."

Between 1910 and 1920, the city's black population had increased 148.2 percent, rising from 44,103 to 109,458, with some 50,000 persons migrating from the South; most of this migration occurred in the years 1916 to 1918. While Chicago blacks enjoyed more freedom than those in many other parts of the country, racial barriers were nevertheless formidable. Most public accommodations were closed to blacks; discrimination in employment was virtually universal, and access to housing outside the ghetto was severely limited. In addition, a whole host of ethnic groups—Italians, Poles, Irish, themselves marginal in status—opposed any expansion of opportunities for blacks.

Racial confrontation is an urban product, and a distinct urban black subculture began to develop for the first time in the immediate post-World War I era. Most of the major cities of the North experienced a dramatic increase in the percentage of blacks in their populations between 1910 and 1920. New York City's black population increased from 91,709 to 152,467, Philadelphia's from 84,459 to 134,229, and Detroit's went up 611 percent, from 5,741 to 40,383. Blacks were moving north, the major cities of the South either remaining stable in terms of percentage of blacks or in five cases actually declining. In northern cities, huge and sprawling ghettoes came into existence, and they represented a new and very different set of conditions.

The blacks of these cities were an urban proletariat rather than a rural peasantry. Rather than being a monolithic system of oppression, the system yielded here and there. These urban blacks absorbed some of the aspirations for political and social mobility from the other ethnic groups they encountered in the cities and, in the somewhat free climate, were more inclined to challenge these other minorities.

In these black ghettoes, nationalist groups began to arise—the Garvey movement in New York, the Abyssinians in Chicago, and, in the early 1930's in Detroit, the Black Muslims.

Civil rights activity, in the modern sense of the word, also developed in these urban settings.

THE CIVIL RIGHTS MOVEMENT

The civil rights movement thrust itself against the restrictions of caste. It focused primarily on the legal and social disabilities visited upon blacks because of their caste-like status. Historically, it had three objectives: (1) it sought to realize elementary civil liberties for blacks; (2) from the turn of the century through the beginning of World War II, it sought to make separate facilities genuinely equal; and (3) following World War II, it increasingly posed a legal challenge to the idea that separate facilities could be equal.

The movement sought to erode caste restrictions placed on blacks, and in many of its specifics this objective did not pose the likelihood of any tangible cost to whites. This can be made clear by briefly discussing some of the struggles of the oldest civil rights organization, the National Association for the Advancement of Colored People. A number of civil rights organizations have fought racism, including the National Equal Rights League, the National League for the Protection of Colored Women, the National Negro Political League, and the National Independent Political League, but the N.A.A.C.P. is the oldest and most enduring.

When it came into existence in 1910, the N.A.A.C.P. confronted a reality in which blacks were denied the protection of some laws and victimized by others. The organization was founded by black intellectuals and white liberals. As was indicated earlier in this chapter, the great mass of blacks at that time were impoverished and rural and were dissuaded by white terror from seeking redress through conventional, interest-group politics. The most respected black leader of the time, Booker T. Washington, counselled accommodation to the system, arguing essentially that blacks should raise themselves by their own bootstraps before becoming concerned with legal and political rights.

The blacks who helped to found the N.A.A.C.P. had distinguished themselves academically or professionally, and the black social base of the organization was primarily middle class. Because they had pulled themselves up by their bootstraps but were still subject to savage mistreatment, the relative militancy of the N.A.A.C.P. probably made more sense to them intellectually and viscerally than the accommodationist position of Booker T. Washington.

The organization became involved almost immediately in antilynching campaigns, seeking to arouse public indignation against this crime and imploring the federal government to ensure its black citizens minimal protection.

The caste-like status of blacks in that era, informally enforced by terror, was also formally secured by law and thus, inevitably, the organization was drawn into what became identified as its major strategy, the contesting of black rights in court. On December 10, 1910, Baltimore, Maryland, enacted the first city ordinance in the United States which would have segregated blacks in certain residential areas *by law*. Richmond, Norfolk, and Roanoke, Virginia, also enacted such laws, as did St. Louis, Missouri, Dallas, Texas, Louisville, Kentucky, and a number of other cities.[20]

In the last decade of the 19th century, the courts had reinterpreted the Fourteenth and Fifteenth Amendments and various civil rights laws in a way that stripped blacks of the legal prerogatives of citizenship. Concurrently, state and local governmental bodies began to pass new laws that defined a new system called "segregation." In this period, following the Supreme Court's "separate but equal" decision of 1896, *Plessy* vs. *Ferguson*, there was a rash of such laws, defining the meaning of segregation in the areas of public accommodation, education, and politics. The ordinances passed by Baltimore and other cities were extending the definition *de jure* to residence, restricting blacks by law to certain areas of a city.

These laws eventually brought the N.A.A.C.P., for the first time, to the Supreme Court. The initial efforts of the organization were primarily defensive, aimed at preventing the caste position of blacks from being frozen into law. It was fighting its first battles in a climate in which undergraduate women at Cornell University in 1913 petitioned the faculty to remove two black girls from the women's dormitory[21] and in which the Harvard Club of Philadelphia in the same year "wrote to class secretaries asking for the names of Negro graduates in each class in order to exclude them from invitations to the annual dinner."[22] It was an era in which many of "the best and the brightest" were vigorous advocates of the caste subordination of blacks.

The organization began to fight in court to ensure that the "separate but equal" facilities the Supreme Court had declared constitutional in its 1896 *Plessy* vs. *Ferguson* decision were in fact equal. This battle led to a series of cases that undermined the legal foundations of caste. It will be instructive to review some of those cases since they involved gains for the organization that entailed no immediate and direct costs to whites.

In 1946, the organization commenced legal action for Ada Louise Sipuel[23] in Oklahoma and, five weeks later, on May 15th, for Hemon Marion Sweatt in Texas.[24] Both cases involved capable blacks who wished to attend law school. Neither Oklahoma nor Texas admitted blacks to their state law schools, nor did they provide law schools for blacks. In both instances, color was the only circumstance barring applicants from institutions which their tax money helped to support, and in both cases the N.A.A.C.P. won a successful decision.

The organization had had similar cases involving blacks seeking graduate education in states which provided no facilities for blacks. Through these cases, the organization began to undermine the belief that the doctrine of "separate but equal" was viable. The changes it began to bring about were of overwhelming importance historically, but at the same time those changes did not involve a threat to the fundamental interests of whites. They were changes which entailed greater personal security and safety for blacks and changes which broadened opportunities for "qualified blacks."

The organization is not to be faulted or criticized in this respect. Given the climate of the times, its actions were seen by most whites and many blacks as "radical." It was widely regarded in the South as a seedbed of militancy, and its members were subjected to threat and harassment. It sought to achieve a situation where blacks enjoyed at least minimal human rights, where there was some minimal respect for their basic humanity.

The direct action phase of the modern civil rights movement, which swelled to immense proportions between the first sit-ins in Greensboro in February of 1960 and the passage of the Civil Rights Act of 1964, dealt largely with issues of caste. Its success is embodied in the 1964 Civil Rights Act, which is concerned principally with caste.

Let us briefly review the Act and its provisions. Title One deals with voting and prohibits registrars from applying differing standards to white and Negro voting applicants. Title Two deals with public accommodations, and Title Three with public facilities, the former stating that race cannot be used to bar an individual from service in motels, hotels, restaurants, etc., and the latter that blacks cannot be barred from publicly owned or operated facilities such as parks, stadia, and swimming pools. Titles Four and Five deal with enforcement and investigation in civil rights cases. Title Six provides that no person shall be subject to discrimination in any program receiving federal aid, while Title Seven bars discrimination by employers or unions with over 100 employees or members, expanding coverage over a four-year period to organizations with only 25 members. The balance of the Act deals with miscellaneous matters.

Significantly, those titles of the Act dealing with the caste issues of public accommodations and public facilities have met with substantial compliance. But those titles of the Act dealing with the class issues of employment and union membership—issues where the substance rather than the symbols of white privilege are at stake—remain very much matters of controversy.

Clearly the Act focused on caste barriers and its major consequence was to reduce those barriers. James Farmer, then Chairman of the Congress of Racial Equality, urged members returning from the annual

C.O.R.E. conference in Kansas City to gauge the seriousness of the legislation in terms of places serving the public. Headlines in the *New York Times* on July 4, the day following the signing of the Act reflect its thrust. "Negroes in South Test Rights Acts, Resistance Light—A steak house in Virginia and a pool in Georgia are Integrated Peacefully, Birmingham Obeying—Chamber of Commerce Asks Compliance in Jackson."

Bayard Rustin, organizer of the 1963 March on Washington for Jobs and Freedom and of New York City's first school boycott in 1964, indicated,

> . . . . we hit Jim Crow precisely where it was mostly anachronistic, dispensable, and vulnerable—in hotels, lunch counters, terminals, libraries, swimming pools, and the like. For in these forms Jim Crow does impede the flow of commerce in the broadest sense; it is a nuisance in the society on the move (and on the make). Not surprisingly, therefore, it was the most mobility-conscious and relatively liberated groups in the Negro community—lower middle-class college students—who launched the attack that brought down this imposing but hollow structure.[25]

Even where the preriot movement focused on employment (ostensibly a class issue), it was primarily in terms of caste questions. For example, in the San Francisco Bay area, a number of rather strong C.O.R.E. chapters flourished in 1963 and 1964. Numerous employers—Sears and Roebuck, Lucky Stores, Safeway, the Bank of America, etc.—were approached and questioned about their hiring policies. In certain cases, direct action—picketing, boycotts, demonstrations—had to be undertaken to persuade an employer to cease discrimination in the hiring of blacks. Negotiations with employers, or direct action against them, invariably met with success. In retrospect, the consequence of C.O.R.E.'s efforts was to open up opportunities for those blacks who were blocked solely because of color. The black girl with a high school education could now become a supermarket clerk; the well-spoken, neatly groomed young black man might get a job as a bank teller. In other words, success came principally in the form of the removal of some of the *caste* barriers to black employment. This was an important and necessary step in the process of improving black status. Once the caste battles receded, however, it became increasingly obvious that there was a huge pool of blacks, products of inferior slum schools, rejects from the draft, persons not even counted by the census taker, for whom success in persuading these employers to remove caste barriers was largely irrelevant.

The 1964 Civil Rights Act and the 1965 Voting Rights Act brought the Civil Rights movement to an impasse. This was not perceived at the time, and indeed it was largely the urban riots which made that fact clear. With the passage of the two acts and with the erosion of the legal supports for caste differentiation, there was the sense that a climatic battle had been won.

The riots began at a time when it was popularly believed that "things were getting better." The Watts riot occurred a year after the passage of the 1964 Civil Rights Act and months after passage of the Voting Rights Act. Watts inaugurated a period of turmoil during which the limited dimensions of the earlier successes became obvious. Between 1965 and 1968, a number of American cities experienced massive rioting. Andrew Kopkind, writing in *The New York Review of Books,* understood the meaning of the riots. "Above all, there is a sense that the continuity of an age has been cut, that we have arrived at an infrequent fulcrum of history, and that what comes now will be vastly different from what went before."[26]

Race violence had occurred earlier in American history. The "Red Summer" of 1919 saw outbreaks in a number of cities. The pattern of such violence differed dramatically from that of the 1960's, however. Previously, whites had attacked blacks, and, occasionally, blacks had fought back. Pogroms took place where blacks were driven from communities and their homes destroyed; where they fought back, as happened in Chicago in 1919, something like "race war" occurred. The riots of the 1960's departed from both these patterns.

The 1960 riots always seemed to begin with a certain kind of encounter between people who lived in the ghetto and people who did not. In terms of the vocabulary of the theater, the escalation of an encounter into a riot hinged on an expansion of the cast. The initial encounter usually brought together the police and one or more residents of the ghetto. A policeman stopped a car he believed to have been speeding, or questioned some juveniles about their activities. At this point, the police and the party or parties stopped constituted the whole cast in the encounter. Under most circumstances, they played out a drama that did not attract public attention. The policeman had a variety of roles he might adopt vis-à-vis the party he had stopped (tough but fair cop, nigger hater, impartial enforcer of the law, etc.), as had the object of his attentions (bewildered party willing to be cooperative, innocent party indignant at being stopped, etc.). Their roles meshed in certain ways to yield an outcome (tough but fair cop lets bewildered party willing to be cooperative go with a warning, nigger hater takes in innocent party indignant at being stopped). Thousands of such little dramas are played out every year and are never reviewed in the press as riots.

The crucial juncture in the riot process occurred when the audience of such dramas become players themselves. If some juveniles smash windows and the police come and arrest them, there has not been a riot. Only when the cast expands, does a riot begin to develop. What constitutes the necessary number of actors varied with the situation. In the incident which precipitated the Detroit riot, it was several dozen patrons of an after-hours drinking spot and a certain number of policemen to arrest them. In the Watts riot, it was two policemen and two individuals suspected of drunken driving.

Expansion of the cast meant that persons not having a role in the original drama decided to become players. Put somewhat differently, it meant that some element of community support developed for the ghetto actors in the original encounter. This collective decision constitutes the key juncture in the transformation of an incident into a riot. It meant that the grievance of an individual citizen of the ghetto became a collective complaint. As the ghetto cast expanded, the character of the drama changed. The specific object of complaint (an abusive cop, an insulting merchant, etc.) was no longer accessible to many of the actors who had mobilized themselves to play some role in the drama of retribution. Therefore meaningful substitutes were found; e.g., white-owned stores were burned, cars driven by whites were stoned.

What began as relative minor theater—off Broadway, so to speak —became a major production with a cast of thousands and costing millions of dollars.

The larger social background of the riots was one in which the realities of day-to-day life for many blacks had not changed at all or had improved only marginally, despite the massive efforts of the movement and the passage of legislation of landmark proportions. The irony was that genuinely important and historic changes had occurred; many of the customs of caste had been breeched.

The riots marked a shift in the character of American race conflict and provided the setting within which groups very different from the earlier civil rights groups came to the fore.

BLACK COMMUNITY WELFARE

In a sense, then, before the man in the ghetto could come to feel that he really did have a right to a better life, the battles of caste had to be fought. Thereafter, an increasing number of blacks, in particular ghetto blacks, became more and more dissatisfied with continued deprivation.

From a certain perspective, issues of symbolic degradation, i.e., discrimination in public accommodations, separate drinking fountains, restroom facilities, etc., are less important than questions of employment or equal access to educational facilities. It may appear to be obvious that opportunities for employment are more central to an individual's life chances than the opportunity to use a public rest room. Yet, from another perspective, this proposition is not quite so obvious.

The practices of symbolic degradation were an assault upon the very humanity of blacks. It was sometimes easier to find overnight lodgings for a dog than for a black. The ban against blacks in certain public accommodations was more absolute than the ban against dogs. or cats. Symbolic degradation compromised the black's very status as a human being. Also, it is unlikely that a white society which had not taken the step of acknowledging the elementary humanity of blacks could take steps in areas that were apparently more practical.

In the postriot era, questions of unequal access to limited resources more clearly became the issue. The struggle began to assume some of the qualities of a zero sum game. Incompatible interests become the locus of conflict.

The New York City teachers' strikes of 1968 will serve as a good example of this kind of conflict. Their impact on the city was enormous and catastrophic. "The . . . teachers strike of 1968 seems to me," the writer Martin Mayer observed, "The worst disaster my native city has experienced in my lifetime—comparable in its economic impact to an earthquake that would destroy Manhattan below Chambers Street, much worse in its social effect than a major race riot."[27] Although the details of the event were exceedingly complex, the basic features of the conflict can be described simply.

Involved in the conflict were: the United Federation of Teachers, led by Albert Shanker, "former junior high school math teacher . . . a product of the socialist wing of the teachers' union, and a civil rights activist";[28] the governing board of the Ocean Hill School project, a body made up of elected parent representatives; for the most part welfare mothers; various community leaders from the black and Puerto Rican Ocean Hill–Brownsville section of Brooklyn; and various city and state politicians and educators.

A significant circumstance is that over 50 percent of the children in the city's schools are black or Puerto Rican, while over 90 percent of the city's teachers are white.

The longer black and Puerto Rican children stay in school, the worse they perform on standardized achievement tests. Consequently, black and Puerto Rican parents are as dissatisfied with the schools as middle- and upper-class white parents, but they do not have the same option of sending their children to private schools. Significantly, among the major protagonists in the confrontation, the members of the Ocean Hill–Brownsville board were probably the only parents whose children were actually attending public schools.

Throughout the 1960's, as David Rogers indicated in *110 Livingston Street*, efforts to promote greater integration in the public school system came mostly to naught.[29] Frances Piven concurred in this judgment: "School personnel effectively defeated school desegregation policies by simply failing to inform ghetto parents of their right to enroll their children in white schools, and by discouraging those parents who tried to do so."[30] Eventually, black parents seeking better education for their children began to talk less of integration and sought alternatives.

For a variety of reasons, in the late 1960's, many black activists began to advocate "community control" of schools. This demand was consistent with the rhetoric of black power and represented a broad response of blacks to the postriot era when integration in areas other than those peripheral to white interests seemed more and more difficult to realize. In effect, blacks were saying, "If we cannot move out of the ghetto or integrate the schools, then let us at least control the institutions and services of the ghetto, including the schools."

In terms of education, this pressure for black community control took the form in New York City of "decentralization." The concept of decentralization had been advocated by other parties simply on grounds of breaking up the massive educational bureaucracy which had developed in the city. Consequently, by the late 1960's, various forms of decentralization were being advocated by a variety of groups, and efforts were being made to establish a few demonstration districts.

From the viewpoint of the parents on the governing board of the Ocean Hill–Brownsville demonstration project, it was a matter of recognizing that their children were not learning in school and of attempting to remove teachers deemed incompetent or bigoted. From the viewpoint of the union, it was a matter of job security.

The governing board demanded the removal of 19 teachers, and insisted, according to Mayer, that the community had the right to hire and fire teachers for the district's schools.[31] The union responded with a series of strikes, its concerns related mainly to establishing job security for its members.

Piven, a perceptive analyst of the social system, placed the conflict in a larger context:

> The emerging conflict is not difficult to explain. Whites and blacks are pitted against each other in a struggle for the occupational and political benefits attached to public employment. Whites now

have the bulk of these benefits, and blacks want a greater share of them. Nor is it only jobs that are at stake. Organized public employees have become a powerful force shaping the policies of municipal agencies, but the policies that suit employees often run counter to ghetto interests. We may be entering another phase in the long and tragic history of antagonism between the black poor and the white working class in America.[32]

At stake was the distribution of wealth and services and the interests of a variety of white groups that had a stake in the status quo. The Central Labor Council, representing 1,200,000 workers, the overwhelming percentage white, voted to support the teachers' union. As Piven pointed out, this body had its own interest in the matter. "The Board of Education disperses over 1 billion dollars annually for construction. Under a system of community control, contracts might be awarded to black businesses or to contractors who hire black workers."[33]

The implications of the teachers' strike were profound. The issue was no longer whether a superlatively prepared black with degrees from Harvard and Yale could get *a* job as a teacher, but whether the black community could effectively influence or even determine the structure of the school system. Consequently, as Piven indicates, "Threatened by the efforts of ghetto parents to free their children from an unresponsive educational system, the [teachers'] union became the major force opposing school decentralization."[34]

On issues of real substance, large numbers of whites, with or without personal hostility, may have a stake in institutional arrangements which work to the detriment of blacks. As they defend these interests against the efforts of blacks to improve their condition, racism may emerge. Thus, Martin Mayer, writing from a perspective sympathetic to the union, nevertheless indicated that eventually the "strike revealed a shocking quantity of racist sentiment in the city and among more teachers than one would have expected."

The leadership of the teachers' union had a history of active support of civil rights; two years before the strike, the union's executive committee had voted 30-2 to support a proposed police civilian review board, a measure strongly supported in the black and Puerto Rican communities and vehemently resisted by the police and an overwhelming percentage of whites. The union also had a stake, however, in the perpetuation of an educational system which did not work to the interest of minority children. Neither the union nor its supporters were opposed to all change in education; they were opposed to those changes which threatened their jobs and their influence, and they were successful in weakening school decentralization policies.

The material white stake in policies detrimental to blacks and other minorities is obviously of long standing. As Piven indicates, "as it stands now, there is only so much in the way of jobs, services, and control over policy to be divided up," and whites have fought to retain control, unions representing firemen, policemen, and sanitation men in New York City going to court "in opposition to changes in civil service procedures which would have increased employment opportunities for blacks and Puerto Ricans."[35]

Why not expand the resources available? As will be indicated, it is not that easy. And while resources are limited, the efforts of black parents to redistribute them have the character of a zero sum game. If there are ten schools in an area and only five can receive libraries, the efforts of black parents to receive one or more mean that the largely white schools receive four or fewer.

The zero sum quality of this kind of struggle gives it a much more intense quality than struggles on the part of whites, say, to maintain segregated amusement parks.

This mode of analysis can be applied to other problem areas. Ultimately, the opposition of trade unions to opening up opportunities for black advancement may be more intense than that of management. In some unions, membership is virtually passed on from father to son like a family legacy. Policies intended to expand opportunities for blacks to participate in apprenticeship programs and acquire union membership have something of a zero sum quality. As Kenneth Clark has indicated, "the interests of the privileged are at stake." These interests involve the distribution of wealth and power, and therefore the battle to effect change will probably be longer and more bitter than the battle to erode caste privilege.

Three kinds of movements have come to the fore in the postriot era: separatist movements, radical movements, and movements representing what might be termed "soul politics." Each is based on a different logic and analysis of American society, yet each in a different way advocates black control over the institutions affecting the quality of black lives. Each is a response to the limits inherent in earlier successes. In the remaining pages of this chapter, the logic and historical background of each is discussed, and in subsequent chapters specific organizations representing each thrust are analyzed. None of these three orientations are new; they have simply gained greater importance in the postriot era. The objectives of the preriot movement could be captured in the phrases "civil rights" and "integration"; those of the postriot movement are defined by the terms "black power" and "community control."

BLACK SEPARATISM

The idea of separation of the races in the United States has been advocated at various times by both blacks and whites. Thomas Jefferson and Abraham Lincoln both suggested the desirability of resettling blacks outside the United States. In the 18th and 19th centuries, various groups of white philanthropists, some motivated by humanitarianism, others by racism, supported black emigration. Liberia and Sierra Leone were created by these groups, the latter inspired by British philanthropists seeking resettlement of New World blacks and their descendants taken by British forces during the Revolutionary War and brought to England.

Black separatism has been an expression of black despair at the possibility of eroding white racism. The Convention of Free Colored People held in Baltimore in 1852 expressed this despair in a statement supporting black emigration.

> . . . *while we appreciate and acknowledge the sincerity of the motives and activity of the zeal of those who during an agitation of twenty years have honestly struggled to place us on a footing of social and political equality with the White population of this country, yet we cannot conceal from ourselves the fact that no advance has been made towards a result to us so desirable; but that on the contrary, our condition as a class is less desirable than it was twenty years ago.*[36]

In 1853 the convention appointed agents to explore opportunities for mass black emigration to Haiti, Central America, and Niger Valley.

Martin Robinson Delaney, a black Harvard-educated physician, was the most prominent emigrationist of the 1850's. In a letter to one of the leading white abolitionists, William Lloyd Garrison, he explained, "more in sorrow than anger," why he had become an advocate of separatism:

> *I am not in favor of caste, nor a separation of the brotherhood of mankind, and would as willingly live among White men as Black if I had equal possession and enjoyment of privileges; but shall never be reconciled to live among them subservient to their will— existing by mere sufferance as we the colored people do in this country . . . . If there were any probability of this [achieving equal rights], I should be willing to remain in the country fighting and struggling on, the good fight of faith, but I must admit, that I have no hopes in this country—no confidence in the American people . . . .*[37]

In 1859, Delaney led an expedition up the Niger River Valley and reached agreement with several tribes whereby they granted settlement rights to American blacks.

The erosion of black liberties in the postreconstruction period provoked a resurgence of separatism. Henry M. Turner, Bishop of the African Methodist Episcopal Church, became its principal spokesman. Turner had served in the Georgia legislature during the reconstruction period and had in his own lifetime seen the loss of black liberties enacted into law after the Civil War and experienced the growth of a racial caste system in the United States.

In the decade following World War I, Marcus Garvey defended separatism in terms of the unlikely prospect that blacks would achieve equal rights in the United States:

> *You and I can live in the United States of America for 100 years, and our generations may live for 200 years or for 5000 more years, and so long as there is a black and white population, when the majority is on the side of the white race, you and I will never get political justice or get political equality in this country.*[38]

Separatist sentiment reasserted itself in the period following the urban riots. Contemporary separatism, like its historical forerunners, rests on three related assumptions:

1. Separatism assumes that racism is an indelible part of the white psyche.

Richard Henry, one of the founders of the Republic of New Africa, articulated this point of view, indicating that his conclusion was "supported directly by the evidence of the Martin Luther King era, during which black people for ten years offered themselves as nonviolent sacrifices to redeem racist whites, only to find whites in America as persistently racist in the end as in the beginning."[39] Robert S. Browne, a theoretician of black separatism, expressed it somewhat differently:

> *The manner in which Germany herded Jews into concentration camps and ultimately ovens was a solemn warning to minority peoples everywhere. The casualness with which America exterminated the Indians and later interned the Japanese suggests that there is no cause for the Negro to feel complacent about his security in the United States.*[40]

2. The second assumption of separatism is that blacks have certain common characteristics arising largely out of the shared experience of oppression and exploitation.

Milton Henry, cofounder of the Republic of New Africa, expressed this point of view: "The more I wrote, spoke and thought, the more I came to see that we were a nation. We had all the criteria: the unity of ideology, the humor, the shared experiences, the community of suffering, the common relationship to the 'master race'—everything."[41] For separatists, a black culture is not only an historical reality but also a psychological necessity. The only way, according to separatists, in which blacks can evade the ego erosion inherent in such things as white standards of beauty is to identify with the norms and values of black culture. Cultural nationalism springs from this source.

3. The third assumption follows from the first two. Given the ineradicable nature of racism and the common identity of blacks, it follows that blacks should seek a separate sovereignty.

In its clearest form, separation involves establishing a separate black nation; in a more muted form, it entails cultural nationalism—a point of view and movement that seek to unify blacks by emphasizing certain cultural characteristics assumed to be unique to them and that demands black control of institutions in the black community.

The Republic of New Africa represents a clear and unequivocal expression of separatism. The Republic demands five southern states as partial reparation for the historical exploitation of blacks, arguing that these are states in any event where a large portion of the black population lives. Robert Browne, an advisor to the founders of the Republic of New Africa, arguing that American blacks culturally are not African, also articulated the case for separatism:

A formal partitioning of the United States into two totally separate and independent nations, one white and one black, offers one way out of this tragic situation. Many will condemn it as a defeatist solution, but what they see as defeatism may better be described as a frank facing up to the realities of American society. A society is stable only to the extent that there exists a basic core of value judgments that are unthinkingly accepted by the great bulk of its members. Increasingly, Negroes are demonstrating that they do not accept the common core of values that underlies America—whether because they had little to do with drafting it or because they feel it is weighted against their interests.[42]

In the next chapter, attention will be given to the oldest, most powerful, and most successful separatist organization, the Lost-Found Nation of Islam in the Wilderness of North America, popularly known as the Black Muslims.

BLACK PROTEST MOVEMENTS AND RADICAL POLITICS

In the postriot period, a number of new black protest groups came to prominence. Among the more important were the Black Panthers. Although they have certain unique characteristics, the Panthers represent an historical approach which seeks to link black protest to radical politics.

In contrast to separatists, whose analysis of American politics focuses solely on race, radical black analysis tends to see the American economic, political, and social systems as exploitative of a number of groups. The Russian Revolution had a profound impact on black intellectuals in the United States as well as upon intellectuals in Asia and Latin America. Claude McKay, the black poet, who visited the Soviet Union in 1922, articulated the perspective of these intellectuals.

With the mammoth country securely under their control, and despite the great energy and thought that are being poured into the revival of the national industry, the vanguard of the Russian workers and the national minorities, now set free from imperial oppression, are thinking seriously about the fate of the oppressed classes, the suppressed national and racial minorities in the rest of Europe, Asia, Africa, and America. They feel themselves kin in spirit to these people. They want to help make them free. And not the least of the oppressed that fill the thoughts of the new Russia are the Negroes of America and Africa.[43]

The Messenger, edited by A. Philip Randolph and Charles Owen, who described their publication as "the only radical black magazine in America," also presented this viewpoint in the period immediately following World War I.

The history of the labor movement in America proves that the employing class recognize no race lines. They will exploit a white man as readily as a black man. They will exploit women as readily as men. They will even go to the extent of coining the labor, blood and suffering of children into dollars . . . . If the employers can keep the white and black dogs, on account of race prejudice, fighting over a bone, the yellow capitalist dog will get away with the bone—the bone of profit.[44]

From this perception there follows a call for unity among the oppressed. The Black Panthers issued this call:

The Black Panther Party stands for revolutionary solidarity with all people fighting against the forces of imperialism, capitalism, racism and fascism. Our solidarity is extended to those people who are fighting these evils at home and abroad . . . our struggle for our liberation is part of a worldwide struggle being waged by the poor and oppressed against imperialism and the world's chief imperialist, the United States of America.[45]

Prior to the rise of the Black Panthers, political radicalism among American blacks, as among American whites, was confined largely to the intelligentsia. For the most part, those blacks active for any period of time in radical politics were intellectuals like Richard Wright, W. E. B. Dubois, and A. Philip Randolph. The Panthers managed to derive more of their active support from the streets than previous radicals. This difference was due partly to style and partly to substance.

The Panthers will be discussed at greater length in the next chapter.

SOUL POLITICS

Radicalism and separatism have less of a grip on the imagination and loyalties of blacks than does conventional interest-group politics. This is not to say that most blacks are intensely political but merely that the greatest proportion subscribe to conventional political strategies.

Soul politics rests on two premises:

1. Blacks should control, or at least strongly influence, those institutions which affect their fortunes.

Black politicians and blacks attuned to politics are, of course, a heterogeneous group. Many, however, implicitly if not explicitly, share some assumptions with the separatists. As was indicated, separatists start with the premise of white incorrigibility as regards racism. Black power politics are not quite so pessimistic. It is no longer assumed that appeals to conscience of the sort which characterized the movement of the early 1960's are efficacious, but there is no assumption of indelible white racism. Instead, the major black politicians adhere to an interest-group model. According to this model, any group in power will take care of its own first. Therefore, for black interests to be promoted, blacks must be in power.

2. The second premise relates to the first. It is assumed that government is an effective mechanism for correcting some of the problems of the black community. It is assumed that the importance of blacks in power is substantive rather than symbolic. Black politicians note that the black population is more dependent on public services than

other populations because of lack of income to buy services privately. Blacks go to public rather than private schools; they and other minority groups are more likely to go to public hospitals than private proprietary hospitals; they are more likely than whites to live in public housing. Public services in black and minority communities have historically been less satisfactory than those in white communities: garbage collection is less certain; in some cities, the police are as likely to be dealing in drugs as arresting drug peddlers. The machinery of government is seen as a mechanism for the melioration of these problems.

In Chapter 3, discussion will be focused on the black-based urban political party as seen in Newark and Gary. The implications for blacks of control of city hall will be examined.

REFERENCES

1. Ben J. Wattenberg and Richard M. Scammon, "Black Progress and Liberal Rhetoric," *Commentary*, 55, No. 4 (April, 1973), p. 35.

2. *Ibid.*, p. 39.

3. Howard Schuman, "Sociological Racism," *Transaction*, 7, No. 2 (December, 1969), p. 44.

4. *Ibid.*, p. 47.

5. Hanes Walton, *Black Politics* (Philadelphia. J. B. Lippincott, 1972), pp. 193, 197.

6. I am indebted for the phrase "classical civil rights movement" to Bayard Rustin, "From Protest to Politics: The Future of the Civil Rights Movements," in *The Radical Papers* (Irving Howe, ed., Garden City, New York: Doubleday and Company, Inc., 1906), pp. 347–362.

7. *Ibid.*, p. 348.

8. Harold Baron, et al., "Black Powerlessness in Chicago," *Transaction* (November, 1968), p. 27.

9. William Lloyd Warner, "American Class and Caste," *American Journal of Sociology*, 42 (September, 1936), pp. 234-237.

10. Walter White, *A Man Called White* (New York: Arno Press and *The New York Times*, 1969), pp. 29–33.

11. *Ibid.*, pp. 163–165.

12. Ralph Ginzburg, *100 Years of Lynching* (New York: Lancer, 1962), p. 94.

13. *Ibid.*, pp. 229–230.

14. *Ibid.*, pp. 238–239.

15. White, *op. cit.*, p. 361.

16. Ginzburg, *op. cit.*, pp. 61, 71, 98.

17. Ray Stannard Baker, *Following the Color Line: American Negro Citizenship in the Progressive Era* (New York: Harper and Row, 1964), p. 8.

18. Baker, *op. cit.*, p. 6.

19. Arthur Waskow, *From Race Riot to Sit-In: 1919 and the 1960's* (Garden City, New York: Doubleday and Co., 1967), p. 10.

20. Charles Flint Kellogg, NAACP: *A History of the National Association for the Advancement of Colored People* (Baltimore: Johns Hopkins Press, 1967), pp. 183–184.

21. *Ibid.*, p. 195.

22. *Ibid.*, pp. 198–199.

23. White, *op. cit.*, pp. 144–148.

24. *Ibid.*, pp. 148–152.

25. *Rustin, op. cit.*, pp. 347–348.

26. Andrew Kopkind, "Soul Power," *New York Review of Books*, 9, No. 3 (1967), p. 6.

27. Martin Mayer, *The Teachers Strike, New York 1968* (New York: Harper and Row, 1969), p. 15.

28. Mayer, *op. cit.*, p. 13.

29. David Rogers, *110 Livingston Street* (New York: Random House, 1968).

30. Frances Fox Piven, "Militant Civil Servants in New York City," *Transaction*, 7, No. 4 (November, 1969), p. 27.

31. Mayer, *op. cit.*, pp. 39–67.

32. Piven, *op. cit.*, p. 24.

33. *Ibid.*, p. 25.

34. *Ibid.*, p. 28.

35. *New York Times*, July 4, 1973, p. 1.

36. "Resolution of the Convention of Free Colored People," in *Black Power: The Radical Response to White America* (Thomas Wagstaff, ed., Beverly Hills: Glencoe Press, 1969), p. 45.

37. Martin Delaney, "I Have No Hope in This Country," in Wagstaff, *ibid.*, pp. 43–44.

38. *Chronicles of Black Protest*, Bradford Chambers, ed. (New York and Toronto: New American Library, 1968), p. 168.

39. Ernest Dunbar, "The Making of a Militant," *Saturday Review Society*, 55, No. 51, 1973, p. 29.

40. Robert S. Browne, "A Formal Partitioning of the United States into Separate and Independent Nations," in *Black Protest Thought in the Twentieth Century* (August Meier, Elliott Rudwick, and Francis L. Broderick, eds., 2nd ed.; Indianapolis and New York: The Bobbs-Merrill Company, Inc., 1971), pp. 522–523.

41. Dunbar, *op. cit.*, p. 29.

42. Brown, *op. cit.*, p. 525.

43. Claude McKay, "Soviet Russia and the Negro," in Wagstaff, *op. cit.*, p. 99.

44. A. Philip Randolph and Chandler Owen, "A Socialist Critique in *The Messenger*," in Meier, Rudwick, and Broderick, *op. cit.*, pp. 81–82.

45. Philip S. Foner, *The Black Panthers Speak* (Philadelphia/New York: J. B. Lippincott, 1970) p. 220.

2

BLACK PANTHERS AND BLACK MUSLIMS

The Muslims and the Panthers both represent reactions to American racism. Both separatism and radicalism gripped the passions of a number of young blacks in the postriot period. The Muslims have been the oldest, best organized, most powerful, and most enduring separatist organization. The Panthers were unique among radical organizations for the extent to which they established a constituency in the ghetto.

Despite their vastly different, even conflicting ideologies, both appeal to young, ghetto, street-corner blacks. The most prominent organizations in the 1960-65 civil rights movement had the sympathy, but not the active participation, of street-corner blacks. The blacks who took part in sit-ins and who picketed the banks and supermarkets in protest against discriminatory hiring practices were, for the most part, middle class in background or aspiration. The Panthers and Muslims developed a style and ideology which was resonant with the style and outlook of a very different segment of the black population, and in the postriot period they began to enjoy the kind of active participation among street-corner blacks that the classic civil rights movement had not had.

This chapter, based in part on interviews and field work, focuses on the structure and ideology of the Muslims and Panthers and on the processes by which their members developed a commitment to them.

THE BLACK PANTHERS

"We Want Freedom, We Want Power to Determine the Destiny of Our Black Community."[1]

In the summer of 1966, the term "black power" was first heard in the land. It came to public attention when used by Stokely Carmichael in the "march against fear," which civil rights leaders took up after James Meredith, the originator of the march, had been shot and wounded on a Mississippi road. Like many terms bandied about in political discourse—"communism," "capitalism," "freedom"—it has no clear meaning, or, more accurately, it means whatever its user intends it to mean. There is no single black-power movement; rather, a number of groups use a rhetoric heavily laden with calls for "black power."

The Panthers as a self-declared radical party achieved an unprecedented degree of popularity among blacks. Twenty-five percent of a nationwide poll of blacks taken in 1970 by the Louis Harris organization indicated that they admired the Panthers "a great deal." Polls taken in New York, San Francisco, Detroit, Baltimore, and Birmingham, Alabama, in 1970 revealed widespread support, as did an investigative report on black opinion in San Francisco, New York, Detroit, Cleveland, and Chicago undertaken for the *Wall Street Journal*.[2] As the historian Philip Foner has observed, "Never before in the history of black Americans has an admittedly revolutionary party won such support in the leading black communities of this country."[3]

The Black Panther Party for Self-Defense was organized in the fall of 1966. It began as a group whose primary purpose was to follow the police around in the ghetto on the lookout for any police mistreatment of blacks. It differed from a similar group in Los Angeles called the Community Alert Patrol in that its members carried and openly displayed weapons, a practice not illegal at that time.

The Panthers first came to public attention on February 1, 1967, when 20 of them, armed with pistols and shotguns, marched through San Francisco's International Airport to escort the wife of the late Malcolm X to a speaking engagement, giving as their reason for the armed escort that the same forces which had assassinated Malcolm X might make an attempt on the life of his widow. "It was not until May, 1967, however, when the California legislature debated a bill calling for a prohibition against the carrying of weapons, that the Panthers achieved national prominence by appearing within the state capital armed to the teeth."[4]

The purpose of this half of the chapter is to attempt an explanation for their popularity and for their downfall.

Politics as Theater and the "Rap" as Politics

To understand the success of the Panthers among certain sectors of the ghetto population, one must analyze the life-style of young black males within that population. The analysis offered here is in terms of the sociological theory on stigma and the presentation of self.

Historically, young ghetto males have had the problem of "managing" social stigma. The norms of society devalue their status, and negative stereotypes about them are widely held. They have what might be referred to as a *status debit*. There is a tendency on the part of others to assume automatically that they are less worthy of respect or deference than other persons.[5]

The process of stigma poses several questions. What are the attributes of the negative stereotype of those who are stigmatized? What functions does the process serve for "normals"? How does stigma manifest itself institutionally; e.g., are the stigmatized denied access to "public" accommodations, are they restricted to certain jobs, etc.? How do the stigmatized handle being stigmatized?

The last question is the focus of this discussion.

Much of the quality of ghetto "street style" can be understood as a response by young black males to a situation in which others, including people in the ghetto, automatically devalue their status. They experience antipathetic distinctions that are made systematically rather than randomly. That is, other people encounter the occasional rude clerk or belligerent taxi driver, but this hostility is a chance element of their experience rather than an aspect of the reaction to them of most other people.

The functions of street style can be understood in this context. Street style is a certain way of presenting self in everyday life. Its object is to establish *status credit*, the right to be taken seriously, to be accorded deference. Street style is virtually a form of theater in which the actor assumes that his audience is hostile. He attempts by a certain element of personal style to establish a claim to their respect and possibly even admiration.

The components of street style involve a good "rap," a distinctive and stylish mode of dress, and any of several postures in relation to others.

Rapping is "distinctively a fluent and lively way of talking, always characterized by a high degree of personal style."[6] That the function of rapping is theatrical is suggested by Kochman's research indicating that one "raps *to* rather than *with* a person. Rapping is to be regarded more as a performance than verbal exchange . . . . the function of rapping . . . . is *expressive* . . . . the speaker raps to project his personality on to the scene or to evoke a generally favorable response."[7] It comes into play "at the beginning of a relationship to create a favorable impression and to be persuasive at the same time."[8] The sociologist John Horton, also a student of black street culture, defined the rap as follows:

> *Although sometimes used synonymously with street conversation, "rap" is really a special way of talking—repartee. Street repartee at its best is a lively way of "running it down," of "jiving" (attempting to put someone on), of trying "to blow another person's mind," forcing him to "lose his cool," to give in or give up something.*[9]

Those street blacks accomplished at rapping use language in a colorful and imaginative manner. They are facile at playing the "dozens" (verbal dueling involving the exchange of imaginative insults) and at presenting an extravagant collection of seriocomic boasts and compliments when confronting women.

Like rapping, the mode of dress is an element of theater among street blacks. Dress styles are colorful and individualistic, again reflecting the process whereby a *persona* is established and a status debit overcome.

Horton, in his study of black street-corner men, observed, "Where there is little property, status . . . is determined by qualities of mind and brawn." He asked his street-corner men, "How does a dude make a rep on the set?" More than half his sample mentioned "style." Style had many dimensions. It meant to "carry one's self well, dress well, to show class." It meant showing respect for others. "Yet one must show respect in such a way that he is able to look tough and inviolate, fearless, secure, 'cool'."[10]

The presentation of self on the part of young street-corner blacks can be described in terms of certain commonly found types. There is a social type found on the street referred to by some as a "bad motherfucker." In this context, the word "bad" really means "exemplary," "extraordinary." The term denotes an individual with a good rap and a distinctive and arresting mode of dress, who relates to others in a manner that is tough but not threatening. The bad motherfucker commands respect and admiration and may be differentiated from the individual referred to by some as a "crazy nigger." With the crazy nigger, toughness shades over into belligerence. Whereas the bad motherfucker is good to be around for his style, sharpness, toughness, and cool, the crazy nigger is dangerous to be near because of his penchant for cruelty and random violence. As we shall see, the Panthers were bad motherfuckers who were mistaken by a white public unfamiliar with the nuances of ghetto social types for crazy niggers.

In the lexicon of the ghetto, the Panthers were "all bad"; that is, they had dash, verve, and style. They had a good rap and a distinctive presentation of self. Eldridge Cleaver captured this appeal in his description of how he reacted when he first saw the Panthers:

> *The most beautiful sight I had ever seen. Four Black men wearing black berets, powder-blue shirts, black leather jackets, black trousers, shiny black shoes—and each with a gun! In front was Huey P. Newton. Beside him was Bobby Seale. A few steps behind him was Bobby Hutton. Where was my mind at? Blown.*[11]

A number of observers commented on the Panther appeal to young black males, all touching on elements of style. Julian Bond, the black legislator, observed.

What the Panthers do more than anything else is they set a stand-ard, that young black people particularly want to measure up to . . . . It's a standard of aggressiveness, of militance, of just force-fulness, the sort of standard we haven't had in the past. Our idols have been Dr. King, who, for all of his beauty as a man, was not an aggressive man, but the Panthers, and I think Malcolm X, have set this new kind of standard that a great many people want to adhere to.[12]

Evord Connor, interviewed in a survey of black opinion, said of the Panthers that "they appeal to young kids and create a sense of black awareness."[13]

The Panthers did not create a new style; they were examples of an already existing street style. Panther style and ghetto style were similar partly because the Panthers were organized by blacks rather than being an offshoot or creation of white radical groups. The historian Philip Foner pointed this out:

. . . the Black Panthers, while by no means the first blacks in the United States to oppose the capitalist system and espouse the cause of Socialism, were the first to do so as a separate organization. Heretofore, blacks who favored a Socialist solution for the evils of capitalist society—and there have been many since the end of the Civil War—did so either through the Socialist Party, the Socialist Labor Party, or the Communist Party. Here they became members of parties made up mainly of whites. The Black Panthers, though favoring Socialism and coalition with other oppressed groups, retain their separate identity as a revolutionary movement.[14]

The black origins of the party reflect the fact that it was organized when the old integrationist emphasis was on the wane. Stokely Carmichael and others in the Student Non-Violent Coordinating Com-mittee had charged that "white liberals" dominated civil rights organi-zations and constrained blacks in them from pursuing certain courses of action. The *geist* in the period in which the party was organized was very much against subordinate black participation in white organizations or white participation in black organizations.

The black organizers of the party were much closer to the street than previous prominent black radicals. James W. Ford, Communist Party candidate for Vice-President in 1932, 1936, and 1940, had come to the party via the labor movement. Benjamin Davis, a Harvard-trained lawyer, moved into the party as an adult. A. Philip Randolph, Chandler Owen, and the black socialists who published *The Messenger* were middle-class intellectuals. Even such prominent civil rights leaders as Walter White, Roy Wilkins, Martin Luther King, and James Farmer either have never participated in black street culture or were far removed from its image and circumstances by the time they became active in organized protest.

By contrast, Bobby Seale, Panther Chairman, was a $650-a-month worker in an antipoverty program during the period when the party was planned and had been a musician, a carpenter, a journeyman sheet-metal worker, and a mechanical draftsman, as well as a student at Merritt Junior College in Oakland. Newton and Seale had gone door to door in the black ghetto in Oakland, querying residents on what they needed and wanted, and the responses—decent housing, an end to police harassment, exemption of blacks from military service, and other felt needs— formed the basis of the ten-point program that the Panthers were to promulgate. Huey Newton, Minister of Defense, was at Merritt Junior College, and Eldridge Cleaver, Minister of Information, who joined the party shortly after its formation, had served nine years in prison.

The Radical Connection

Bobby Seale and Huey Newton were deeply influenced by what they had read of Malcolm X. ". . . Newton viewed himself as Malcolm's heir and the Black Panther Party as the successor to his Organization of Afro-American Unity."[15] They were aware that Malcolm had broken with Black Muslim doctrine and repudiated hatred of all whites, calling instead for coalitions with whites "whenever it would be useful for black people to do so—provided the power to decide policy and action alternatives lay in black hands."

Seale and Newton were also familiar with some of the writings of revolutionaries such as Lenin, Mao Tse-Tung, Marx, and Engels.

Thus, as many black political organizations in 1966 and 1967 began to repudiate whites and to eschew collaboration or coalitions with whites, the Panthers were the only major black organization to the left of the old-line integrationist-minded civil rights organizations that was not inhospitable to whites.

It was inevitable, then, that white radicals and black Panthers would come into association and that their fates would become entangled.

Many young white radicals had first become involved in politics in the civil rights movement in the South and had been radicalized by the experience. They had come to believe that more than civil rights bills were needed in order to do away with poverty and exploitation, and they saw the nation's opposition to left, revolutionary regimes abroad (e.g., Cuba) as an extension of opposition to progressive change at home. After all, if revolutionary, third world countries succeeded in establishing a measure of justice and economic security for their people, might it not become impossible to rationalize and perpetuate injustice and deprivation at home? Many young radicals had come to believe that revolutionary change was both necessary and possible in the United States.

Involvement with blacks was important in two ways for many white radicals. First, a black connection helped legitimatize their identity as radicals. Most young white radicals of that period were middle or upper-middle class in background (see Chapter 8 for further discussion of this point) and it was, perhaps, difficult for them to be wholly confident of their own commitment to radical change, wholly confident that they were not playing charades, wearing workshirts and dungarees, and calling themselves radical. An association with black militants helped reinforce a conviction that their radicalism was real, that it consisted of actions as well as words. After all, if they were taken seriously by people whose radical credentials could not be challenged, then they could take themselves seriously as radicals.

Second, blacks were considered fundamental to any kind of mass-based political movement in the United States. Radical white organizations that did not have access to blacks were shut off from the most militant sector of the working class.

It was the second factor which brought the Panthers into a coalition with the Peace and Freedom Party. The PFP was a coalition of white radicals and left liberals seeking in California to offer a third party's electoral alternatives. Faced with being unable to obtain enough signatures to place candidates on the ballot, the PFP (over the objections of its liberals) approached the Panthers seeking access to the black community. "The basis of the coalition with the PFP was that the Panthers would set the PFP line on all issues related to the black community."[16] PFP petitions were circulated in the black community, and PFP candidates, including Panthers running on the PFP line, appeared on the ballot. The radical connection gave the Panthers access to funds for organizing and for various programs, and eventually provided them with a broader constituency in the campaigns to free Huey Newton and Bobby Seale after these two leaders had been jailed. The political scientist, Ross Baker, observed, "The importance of the Panthers to the radical community at this point cannot be overstated. For virtually every white radical group they possessed a moral superiority, an almost incandescent purity of motive and idiom."[17]

Reservations were expressed by some white radicals, by progressive labor, charging that Panther concentration on blacks was at variance with notions of working class solidarity, and by some Panthers, contending that the radical connection would draw the Party away from its base in the black community.

The association continued, however, until mounting troubles with the authorities began to overwhelm both.

The fall of the Panthers came not from their involvement with radical white groups, but primarily from what they were perceived to be by the white public. Although the Panthers called for solidarity among the oppressed, their activities were aimed mainly at developing a ghetto constituency. The success of the Panthers among street-corner blacks had an adverse effect among whites. Again, an analogy with the theater may help to clarify the process.

Black Theater: White Audience

Every social movement plays to a certain audience. The classical civil rights movement played to a national white audience. Its objective was to arouse the sympathy and support of that audience by projecting an image of blacks which ran counter to negative stereotypes, an image of blacks as essentially average Americans, except for darker skin, and indeed many of the black activists and much of the black leadership were middle class. The classic movement did succeed in engaging white support, partly by eroding stereotypes, but at the cost of a style at variance with that found among many ghetto blacks. The image the Panthers sought to project was intended to appeal to ghetto blacks, not to counter negative stereotypes held by whites. They succeeded, partly by virtue of stylistic affinity, in engaging a certain ghetto constituency, but at the price of arousing white fear and hostility.

In a sense, whites genuinely could not "see" the Panthers. Lack of familiarity with ghetto social types did not allow them to understand who the Panthers were or what they were about. Few whites have experienced the ghetto or interacted with its residents. Those few who have had direct experience there are in roles that do not encourage insight into the nature of the social system. They come as agents of various kinds of bureaucracies—as policemen, social workers, or teachers. If most whites free-associate on the term "black ghetto," a variety of images suggesting danger and degradation probably spring to mind. The Panthers were obviously not civil rights blacks of the Martin Luther King, Roy Wilkins type with whom whites could identify, nor were they long-suffering victims of the freedom-rider type, with whom whites could sympathize. They were sharply though exotically dressed blacks who carried guns; and, lacking the right category, whites placed them in the only category they had, one which happened also to exist in the ghetto but which was inaccurate. They were placed in the category of "crazy niggers."

The Condemnation and Persecution of the Panthers

Condemnation: "To pass an adverse judgment on; disapprove of strongly; censure; to give a judicial decision against; inflict penalty upon; doom."

The police were the Panthers' immediate antagonists, and in the drama these two groups played out, the police were perceived by most whites as heroes, as defenders of the community against a savage horde. Whereas police chief Eugene "Bull" Connor was viewed as a sadistic Neanderthal for turning water hoses and dogs on black civil rights marchers in the early 1960's, Edward V. Hanrahan was lauded by whites a decade later after directing a raid by Chicago police on an apartment in which two Panthers were killed and four wounded under circumstances strongly suggesting that the police met little or no resistance.

Ideologically, the Panthers were radical, but other radical groups were not subjected to attack, and, in any event, there is little evidence that Panther ideology was even remotely understood by the public. They were repeatedly called racist although they repudiated black separatism and called for a coalition of the oppressed and of those opposed to capitalism. They identified capitalism as "the problem" rather than whites.

> *One aspect of American society consists of the oppressor-oppressed relationships. As we live in a capitalist environment the masses of the public are exploited at the hands of a few individuals that control and hold all of this nation's wealth. More people are waking up to the facts of capitalism's true nature, and as these people do so, they see that capitalism is the oppressor. Once this is realized these aware segments of our communities then move to further the destruction of this capitalist state. That puts them in direct opposition to the government, which perpetrates and tries to spread capitalism and imperialism throughout the world.[18]*

Panther Connie Matthews, in a speech given at a California State University at San Jose, said:

> *We understood there are Black people who are pigs and we understood that there are White people who are pigs. What we are trying to say is that we want a United Front of all ethnic oppressed groups, regardless of race, color, creed or what have you, because the ultimate aim is to overthrow this establishment.[19]*

Their analysis of American society led them to repudiate black racism explicitly. In their view, whites as well as blacks were victimized by a rapacious and cynical capitalist ruling class. Their willingness to enter into coalitions with white radicals brought them into conflict with black separatists and led to bitter exchanges.

Panther Linda Harrison commented on cultural nationalism, a variant of black separatism:

> Cultural nationalism manifests itself in many ways but all of these manifestations are essentially grounded in one fact: a universal denial and ignoring of the present political, social and economic realities and a concentration on the past as a frame of reference. . . . Those who believe in the "I'm Black and Proud" theory— believe that there is dignity inherent in wearing naturals; that a buba makes a slave a man; and that a common language, Swahili, makes all of us brothers. These people usually want a culture rooted in African culture; a culture which ignores the colonization and brutalization that were part and parcel, for example, of the formation and emergence of the Swahili language. In other words, cultural nationalism ignores the political and concrete, and concentrates on a myth and fantasy.[20]

For the most part, Panther activities were unexceptional. Other groups had engaged in the same community activities without drawing the ire of the powerful. The programs developed by the Panthers were intended to extend to the black community services not being adequately provided by public agencies. Thus, they developed a breakfast program, medical assistance programs, and "liberation" schools. These programs were intended, of course, to inspire community support for the Panthers, but they also touched areas of genuine need. For example, the free breakfast program was intended to demonstrate Panther service to the community, but there were in fact black children who needed breakfast. Eldridge Cleaver commented on the larger, political objectives of the breakfast program:

> Breakfast for Children pulls people out of the system and organizes them into an alternative. Black children who go to school hungry each morning have been organized into their poverty, and the Panther program liberates them, frees them from that aspect of their poverty. This is liberation in practice. . . . If we can understand Breakfast for Children, can we not also understand Lunch for Children, and Dinner for Children, and Clothing for Children, and Education for Children, and Medical Care for Children. And if we can understand that, why can't we understand not only a

People's Park, but People's Housing and People's Transportation, and People's Industry and People's Banks? And why can't we understand a People's Government?[21]

Social science research has revealed that many slum children do come to school without having had breakfast and that this fact may affect their academic performance. Without evidencing an awareness of social science literature on the matter, the Panthers nevertheless express a similar view.

It is a beautiful sight to see our children eat in the morning after remembering the times when our stomachs were not full, and even the teachers in the schools say that there is a great improvement in the academic skills of the children that do get the breakfast. At one time there were children that passed out in class from hunger, or had to be sent home for something to eat. But our children shall be fed, and the Black Panther Party will not let the malady of hunger keep our children down any longer.[22]

Persecution: "To afflict or harass constantly so as to injure or distress; oppress cruelly, especially for reasons of religion, politics, or race; to trouble or annoy constantly."

The persecution of the Panthers was a fairly straightforward matter. On October 28, 1967, Huey Newton was arrested after a shooting incident in Oakland and charged with kidnapping and killing a policeman. Newton was acquitted of the kidnapping charge but found guilty of "voluntary manslaughter" and sentenced to 2 to 15 years. On January 16, 1968, police raided the home of Eldridge Cleaver, and on September 17 Cleaver's parole was revoked and he was ordered to return to prison. In November, Cleaver fled abroad. Judge Julius Hoffman sentenced Bobby Seale to 48 months in jail, three months on each of 16 charges, this device allowing an evasion of the Supreme Court decision that any person imprisoned for more than six months is entitled to a jury trial. Seale was later charged with complicity in a murder committed in Connecticut and put on trial. In New York City, a number of Panthers were arrested and held in jail on very high bail for over a year and finally put on trial for a variety of offenses. On December 6, 1969, Panthers Fred Hampton and Mark Clark were killed and four other Panthers injured in a Chicago police raid. Physical evidence suggested little or no Panther resistance.

Newton's conviction was reversed on appeal after he had spent two years in prison. Seale eventually regained his freedom, as did many other Panthers after spending months or even years in jail on charges found not to have substance. The effect of the legal onslaught, however, was to erode the organization's capacity for action.

Rising From the Ashes

Early in May, 1973, Bobby Seale, chairman of the Black Panther Party, came in second in a crowded field of candidates for the office of mayor of Oakland and entered a runoff with the incumbent, John Reading. Two weeks later, Seale lost the runoff but pronounced the effort a success because it had demonstrated that the Panthers were able to organize the black community and to establish themselves as important spokesmen for that community.

Seale's impressive electoral performance also demonstrated that the Panthers had risen from the ashes.

Persecution of the organization had had two important consequences. First, it nearly led to its extinction. Second, it precipitated a schism between those who wanted the organization to hold to its radical dogmas and go underground and those who wanted it to reemphasize the reformist aspects of its program and deemphasize revolutionary rhetoric.

The Party's program has always combined revolutionary calls for solidarity of the oppressed with specific proposals that are essentially reformist in character. In response to the repression, Huey Newton sought to orient the party towards community service while Eldridge Cleaver called for fidelity to the rhetoric and goals of revolution.

> *The Cleaverites argued that the Newtonites, in order to maintain the cohesion of the party in this difficult period, were forcing it to back down from its position as the revolutionary vanguard. They argued that rather than betray those principles of armed revolution that Cleaver saw as the basis of the party, it was preferable to take the Panthers underground. The Newtonites responded that to persist in an overtly revolutionary path was to expose the party to annihilation, and to go underground was to mean severance of the party from its community base.*[23]

The different positions of Newton and Cleaver reflected differences both of background and of existential circumstance. While both had roots in the black community, Cleaver had had a great deal more involvement with white radicals. Cleaver, while in prison, had been "discovered" by white radicals and his writings were first published by them. On release from prison, he became a journalist for the muckraking periodical *Ramparts,* and moved in white left circles. Newton had not had this experience. More important, while Newton has been released from prison and the charges against him have been dropped, Cleaver is in exile and faces prison if he returns to the United States. Newton therefore has a stake in attempting to reorient the party along lines which will allow it to be effective but less threatening, while Cleaver has little to lose in calling for revolution.

The schism led to a purge of Cleaver's followers with a splinter group of Cleaverites surviving in New York City. In late 1971, they became the Black Liberation Army and launched a series of attacks against the police.[24] The Newton-Seale group, on the other hand, moved toward an emphasis on community service that included lunch programs, medical programs, free groceries, and small-scale industries. Establishing links with the black churches and entering electoral politics, they announced that they were engaging in a strategy of survival while waiting for the revolution.

Conclusions

The persecution of the Panthers suggests that illusion is more powerful than reality. Their actions focused, for the most part, on genuine ghetto needs for social services; their ideology made use analytically of class as well as race. Neither of these characteristics placed them outside the boundaries of radical political groups in the United States. They were persecuted for what they appeared to be rather than for what they were. They appeared to be "crazy niggers," largely because the "bad motherfucker" social type was unknown to naive viewers.

The political scientist Ross Baker writes:

> It is well to recall that the great ethnic urban political machines of the past began in much the same fashion as have the transformed Panthers. How different, after all, are the Panther shopping bags of free food from the bags of coal and the Thanksgiving turkeys that served to build the urban machines of the Irish and Italians. The defeat of Bobby Seale for mayor of Oakland constitutes a minor temporary setback.[25]

The Panthers managed to develop certain loyalties among blacks who are not ordinarily participants in the electoral process. It remains to be seen whether they can convert the enthusiasm and support of that group into long-term commitment to mainstream electoral politics. If they can, the ultimate irony in the Panther drama will be that persecution condoned by persons fearful of Panther power will have led the Panthers to bring their vast constituency of motherfuckers into electoral politics.

THE BLACK MUSLIMS

*"You were black enough to get in here. You had the courage to stay.
Now be man enough to follow the honorable Elijah Muhammad.
You have tried the devil's way. Now try the ways of the Messenger."*
Minister William X, in a
West Coast Black Muslim Mosque

The Lost-Found Nation of Islam in the Wilderness of North
America, commonly known as the Black Muslims, claims a small but
devoted membership among blacks in the cities. They are the most
enduring of black separatist groups, having been founded in the early
1930's. The tensions of the postriot era have given them a new prominence. The way of the "Messenger" is rigorous for those who follow it.
The man or woman who becomes a Muslim accepts not only an ideology but an all-encompassing code that amounts to a way of life.

A good Muslim does a full day's work on an empty stomach. When
he has his one meal of the day in the evening, he cannot eat pork, nor
can he have a drink before or a cigarette after; strict dietary rules are
standard procedure, and liquor and smoking are forbidden under any
circumstances. His recreation is likely to consist of reading the Koran,
participating in a demanding round of temple-centered activities, running public meetings, or aggressively proselytizing on the streets by
selling the Muslim newspaper, *Muhammad Speaks.*

Despite allegations of Muslim violence (adverse publicity from the
slaying of Malcolm X supports the erroneous notion that Muslims
preach violence), the member's life is basically ascetic. Why, then, in a
nonascetic, hedonistically oriented society, do people become Muslims?
What is the life of a Muslim like?

What perspective on life makes membership in such an organization attractive? Under what conditions does the potential recruit develop those perspectives? How does he happen to come to the door of
the temple for his first meeting? The Black Muslims are a deviant organization even within the black community; the parents or friends of
many members strongly objected to their joining. How, then, does the
recruit handle pressures that might erode his allegiance to the organization and its beliefs?

When the author conducted in-depth interviews with 19 West
Coast recruits, two factors emerged as having the greatest appeal for
Muslim recruits—black nationalism and an emphasis on self-help. Some
recruits were attracted primarily by the first, and some by the second.
The 14 interviewees who joined the organization for its aggressive black
nationalism will be called "Muslim militants." The remaining five, who

were attracted more by its emphasis on hard work and rigid personal morality, may be aptly termed "Protestant-ethic Muslims."

Of the 14 Muslim militants, some came from the South, some from border states, and some from the North. All lived in California at the time of the interview; some migrated to the state as adults, others were brought out by their families as children. They varied in age from 24 to 46, and in education from a few years of grade school to four years of college. Regardless of these substantial differences in background, there were certain broad similarities among them.

At some point, each one had had experiences that led away from the institutional ties and commitments that lend stability to most people's lives. Nine had been engaged in semilegal or criminal activities. Two had been in the military, not as a career but as a way of postponing the decision of what to do for a living. None had a stable marital history. All of them were acutely aware of being outsiders by the standards of the larger society—and all had come to focus on race bias as the factor which denied them more conventional alternatives.

Leroy X came to California in his late teens, just before World War II:

> *I grew up in Kansas City, Missouri, and Missouri was a segregated state. Negroes in Kansas City were always restricted to the menial jobs. I came out here in 1940 and tried to get a job as a waiter. I was a trained waiter, but they weren't hiring any Negroes as waiters in any of the downtown hotels or restaurants. The best I could do was busboy, and they fired me from that when they found out I wasn't Filipino.*

Leroy X was drafted and, after a short but stormy career, was given a discharge as psychologically unfit.

> *I tried to get a job, but I couldn't so I started stealing. There was nothing else to do—I couldn't live on air. The peckerwoods didn't seem to give a damn whether I lived or died. They wouldn't hire me and didn't seem to worry how I was going to stay alive. I started stealing.*
> *I could get you anything you wanted—a car, drugs, women, jewelry. Crime is a business like any other. I started off stealing myself. I wound up filling orders and getting rid of stuff. I did that for fifteen years. In between I did a little time. I did time for things I never thought of doing and went free for things I really did.*
> *In my business you had no friends, only associates, and not very close ones at that . . . . I had plenty of money. I could get anything I wanted without working for it. It wasn't enough, though.*

Bernard X grew up in New York City:

As a kid . . . you always have dreams—fantasies—of yourself doing something later—being a big name singer or something that makes you outstanding. But you never draw the connection between where you are and how you're going to get there. I had to—I can't say exactly when, 13, 14, 15, 16. I saw I was nowhere and had no way of getting anywhere.

Race feeling is always with you. You always know about the Man but I don't think it is real, really real, until you have to deal with it in terms of what you are going to do with your own life. That's when you feel it. If you just disliked him before—you begin to hate him when you see him blocking you in your life. I think then a sense of inevitability hits you and you see you're not going to make it out—up—away—anywhere—and you see the Man's part in the whole thing, that's when you begin to think thoughts about him.

Frederick 2X became involved fairly early in a criminal subculture. His father obtained a "poor man's divorce" by deserting the family. His mother had children by other men. Only a tenuous sense of belonging to a family existed. He was picked up by the police for various offenses several times before reaching his teens. The police patrolling his neighborhood eventually restricted him to a two-block area. There was, of course, no legal basis for this restriction, but he was manhandled if seen outside that area by any policeman who knew him. He graduated in his late teens from "pot" to "shooting shit" and eventually spent time in Lexington.

William 2X, formerly a shoeshine boy, related the development of his perspective this way:

You know how they always talk about us running after white women. There have always been a lot of [white] servicemen in this town—half of them would get around to asking me to get a woman for them. Some of them right out, some of them backing into it, laughing and joking and letting me know how much they were my friend, building up to asking me where they could find some women. After a while I began to get them for them . . . . I ran women—both black and white . . . . What I hated was they wanted me to do something for them [find women] and hated me for doing it. They figure "any nigger must know where to find it . . . ."

Amos X grew up in an all black town in Oklahoma and attended a black college. As a result, he had almost no contact with whites during his formative years.

One of my aunts lived in Tulsa. I went to see her once when I was in college. I walked up to the front door of the house where she worked. She really got excited and told me if I came to see her anymore to come around to the back. But that didn't mean much to me at the time. It is only in looking back on it that all these things begin to add up.

After graduating from college, Amos joined the Marines. There he began to "see how they [the whites] really felt" about him; by the end of his tour, he had concluded that "the white man is the greatest liar, the greatest cheat, the greatest hypocrite on earth." Alienated and disillusioned, he turned to professional gambling. Then, in an attempt at a more conventional way of life, he married and took a job teaching school.

I taught English. Now I'm no expert in the slave masters' language, but I knew the way those kids talked after being in school eight and nine years was ridiculous. They said things like "mens" for "men." I drilled them and pretty soon some of them at least in class began to sound like they had been inside a school. Now the principal taught a senior class in English and his kids talked as bad as mine. When I began to straighten out his kids also, he felt I was criticizing him . . . . That little black man was afraid of the [white] superintendent and all those teachers were afraid. They had a little more than other so-called Negroes and didn't give a damn about those black children they were teaching. Those were the wages of honesty. It's one thing to do an honest job and another thing to be able to . . . .

With the collapse of his career as a public school teacher and the break-up of his marriage, Amos went to California, where he was introduced to the Muslim movement.

I first heard about them [the Muslims] in 1961. There was a debate here between a Muslim and a Christian minister. The Muslims said all the things about Christianity which I had been thinking but which I had never heard anyone say before. He tore the minister up.

Finding an organization that aggressively rejected the white man and the white man's religion, Amos found his own point of view crystallized. He joined without hesitation.

Norman Maghid first heard of the Muslims while he was in prison:

I ran into one of the Brothers selling the paper about two weeks after I got out and asked him about the meetings. Whether a guy could just go and walk in. He told me about the meetings so I made it around on a Wednesday evening. I wasn't even bugged when they searched me. When they asked me about taking out my letter (joining the organization), I took one out. They seemed to know what they were talking about. I never believed in non-violence and love my enemies, especially when my enemies don't love me.

Muhammad Soule Kabah, born into a family of dept-ridden Texas sharecroppers, was recruited into the Nation of Islam after moving to California:

I read a series of articles in the Los Angeles Herald Dispatch, an exchange between Minister Henry and a Christian minister. It confirmed what my grandfather had told me about my African heritage, that I had nothing to be ashamed of, that there were six thousand books on mathematics in the Library of the University of Timbucktoo while Europeans were still wearing skins. Also my father had taught me never to kow-tow to whites. My own father had fallen away. My parents didn't want me to join the Nation. They said they taught hate. That's funny, isn't it? The white man can blow up a church and kill four children and the black man worries that an organization which tells you not to just take it is teaching hate.

The Protestant-ethic Muslims all came from backgrounds with a strong tradition of Negro self-help. In two cases, the recruit's parents had been followers of Marcus Garvey; another recruit explicitly endorsed the beliefs of Booker T. Washington; and the remaining two, coming from upwardly mobile families, were firm in the belief that Negroes could achieve higher status if they were willing to work for it.

When asked what had appealed to him about the Muslims, Norman X replied:

They thought that black people should do something for themselves. I was running this small place [a photography shop] and trying to get by. I've stuck with this place even when it was paying me barely enough to eat. Things always improve and I don't have to go to the white man for anything."

Ernestine X stressed similar reasons for joining the Muslims:

You learned to stand up straight and do something for yourself. You learn to be a lady at all times—to keep your house clean—to teach your children good manners. There is not a girl in the M-G-T who does not know how to cook and sew. The children are very respect-

*ful; they speak only when they are spoken to. There is no such thing
as letting your children talk back to you the way some people believe. The one thing they feel is the Negro's downfall is men and
sex for the women, and women and sex for the men, and they
frown on sex completely unless you are married.*

Despite their middle-class attitudes in many areas, Protestant-ethic
Muslims denounced moderate, traditional civil rights organizations, such
as the N.A.A.C.P., just as vigorously as the militant Muslims did. Norman X said that he had once belonged to the N.A.A.C.P. but had
dropped out: "They spent most of their time planning the annual
brotherhood dinner. Besides, it was mostly whites—and the colored
doctors and lawyers who wanted to be white. As far as most blacks were
concerned, they might as well not have existed."

Lindsey X, who had owned and run his own upholstery shop for
more than 30 years, viewed the conventional black bourgeoisie with
equal resentment: "I never belonged to the N.A.A.C.P. What they
wanted never seemed real to me. I think blacks should create jobs for
themselves rather than going begging for them. That's why I never
supported C.O.R.E."

In this respect Norman and Lindsey were in full accord with the
more militant Amos X, who asserted: "They [the N.A.A.C.P. and
C.O.R.E.] help just one class of people . . . . Let something happen to
a doctor and they are right there; but if something happens to Old Mose
on the corner, you can't find them."

The interviews made it clear that most of the Protestant-ethic
muslims had joined the Nation because, at some point, they began to
feel the need of organizational support for their personal systems of
value. For Norman and Lindsey, it was an attempt to stop what they
considered their own backsliding after coming to California. Both
mentioned drinking to excess and indulging in what they regarded as a
profligate way of life. Guilt feelings apparently led them to seek Muslim
support in returning to more enterprising habits.

The Nation of Islam is a deviant organization. As such, it is subject
to public scorn and ridicule. Thus it faces the problem of consolidating
the recruit's allegiance in an environment where substantial pressures
operate to erode this allegiance. How does it deal with this problem?

To begin with, the ritual of joining the organization itself stresses
commitment without questions. At the end of the general address at a
temple meeting, the minister asks those nonmembers present who are
"interested in learning more about Islam" to step to the back of the
temple. There they are given three blank sheets of ordinary stationery
and a form letter addressed to Elijah Muhammad in Chicago:

> *Dear Savior Allah, Our Deliverer:*
> *I have attended the Teachings of Islam, two or three times as taught by one of your ministers. I believe in it. I bear witness that there is no God but Thee. And, that Muhammad is Thy Servant and Apostle. I desire to reclaim my Own. Please give me my Original name. My slave name is as follows:*

The applicant is instructed to copy this letter verbatim on each of the three sheets of paper, giving his own name and address unabbreviated at the bottom. If he fails to copy the letter perfectly, he must repeat the whole task. No explanation is given for any of these requirements.

Formal acceptance of his letter makes the new member a Muslim, but in name only. Real commitment to the Nation of Islam comes gradually—for example, the personal commitment expressed when a chain smoker gives up cigarettes in accordance with the Muslim rules even though he knows that he could smoke unobserved. "It's not that easy to do these things." Stanley X said of the various forms of abstinence practiced by the Muslims. "It takes will and discipline and time . . . but you're a much better person after you do." Calvin X told of periodic backsliding in the beginning, but added, "Once I got into the thing deep, then I stuck with it."

"Getting into the thing deep" for a Muslim usually comes in three stages:

1. Participation in organized activities—selling the Muslim newspapers, dining at the Muslim restaurant, attending and helping run Muslim meetings.
2. Isolation from non-Muslim social contacts—drifting away from former friends and associates because of divergent attitudes or simply because of the time consumed in Muslim activities.
3. Assimilation of the ideology—making full commitment, when a Muslim has so absorbed the organization's doctrines that he automatically uses them to guide his own behavior and to interpret what happens in the world around him.

The fact that the organization can provide a full social life furthers isolation from non-Muslims. Participation is not wholly a matter of drudgery—of tramping the streets to sell the paper and studying the ideology. The organization presents programs of entertainment for its members and the public. For example, in two West Coast cities a black theatrical troupe called the Touring Artists puts on two plays, "Jubilee Day" and "Don't You Want To Be Free." Although there is a large element of humor in both plays, the basic themes—white brutality and hypocrisy and the necessity of developing black self-respect and courage —are consonant with the organization's perspective. Thus, the organization makes it possible for a member to satisfy his need for diversion without going outside. At the same time, it continually reaches him with its message through the didactic element in such entertainment.

Carl X's experiences were typical of the recruit's growing commitment to the Nation. When asked what his friends thought when he first joined, he replied: "They thought I was crazy. They said, 'Man, how can you believe all that stuff?'" He then commented that he no longer saw much of them, and he added:

> *When you start going to the temple four or five times a week and selling the newspaper, you do not have time for people who are not doing these things. We drifted—the friends I had—we drifted apart . . . . All the friends I have now are in the Nation. Another Brother and I get together regularly and read the Koran and other books, then ask each other questions on them like, "What is Allah's greatest weapon? The truth. The devil keeps it hidden from men. Allah reveals it to man." We read and talk about things we read and try to sharpen our thinking. I couldn't do that with my old friends.*

What is the "stuff" that Carl X had come to believe? According to the official Muslim ideology, the American black man is lost in ignorance. He is unaware of his own past history and the future role which history has destined him to play. Elijah Muhammad has come as the Messenger of Allah to awaken the American black man. The American black man finds himself now in a lowly state, but that was not always his condition. The original men, the first men to populate the earth, were non-white. They enjoyed a high level of culture and reached high peaks of achievement. A little over 6,000 years ago, a black scientist named Yakub, after considerable work, produced a mutant, a new race, the white race. This new race was inferior mentally, physically, and morally to the black race. Their very whiteness, the very mark of their difference from the black race, was an indication of their physical degeneracy and moral depravity. Allah, in anger at Yakub's work, ordained that the white race should rule for a fixed amount of time and that the black man should suffer and, by his suffering, gain a greater appreciation of his own spiritual worth by comparing himself to the whites.

According to Muslim ideology, the time of white dominance is now drawing near its end. It is foreordained that this race shall perish, and, with its destruction, the havoc, terror, and brutality which it has spread throughout the world shall disappear. The major task facing the Nation of Islam is to awaken the American black man to his destiny, to acquaint him with the course of history. The Nation of Islam, in pursuing this task, must battle against false prophets, in particular those who call for integration. Integration is a plot of the white race to forestall its own doom. The black bourgeoisie, bought off by a few paltry favors and attempting to ingratiate themselves with the whites, seek to spread this pernicious doctrine among so-called Negroes. The Nation of Islam must encourage the American black man to begin now to assume his proper role by wresting economic control from the whites. The American black man must gain control over his own economic fortunes by going into business for himself and becoming economically strong. The Nation of Islam must encourage the so-called Negroes to give up those habits which have been spread among them by the whites as part of the effort to keep them weak, diseased, and demoralized. The so-called Negro must give up such white-fostered, dissolute habits as drinking, smoking, and eating improper foods. The so-called Negro must prepare himself in mind and body for the task of wresting control from the whites. The Nation of Islam must encourage the so-called Negro to seek his own land within the continental United States. This land is due him and frees him from the pernicious influence of the whites.

Commitment to the Nation can diminish as well as grow. Four of the members I interviewed later defected. Why?

These four cases can be explained in terms of a weak point in the structure of the Nation. The organization has no effective mechanism for handling grievances among the rank and file. Muslim doctrine assumes that there is a single, ultimate system of truth. Elijah Muhammad and, by delegation, his ministers are in possession of this truth. Thus, only Elijah Muhammad himself can say whether a minister is doing an adequate job. It follows that there is nothing to be adjudicated between the hierarchy and its rank and file.

Grievances arise, however. The four defectors were, for various reasons, all dissatisfied with Minister Gerald X. Since there were no formal mechanisms within the organization for expressing their dissatisfaction, their only solution was to withdraw.

For most members, however, the pattern is one of steadily growing involvement. And once the ideology is fully absorbed, there is virtually no such thing as dispute or counter evidence. If a civil rights bill is not passed, this proves the viciousness of whites in refusing to recognize Negro rights. If the same bill is passed, it merely proves the duplicity of whites in trying to hide their viciousness.

The ideology also provides a coherent theory of causation, providing one is willing to accept its basic assumptions. Norman X interpreted his victory over his wife in a court case as a sign of Allah's favor. Morris X used it to account for the day-to-day fortunes of his associates.

Minister X had some trouble. He was sick for a long time. He almost died. I think Allah was punishing him. He didn't run the

*temple right. Now the Brothers make mistakes. Everyone does—
but Minister X used to abuse them at the meetings. It was more a
personal thing. He had a little power and it went to his head. Allah
struck him down and I think he learned a little humility.*

When a man reasons in this fashion, he has become a fully committed
member of the Nation of Islam. His life revolves around temple-centered activities, his friends are all fellow Muslims, and he sees his own
world—usually the world of an urban slum-dweller—through the framework of a very powerful myth. He is still doing penance for the sins of
Yakub, but the millennium is at hand. He has only to prepare.

The Nation of Islam does not in any real sense convert members.
Rather it attracts blacks who have already, through their own experiences
in white America, developed a perspective congruent with that of the
Muslim movement. The recruit comes to the door of the temple with
the substance of his ideas already formed; the Black Muslims only give
this disaffection a voice.[26]

The Niebuhr Hypothesis

H. Richard Niebuhr, in *The Social Sources of Denominationalism*,
discussed the origins of various contemporary Protestant denominations.
His research indicated that many started as "religions of the dispossessed,"
as millennialist sects among the poorest, most distressed segments of
the population of England in the 18th and 19th centuries.[27]

These sects were millennialist in the sense of holding that a utopia, a
state of social and collective perfection under the rule of God and
Christ, could be reached if people shed their sinful ways and lived a
God-fearing life. Millennialism and asceticism were linked by the
doctrines of these sects, in that the sufferings of the dispossessed were
"explained" in terms of their sinful behavior, i.e., drinking, licentious-
ness, and the like. It was held that the believer should give up sinful
behavior and follow a life of hard work and frugality, a life free of
pleasures of the flesh.

It happened, however, that the hard work and asceticism of members of these sects led to a collective accumulation of wealth. The wealth
was not spent on personal consumption but was plowed back into collective or personal enterprises, and thus over time collective social
mobility began to occur; what had started as sects of the dispossessed
became respectable denominations with bourgeois membership. The
more chiliastic elements of doctrine were gradually dropped, services became more staid, and religious enthusiasm came to be frowned upon.

In certain respects, the Muslims provide a contemporary example of this process. They pose a millennium, a world free of whites, or at least of white domination over nonwhites. They account for the sufferings of blacks partly by reference to dissipation, drinking, whoring, and the like. They impose a strict asceticism. And, most significantly, there may be the beginnings of a collective accumulation of wealth. As with the earlier religions of the dispossessed, this accumulation is an unintended consequence of the behavior mandated by the doctrines.

The Muslims are a semisecret organization; therefore, it is difficult to produce hard data on the state of their finances. The author did research on the organization in 1963-64, however, and again in 1972-73. In that eight-year period, the organization appeared to have prospered greatly. It had a larger number of enterprises in the early 1970's than it had had in the early 1960's. The organization itself appeared to have become a much more substantial employer. It advertised in its newspaper for offset pressmen, offset printers, and press foremen, and sought bakers for its bakeries. Meetings with black professionals and businessmen were held in New York and other major cities to solicit them for employment with the Nation. These efforts suggested that ideological fervor was coming to be seen as less important than technical competence.

It ran its own foodstores, cleaners, clothing stores, printing press, and restaurant. It had sought expansion by buying farmland to produce the food sold in its stores and used in its restaurant. In short, the asceticism, frugality, and tithing seem to have resulted in the accumulation of capital, and the separatist ideology seems to have provided guidelines for the investment of this capital. As the scope of the Nation's entrepreneurial activities expands, however, it feels compelled to substitute skill for doctrinal orthodoxy in the assignment of tasks.

Judging from the analogy between the Muslims and the religions of the dispossessed discussed by Niebuhr, it seems likely that the membership of the Nation will, over time, become increasingly middle-class and that its doctrines will become less extreme.

REFERENCES

1. This is point number one of the Panther's Ten-Point Program.

2. Philip S. Foner, ed., *The Black Panthers Speak* (Philadelphia: J. B. Lippincott, 1970), p. XII.

3. *Ibid.*, p. XIV.

4. Ross K. Baker, "Panthers Outgrow Their Rhetoric," *Nation* (July 16, 1973), p. 48.

5. Indeed, Daniel Moynihan in a memo to Richard Nixon stated that "apart from white racial attitudes . . . the biggest problem black Americans face is the

'anti-social' behavior among young black males." Quoted in Raymond Franklin and Solomon Resnik, *The Political Economy of Racism* (New York: Holt, Rinehart, & Winston, 1973), p. 141.

6. Thomas Kochman, "Rapping in the Black Ghetto," *Transaction*, 6, No. 4 (February, 1969), p. 27.

7. *Ibid.*, p. 28.

8. *Ibid.*, p. 27.

9. John Horton, "Time and Cool People," *Transaction* (April, 1967), p. 6.

10. *Ibid.*, p. 11.

11. Foner, *op. cit.*, p. XX.

12. *Ibid.*, p. IX.

13. *Ibid.*, p. XIII.

14. *Ibid.*, p. XIX.

15. *Ibid.*, p. XVI.

16. *Ibid.*, p. XXIII.

17. Baker, *op. cit.*, p. 48.

18. Foner, *op. cit.*, p. 35.

19. *Ibid.*, p. 156.

20. *Ibid.*, p. 151.

21. *Ibid.*, p. 167.

22. *Ibid.*, p. 168.

23. Baker, *op. cit.*, p. 49.

24. *Ibid.*, p. 51.

25. *Loc. cit.*

26. For a discussion of the Muslims, see "Becoming a Black Muslim: A Study of Commitment Processes in a Deviant Political Organization," unpublished Ph.D. dissertation, John R. Howard, Stanford University, 1965; and "The Making of a Black Muslim," John R. Howard, *Transaction* (December, 1966), pp. 15–21.

27. H. Richard Niebuhr, *The Social Sources of Denominationalism* (New York: Meridian Books, 1960.)

3

SOUL POLITICS:

The Political Meaning of Black Power

Politics can be seen as a deadly serious game in which winning or losing can materially affect the fortunes of a group. Political activism has increasingly come to be the black style in the postriot era. The radicalism represented by the Black Panthers has been redirected into electoral politics at the municipal level, and, in numerous cities other than Oakland, black political organizations contemplate making a bid for the control of city government.

The central question for urban blacks is whether control of the machinery of city government can yield the capacity to deal effectively with ghetto problems. Writing in reaction to the 1968 *Report of the National Commission on Civil Disorders*, Jewel Prestage commented that "it now seems incumbent upon black men to decide if politics, in the traditional sense, is now more of an irrelevancy than an imperative in the search for solutions to their problems."[1] The decision seems to have been made that electoral politics is relevant.

In this chapter, attention is given to the historical facts of black political power and then to an analysis of contemporary urban black politics and political movements.

BLACKS WITHOUT POWER

Black rewards from political participation up to the present can be summarized in the following four propositions:

1. At the national level, blacks have been rewarded largely in the form of offices having only symbolic and ceremonial meaning.

2. At the local level, blacks have been rewarded largely in the form of offices having little power, regardless of whether those rewards come from support of a political machine or from competition by white political organizations for black votes.

3. There has been no correlation between the number of councilmanic or similar offices blacks hold at the municipal level and the condition of blacks in a city. In other words, the condition of blacks in a city has not been better where they have had representation on the city council or equivalent body. Apparently, control, rather than mere

participation, is necessary before the machinery of city government can be used to meliorate ghetto problems.

4. Black rewards from politics have not included political power. Regardless of their numbers in a community, blacks have not occupied offices affording control over those community resources crucial to black welfare.

Below, these propositions are discussed in greater detail.

Black Participation and Federal Patronage

There is not only "colored people's time" and "white people's time," but also colored people's history and white people's history. In terms of white people's history, Woodrow Wilson is popularly regarded as a great humanitarian, who wept for Europe's oppressed. Colored people's history notes that he turned the screws tighter on black Americans by reducing the meager rewards accruing to them from the political system.

From the end of reconstruction in 1876 through 1913, when Wilson was sworn in as President, certain appointive federal jobs were traditionally given to blacks. Within a short period after Wilson took office, 29 blacks in high positions were turned out and their places filled by white appointees.[2] There was a cry of outrage heard from blacks, and a delegation visited the White House to protest both this and an executive order signed by Wilson segregating Negro federal employees in their use of eating and rest room facilities.[3] Only a small number of minor bureaucratic posts were at stake, but these jobs were all that blacks had at that time. Black patronage rewards had included such offices as Recorder of Deeds for the District of Columbia, Register of the Treasury, and Marshal of the District of Columbia. In addition, blacks had received ambassadorial posts to all-black nations, such as Haiti and Liberia, and minor consular appointments to Central American countries.[4]

These federal appointive offices were utterly meaningless in terms of power. They constituted only symbolic recognition, as a medal does for a serviceman. But just as the Congressional Medal of Honor received by Ira Hayes, the Pima Indian, was not negotiable to obtain water rights for his tribe as they scratched out a living on their parched southwestern land, the office of Recorder of Deeds for the District of Columbia was worthless in terms of real power to improve the social and economic conditions of blacks.

In the area of federal patronage, Blacks have had to work harder to gain less. In the century following the Civil War, there were only 30 black judicial appointments to United States Courts, 16 of these being to the Municipal Court in the District of Columbia; otherwise, there were nine blacks appointed to District Courts, three to United States Custom Courts, and two to Circuit Courts of Appeal.[5]

Only in the 1960's, with the appointment of Thurgood Marshall to the post of Solicitor General and later to the Supreme Court, and with Robert Weaver's appointment to the Cabinet as Secretary of Housing and Urban Development, was there a major departure from past practice.

Black Participation and Local Patronage

At the local level, black rewards have also been meager. Harold Baron, in a study of the distribution of power in Chicago, has indicated that in 1965 20 percent of the people in Cook County were black and 28 percent of the people in Chicago but that "in government, out of a total of 1088 policy-making positions, Negroes held just 58."[6] Blacks in Chicago sat on the Mayor's Commission for Senior Citizens, the Civil Service Commission, and a variety of other bodies, but they had little power to change policy or allocate greater resources to the ghetto.

Two factors account for the relative meagerness of the rewards blacks have received from local politics. First, in the racist assumptions which underlie much of popular thinking, there was the conception of the blacks' "place." Just as the caste system of India was based, in part, on occupational differentiation, so, in the United States, there was a feeling that only certain kinds of jobs should be available to blacks, even "good," prominent, or politically faithful blacks. Wilson commented on this principle in terms of Chicago politics:

> *Resistance to Negroes is not, in part, different from the general resistance put up by [for example] the Irish political leadership of the big city to the demands for political recognition expressed by Poles, Italians, or Germans . . . In the case of the Negro, however, this resistance was intensified by the frequent operation of personal hostility and prejudice.*[7]

Second, blacks have simply not had the numbers to force an improvement in patronage or in legislation affecting ghetto conditions. They have had the numbers to get onto the city council in many cities, but not the numbers to control council action.

Cleveland had three blacks on its city council as early as the mid-1940's. A number of cities, including Canton, Ohio, Toledo, Ohio, and Winston-Salem, North Carolina, had black councilmanic representation as early as the 1940's[8] without the black circumstance having been noticeably improved by it.

Given their peculiar class needs, it is likely that control rather than simple participation in municipal decision making is necessary to bring forth action addressed to ghetto ills. Without the ability to shape and direct policy, membership on various municipal bodies seems to yield little more than does lack of membership.[9]

BLACK CITIES: BLACK POWER

The black movement has sought in the postriot era to emphasize the importance of black control over those institutions which shape black life. In the urban context, this means black control of the machinery of city government. Three questions form the substance of discussion in the balance of this chapter:

1. What are the prospects of black control of city government in those cities having a substantial black population?

2. What forms has black political activity taken in the postriot era? Gary, Indiana, and Newark, New Jersey, two cities where blacks have been elected mayor, will be examined as models of the pattern black political organization is likely to take in many cities.

3. To what extent is city government an effective instrument for meliorating the ills of the black population?

Race, Urban Population Trends, and Black Political Power

The numbers are deceptively simple. The populations of a dozen major cities are now, or will by the early 1980's be, more than 50 percent black.[10] These figures mask a fairly complicated situation, and in order to understand the prospects for soul politics it is necessary to discuss that situation.

In the period following World War II, the black population living in cities increased dramatically. The mechanization of agriculture in the South displaced thousands of blacks. The "push off the land" occurred in two phases. Right after the war, the introduction of tractors and herbicides displaced the field hands from full-time to seasonal work at summer weeding and harvest. The now part-time workers moved from the farms to hamlets and small towns. During the 1950's, mechanization of the harvest eliminated most of the black peasantry from agricultural employment and forced them to move to the larger cities for economic survival.[11]

The migration resulted in substantial changes in the racial composition of the population of many cities. In 1950, one person in every eight in the central cities was black; by 1969, this had become one in four in the central cities of metropolitan areas in excess of 1,000,000 in population. The proportion of blacks in the suburbs remained constant at one in twenty.[12]

The blacks migrating north encountered an already existing black housing market, black labor market, black school system, and black welfare system, "not as part of a self-determining community, but as institutions to be controlled, manipulated and exploited."[13] And as the black population grew, these segregated institutions became less and less adequate to sustain even the semblance of a community life. Substantial increases in the black population occurred in a context in which the decisions affecting that population were made by persons outside the community who had interests not consonant with those of the community. This was discussed in Chapter 2 in terms of the New York City teacher's strike. In every city, a variety of groups—trade unions, education bureaucrats, real estate interests, employers, organized crime—had a stake in black subordination. Discrimination in employment saved white trade unionists from having to compete with blacks for jobs and provided employers with a steady supply of cheap labor for the more unpleasant jobs. Residential segregation provided realtors with a captive market for substandard housing. Organized crime siphoned off money via the number's game and the sale of heroin.

At a certain point, in Gary and Newark, the increase in the number of blacks created a potential for black control at the municipal level, and the multiple grievances of the black community provided the issues on which political campaigns could be based. It remained, however, to translate numbers and grievances into a bid for political office.

The Quest for Office: Newark and Gary

Newark, New Jersey, and Gary, Indiana, are not typical of all American cities. Indeed, were they typical, the fortunes of the republic would be bleaker than they are. They are, however, two major cities in which blacks have been elected mayor. Cleveland, Los Angeles, Detroit, and Atlanta are other cities in which this has occurred.[14] Los Angeles is a special case and will be discussed at a later point in this chapter. Future work on black politics will probably yield a threefold classification of cities with elected black leadership: those with a substantial plurality or a majority black population and with a small black middle class and a large black lower class in need of a variety of social services, and with an inadequate tax base (Newark, Gary); those with a substantial black population and with a large black middle class and strong economic foundations (Atlanta, Detroit); and those with a small black population, a white majority, and a strong economic base (Los Angeles). Newark and Gary suggest the probable pattern of black politics in the immediate future in many of the cities with substantial black populations and are, therefore, appropriate cases for analysis.

In both cities, black political organizations were formed independent of existing white political organizations. This process was partly a consequence of the effort to mobilize black support and partly a response to the severe hostility of entrenched white political interests to a black bid for city hall. White political interests saw the spoils of office as sufficiently important to fight fiercely to retain them. There was discontinuity between traditional black political leadership in each city and those blacks who organized to seek city hall. Traditional black political leaders were, for the most part, members of the white political apparatus and found themselves, for reasons to be discussed, opposed to the new, more militant black leadership. The electoral base of the black bid for office was a combination of blacks and middle-income, liberal whites. The electoral base of the opposition, mobilized in Gary by the local Democratic party and in Newark by white office-holders, was composed of lower-middle-class and low-income whites. The black effort in both cities was supplemented by support from national liberal elites.

This situation will now be examined in greater detail.

The Ins and the Outs

Similar processes were seen in both Gary and Newark in terms of the relationship between the black community and the political system. Traditionally, in both cities the political system was an instrument for distributing benefits. Despite black participation in politics, benefits went almost entirely to whites. Some of the benefits were illegal, some were legal. In Gary, "the mayor . . . in association with the county officials would supervise the organized crime (mostly gambling, liquor, and prostitution) within the community. In effect, the police force and the prosecutor's office were used to erect and centralize a protection racket with the mayor as its director and organized crime as its client."[15] In addition, "there were almost 1,000 patronage jobs to distribute to supporters or sell to friends. There were proceeds from a myriad of business transactions and contracts carried out under municipal authority. . . . Every aspect of municipal activity was drawn into the cash nexus."[16]

Within this system, blacks received meager rewards both in graft and in legitimate services. According to Greer, a white paid a $1,200 bribe to obtain a contractor's license to do repair and construction work within the city limits, while a black paid $1,500; he has also indicated that following the election of black mayor Richard Hatcher, "one of the major complaints of the white citizenry was concerned with the sharp decline in the frequency of garbage collection. This resulted, not from a drop in efficiency of the General Services division, as was often charged, but from the fact that the garbage routes were finally equalized between white and black areas."[17]

In Gary, as in Newark, the system became increasingly unstable. In both cities, the black population became a numerical majority but with no commensurate redistribution of public services or political rewards.

Entrenched white political interests in Gary were motivated partly by racism and partly by fear of losing control of a lucrative system, and they strongly resisted black candidate Richard Hatcher's efforts to become mayor. Hatcher won the Democratic primary in 1967 because he had the black vote and a large share of the Spanish-speaking vote, and because the white vote split when a backlash candidate entered the race. Becoming the candidate of the Democratic party, Hatcher, theoretically, was entitled to support in both money and manpower. Support was not forthcoming, however. "The county democratic machine offered Hatcher a bargain: its support and $100,000 for the general election campaign in return for naming the chief of police, corporation council, and controller. . . . [upon Hatcher's refusal] the county machine declared itself for, and campaigned for the Republican."[18]

Building on his base of support in the primary, Hatcher "developed what can best be described as a black united front, inasmuch as it embraced all sectors of the black community by social class, occupation, ideology and temperament. The basis of this united front was a commonly held view that black people as a racial group were discriminated against by the politically dominant forces."[19]

The processes by which black candidate Kenneth Gibson's bid was launched in Newark were similar. In Newark, as blacks made their bid for the mayor's office, entrenched political interest was represented by Mayor Hugh Addonizio and his associates. At stake were certain benefits of office, some legal, others illegal. The mayor appointed the police chief, and members of the police force were deeply involved in various illegal activities. The value of the office of police chief was suggested by the $15,000 offer to newly elected Mayor Gibson by private interests to permit them to name the holder.[20] City government itself was a source of business, entering into contracts with a variety of builders, suppliers, and the like. Millions of dollars were at stake, and contracts were often let on the basis of bribery.

Newark's system of nonpartisan elections made the formation of independent organizations for pursuit of office less unusual than it was in Gary. To understand the black quest for office, it will be useful to look at the structure of electoral systems. The literature on political representation suggests that nonpartisan elections are less favorable to black participation than elections where party label is indicated for the candidates. Fred Barbaro, a student of community organization, has written about Newark's system:

> "The non-partisan election is biased against the poorly educated voter. Its rationale is based on the assumption that all voters can discriminate among candidates—a most difficult chore, even for the educated, especially where the candidates may number over 50 in the city council elections. Most voters don't even know candidates' names, let alone their policy position. In the absence of political party identification, voters are left to choose at random, to not vote at all for that office or to base their discussions on the ethnicity of one or the other of the candidates' names."[21]

Whatever the effects of nonpartisan systems on voter participation, it can be argued that such systems increase the likelihood that black insurgent candidates will obtain a place on the ballot. In the pursuit of office, it is necessary first of all to appear on the ballot. The probability of appearing on the ballot will depend partly on the structure of the electoral system. Where partisan elections are held, candidates conventionally run as the nominee of a party. To run with the party label requires the vote of an authorized body of the party, i.e., district leaders, county chairmen, elected representatives to a party caucus, etc. In a partisan system, the party is a mechanism limiting access to the ballot, and an individual wishing to stand for office with the party label generally has to work his or her way up through the party structure, from doorbell ringer to district leader to county committee and so on. Even hard work and loyalty may not be enough for party leaders to nominate blacks or women or other people whom they deem probable losers or whom they see as being members of subordinate groups not fully entitled to share in the spoils of office.

An insurgent candidate may run as an independent, but at a severe disadvantage. The party has an apparatus to support its candidates that includes party workers and district leaders who will work for the party's candidate, ringing doorbells, circulating literature, telephoning potential voters, and the like. An independent candidate must attempt to put together an organization to compete with the experienced organization of the party. This is difficult to do successfully. Thus, in a sense, Richard Hatcher's task in simply getting on the ballot was more difficult than Kenneth Gibson's.

Where nonpartisan systems exist, organizations tend to be looser and more *ad hoc*. An independent candidate with an *ad hoc* organization does not confront an experienced party apparatus. Instead, politicians form personal organizations. In Newark, these had an ethnic base, being Irish-American with Leo Carlin and Italian-American with Hugh Addonizio.

The instrument of Gibson's nomination was the black and Puerto Rican convention. Approximately 700 blacks and Puerto Ricans, representing a wide spectrum of the active and the influential in the black and Puerto Rican communities, attended the 1969 convention for the express purpose of selecting a slate of candidates and developing a viable campaign structure. Gibson and a black–Puerto Rican slate were selected to seek the mayor's office and city councilman seats. The convention deemed itself the spokesman for minority interests, and whites were excluded from its deliberations. Its participants were regarded by most white politicians as upstarts, and the convention predictably was attacked as racist.

Black political organizations, formed to mobilize black support and in response to the resistance of white political organizations to black political aspirations, characterized black politics in both Gary and Newark. Undoubtedly, this same process will take place in many of the other cities where there are rising political aspirations among blacks.

Old Black Politicians and New

As these new black political organizations were formed, they were attacked by many older, local black politicians. The conflict between these politicians and the younger activists represented differences both of generation and of world view. The older black politicians were, for the most part, members of white political organizations. They had served as conduits channeling meager rewards from these organizations into the black community. They enjoyed a certain amount of prestige and influence in the black community because they could dispense small favors, and the desperate circumstances of the ghetto made even meager rewards important.

Their political role can be better understood by drawing an analogy from the administrative organization of the British colonial system in Africa. In certain parts of Africa, the British employed what was called "indirect rule." Under that system, a "chief," often selected by the British, ruled over a community. His power rested ultimately on the support of the British since they could depose him if they wanted to or they could keep him in power even if most of the community were unhappy with him. His functions were to prevent unrest and disturbances from developing and to insure that the various needs of the British, for field hands, house servants, gun bearers, soldiers, purchasers of British goods, etc., were adequately met by his charges. The various black politicians affiliated with white political organizations functioned essentially in this manner. Their task was to insure the black vote for the organization's candidates. In return, they secured influence among blacks by being able to dispense small favors. They also had personal access to the spoils, although their share was less than that of white politicians.

In Gary, Hatcher's black alliance excluded "those local black politicians who were lackeys of the democratic machine."[22]

In Newark, Irving Turner and George Richardson, both long-time participants in municipal politics, were compromised by lengthy association with white political organizations. Ron Porambo, in *No Cause for Indictment*, an analysis of the problems of Newark, has observed that "like the house Negroes before him, Richardson had offered himself for sale. He had looked the other way for slumlords. He had traded his State Assembly vote for the corrupt Kenny machine of Jersey City. He had deserted the people he lived among for white bourgeois success."[23]

The new leadership was made up of people who had not had similar ties with existing white political organizations. Robert Curvin, organizer of the black and Puerto Rican convention, had been a civil rights activist. Kenneth Gibson, a civil engineer, had made a belated run for mayor in 1966 against Hugh Addonizio. Le Roi Jones, a major force in organizing Newark blacks, had returned to the city after having achieved fame as a playwrite in New York. For years, he had moved in literary, intellectual, and bohemian circles in New York. They were younger men and their political roots lay in the civil rights activism of the early 1960's and the black power movement. The blacks aligned with white political organizations were from an earlier era. They had entered politics when the only role available to a black was as surrogate and spokesman for white political organizations. They secured the votes of the black community and offered the community individual payoffs in return (a parking ticket fixed here, a son sprung from juvenile detention there), while the community was subjected to systematic exploitation. They had no impact on public policy affecting the ghetto. They were unable to have garbage picked up in black neighborhoods as frequently as it was in white. They could not prevent urban renewal from clearing black neighborhoods to erect middle-income housing for whites. They could not prevent police abuse of authority in black areas.

When the black power movement developed, it was revealed that they really had no strong roots in the black community nor faithful constituents. Their influence had been based on being the only power brokers in the community.

Getting Elected

For a variety of reasons, the black vote alone has not been sufficient to insure black electoral success at the municipal level.

Even where blacks are in the majority, the age composition of the black population may deny them electoral supremacy. In Newark, more than half of the black population in 1967 was under 21, whereas only 32 percent of whites fell into that category. "Among the potential voting population, whites still outnumbered blacks by 47 percent to 45 percent. . . ."[24] In addition, the level of political awareness has often been low. Prior to the 1970 mayoralty election, 31 percent of blacks in Newark did not know Kenneth Gibson was black.[25]

Electoral success at the municipal level, even where the majority of the population has been black, has always hinged on support from nonblack segments of the population. The nature of this support has varied depending on its source. It has involved the backing in both Gary and Newark of the Spanish-speaking population. In Newark, this support arose from the effort to form a black–Puerto Rican coalition. In both elections, the Spanish-speaking population was essential. As will be shown later, inability to obtain a significant share of the Mexican vote in Los Angeles cost Bradley the 1969 mayoralty race.

In neither city is the Puerto Rican vote large enough to make Puerto Ricans an independent minority bloc in competition with blacks. Had the white machines made a successful effort to add Puerto Ricans to their ethnic bloc, the electoral success of blacks would have been prevented. In other words, had white politicians approached Puerto Ricans as another ethnic group (entitled therefore to a fair share of the spoils) rather than as a racial group (entitled only to leftovers), they might, at least for two or three more elections, have been able to retain power.

In New York and Los Angeles, the Spanish-speaking population is sufficiently large to constitute an independent political bloc. Political relations between blacks and Puerto Ricans in New York have been smoother than between blacks and Mexicans in Los Angeles. In the first electoral test at the mayoralty level of black–Puerto Rican relations in New York, 75 percent of black voters joined over 90 percent of Puerto Rican voters in bringing Puerto Rican candidate Herman Badillo through a primary and into a runoff. In Los Angeles, on the other hand, Mexican–black relations have often been strained, the division of jobs and money from the poverty program being one major source of tension.

In Newark, 8 percent of the voting-age population is Spanish-speaking, and in the 1970 runoff election between Gibson and incumbent Hugh Addonizio, they voted overwhelmingly for Gibson.

In Gary, Richard Hatcher received over 90 percent of the black vote and a large majority of the Spanish-speaking vote. Almost 90 percent of Gary's overwhelmingly Democratic white voters opted for the Republican candidate, however. Only in the Jewish professional and business section of town did Hatcher do well among whites.[26]

This suggests a second important element in black electoral success at the municipal level. The support of certain traditionally liberal segments of the electorate has been essential. In Newark, Gibson, endorsed by John Caulfield, former Newark fire director who had run as a moderate candidate in the primary, received some moderate white support in defeating Addonizio 55,097 to 43,086. Porambo indicated, "Gibson's win was decisive, topping Addonizio by 12,000 votes, and it was white support that made it possible. A black man was elected mayor of Newark by some 10 percent of the white voters who were fed up with corruption."[27]

In both Newark and Gary, the assistance of national liberal elites was essential to victory for three reasons. First, it helped sensitize the black population to the election. It drew their attention to it, familiarized them with the candidates, and increased the probability of actually voting. Second, these elites provided technical assistance in the mechanics of large-scale campaigning, i.e., they helped in establishing voter lists, canvassing, and so forth, and, third, they gave financial support in meeting the costs of campaigning.

In both cities, various nationally prominent blacks appeared. In Newark, black congresswoman Shirley Chisholm, Julian Bond, black state representative from Georgia, and the show business personalities, Ossie Davis and Dick Gregory, appeared at the black and Puerto Rican convention. In Gary, Muhammed Ali campaigned for Richard Hatcher as did liberal Democrats, and various foundations provided financial support.

In summary, in Newark and Gary blacks have formed their own political organizations—in one case outside the framework of existing parties, in the other within a nonpartisan system. In both cities, there has been discontinuity between older, more traditional black leadership aligned with the exploitative white political organizations and younger leadership often coming out of the civil rights and black power movements. In these two cities, more than 90 percent of blacks supported the black candidate. In addition, the Spanish-speaking vote and that of a small percentage of white liberals proved important in securing victory, as did the support of liberal, national elites. The ethnic, lower-middle-class, and lower-class vote, on the other hand, went overwhelmingly against the black candidate.

The Fruits of Victory

Kenneth Gibson was elected mayor of a city in physical and social decay. One writer observed that the "schools were so crowded that if all students appeared at school on a given day, 10,000 would be without seats."[28] One person in every three receives some form of public assistance; 40 percent of the work force is either unemployed, or underemployed, and one person in every 19 is a drug addict.[29]

Newark is simply an extreme case of the conditions likely to face blacks assuming office in some of the older cities. They encounter demand for, and need of, public services coupled with inadequate resources to meet those demands. In other words, the black population depends to a greater extent than the white population on public services, e.g., public housing, public hospitals, and a public rather than a parochial or private school system. A much greater percentage of blacks find their employment in the public sector. At the same time that these needs exist, the revenues available to city government prove increasingly inadequate and the strategic options open to the new black mayors for increasing revenues and improving services prove to be limited.

Central to an understanding of these problems is an understanding of the relationship between city and suburb. This relationship has four characteristics:

1. Racism allows suburbanites to account for the problems of cities in terms of the presumed inadequacies of blacks rather than by reference to the actions of prior administrations and the exploitative relationship between city and suburb.

2. The city provides a variety of public services for the suburbs at the cost of shrinking its own tax base.

3. Business finds tax advantages in the city which allow it to avoid its share of the cost of adequate services.

4. Business in the city provides a major source of employment for suburbanites, and the labor force in the city provides a source of cheap labor for the suburbs. Each of these propositions is discussed below.

White racism has a great impact on black urban politics. Racism plays a role in two ways; it affects white explanations for urban problems, and it shapes the thinking of whites with regard to appropriate responses to these problems.

It is clearly perceived that many cities have problems; indeed, talk of "the urban crisis" has been common for years. Explanations for the urban crisis are myriad, but racism leads many whites to define the problem of cities as "niggers." Within that perspective, black criminals have made the streets unsafe; black welfare recipients, too lazy to work, have driven the tax rate up; blacks move into the neighborhood and property values fall; teenage black hoodlums rob white students of their lunch money in high school restrooms. From this perspective, urban decay is a consequence of an increase in the black population in a city and of presumed black failings. Those whites who have the financial wherewithal leave the city, while those who remain behind develop a fortress mentality that is preoccupied with preserving the whiteness of the neighborhood.

Solutions offered to the urban crisis frequently reflect this view that the cause of that crisis is "niggers." Political campaigns among white politicians at the municipal level come to be waged in terms of "law and order" or, in other words, in terms of "nigger control." Competing claims are made about who will be able to put more policemen on the street and who will be tougher on "the criminal elements."

Racism, then, is an explanatory system that affects urban black politics by shaping white policy responses to urban problems.

The capacity of the cities to meet the increasing demands of their black populations for public services is undermined by the major subsidies which these cities are providing to the white suburbs and to business. Newark is an example. "In Newark, over 61 percent of the city's land is tax exempt, due to its being used for public purposes. That means that barely one third of the city's land must bear the tax burden of providing municipal services not only for its residents but also for the 200,000 commuters who use the city each day."[30] Cornelius Bodine, business administrator for the city, in his budget statement for 1973, commented on the consequences of this imbalance. "With less land and less value to tax, the tax rate on the remaining property must be high to yield enough revenue to finance local governments."[31] Much of this nontaxable land provides services which are used primarily by suburbanites. For example, this land includes Newark International Airport, limited access highways, Symphony Hall, and the library.

In effect, a black or Puerto Rican or Italian worker, with a wife and three children, struggling to meet the mortgage on a $30,000 home in the city, pays about $225 a month in taxes to support the airport and the access roads which take the $60,000-a-year executive to and from it.

Moreover, the city serves as a reservation for the poor, thereby relieving suburbanites of that financial obligation. As indicated, low-income populations depend heavily on publicly supported services, services that are paid for out of taxes.

Through zoning practices which exclude multifamily dwellings and public housing from their communities, the suburbs effectively keep low-income people in the city. Requirements with regard to minimum lot size and regulations barring multifamily dwellings keep the price of single family homes in the suburbs immediately surrounding Newark at such a high level that the family making $10,000 to $12,000 a year cannot afford to leave the city. At the same time, the suburbs resist public housing.

> *In contrast to the high-cost, single family homes in the suburbs which pay their own way through tax monies, public housing costs the city more than it brings in. Newark has 12,720 units of public housing which hold . . . more than 10 percent of the city's population. Public housing takes up . . . one sixth of the city's total land. This land is off the taxroles; at the same time low-income people in public housing require high levels of service from the city.*[32]

In effect, then, the city both provides certain direct subsidies to the suburbs and provides an indirect subsidy in bearing alone the cost of certain social responsibilities which might be shared by city and suburb.

Franklin and Resnik in their study, *The Political Economy of Racism*, suggest that this kind of relationship is not confined to Newark and its suburbs.

> *The split between city and country has been a consistent theme in American history. It now takes on an added importance, since middle-class people who escape to the suburbs often feel no responsibility to the city. They use many of the services of the city, but they are not willing to pay to support them.*[33]

In addition to providing certain kinds of direct and indirect subsidies for the suburbs, the city is also a major source of suburban employment, to the detriment of the city's population. Of Prudential's 8,300 employees, only 18 percent live in the city,[34] and while the city unemployment rate hovers around 15 or 20 percent, 55 percent of the city's work force is made up of suburbanites. In effect, the suburbs send a skilled white-collar work force into the city, while the city sends a less skilled work force to the suburbs.

In neither Gary nor Newark does business carry its proportionate share of taxes to the city.

> *According to the research findings of Robert Curvin, who was active in the Gibson campaign, the effect of the Bergen-Reiffin Act, passed by the state legislation in the 1940's, was to relieve business from paying certain kinds of taxes on property it owned in the city. Prudential and Mutual Benefit Insurance Companies were in the forefront of the lobbying effort for the bill. By 1949 the last point when Curvin traced it, this bill had lost the city $4 million. It was projected to cost $17 million by 1970.[35]*

In Gary, the problem of financing city services is compounded by the ability of the United States Steel Corporation to remain grossly under-assessed, a greater share of the cost of essential services thereby being shifted to the local population.[36]

Since 1950 jobs in manufacturing in Newark have declined and have been replaced largely by jobs in "transportation, services, contract construction, finance, communications and utilities. A large share of the jobs in these fields require a higher level of skill and education than the jobs which have gone from the city."[37] Thus, the trend in the city has been toward a job market from which many local residents are excluded. Taylor, commenting on the disjuncture between jobs and skill level of the population, observes that "Newark residents who have low skill and education levels are forced to drive long distances to jobs or are forced out of work altogether. They return with lower wages [partially spent on transportation] to pay high city taxes, while suburban commuters take the higher wages to pay lower taxes."[38]

Newark and Gary will not be found in exact replica in other cities in which blacks occupy city hall, but neither are their problems unique. Challenges of the same general character are likely to face other urban black politicians who acquire administrative responsibility for municipal affairs.

The problems are difficult and subtle and could become even more severe. The suburbs would like to acquire businesses that add to their tax roles without adding to their tax burden by significantly increasing the school age population. Surburban communities around Newark might, therefore, try to induce corporations now in the city to move. From the standpoint of the corporation, it might make sense to be closer to its work force while not having the fears about public order which attend being in the city. On a national basis this kind of movement has occurred. The economist William Tabb has observed that:

> *From 1960 to 1966 white central city population for the nation as a whole declined by 1.3 million. At the same time there has been a concentration of new employment on the periphery of the cities.*

*New construction of factories, commercial buildings, and a relative-
ly large part of public buildings, as shown in data on the value of
building permits issued, is in suburban or periphery areas as opposed
to central city locations.*[39]

This movement of corporations to the suburbs, in addition to involving
corporate evasion of tax responsibilities, would make the city's problems
even worse.

We are now ready to explore the potential of city government for
the melioration of ghetto problems.

In Power

When Gibson was elected in Newark and Hatcher in Gary, blacks
danced in the streets. They believed that conditions in these cities
would be fundamentally improved. In neither case was this belief correct.
Again, the factors and processes which limited the potential for change
are not unique to Gary and Newark but are found in most of the cities
where blacks are likely to make a bid for the highest municipal office.

As blacks assumed office, they discovered that the powers inherent
in municipal government are limited.

First, services at the municipal level are delivered through various
bureaucracies—the welfare department, the department of sanitation, the
police department, and so on. The employees of these bureaucracies are
protected both by civil service regulations and, increasingly, by unions.
Thus, the mayor's freedom to make sweeping changes in personnel or
dramatic changes in policy are rather limited. Blacks in power are constrained simply by the need to continue essential services. In Gary, " . . .
it was always a premise of the administration that vital municipal services (police and fire protection, garbage collection, education, public
health measures) had to be continued . . . it also appeared that with a
wholesale and abrupt transition to a totally new work force it would be
impossible to continue these services . . . ."[40]

Second, the fiscal fortunes of the city are often determined by
others since the state legislature determines the types and rates of taxation open to the city.

Third, cities depend increasingly on the federal government for
financial support via a range of programs designed to deliver a variety
of services to the public in education, health care, and other fields.

Blacks in city hall can make appointments to certain posts not
protected by civil service, but, despite pressure from their black constituencies, both Gibson and Hatcher refrained from filling these posts
entirely with black appointees, fearing this would further frighten and

alienate whites. Thus, Gibson, under intense pressure to appoint a black as police director, filled the post with a white officer. Whites continued to hold posts as director of the fire department and director of public works, and a white was recruited as business director.

The position of blacks in Gary and Newark was not unlike that of blacks in some newly liberated African countries. As Greer points out, having been excluded by the white organizations from any positions of responsibility, few blacks in either city had any experience in the administrative affairs of cities. Of necessity, then, at least some whites had to occupy positions of responsibility in the bureacracies of these cities, either as holdovers from previous regimes or as recruits to the black regimes. In the same way, representatives of the former colonial power, with few exceptions, have retained many posts when a colony has gained its independence.

The options open to black politicians at the municipal level, then, have been limited. Possibly because the problems were so overwhelming, neither Gibson nor Hatcher retained a strong political organization after winning office. Another explanation is that the fruits of office were too meager to sustain such an organization. A black might have felt it important to participate in organized activities to get Gibson or Hatcher elected, but once the candidates were in office there was relatively little (assuming that both men are honest) that could be distributed through the organization to its faithful members. Rather, the goals of the candidates and their organization were to improve the delivery of services to everyone. Thus, there was little incentive for elaborate organizations to continue to exist.

Basically, there are three options open to black mayors. First, they may provide impetus and direction in formulating more progressive federal-local programs, e.g., family allowances, a national health insurance plan; second, they may be able, to introduce marginal changes in the way city government operates, opening a limited number of job opportunities to blacks; and, third, they may be able to give the ghetto a sense that its voice is heard and its interests represented in the councils of power.

In summary, the urban black quest for power at the municipal level is an expression of black power, and for those seeking black power, urban electoral politics is the only game in town. Given the distribution of blacks geographically, as many as 18 to 20 could be elected to Congress. At the state and county levels, an increasing number of blacks have won office. At all three levels, however, they function as members of very large bodies and, of necessity, have little or no independent power. In 1972, there were 1,486 state senators in the nation, of whom 34 were black, and 4,058 state representatives, of whom 170 were black. Black power at the state or federal levels, defined in terms of holding office, is simply not likely.

While black political organizations cannot make dramatic positive changes at the municipal level, they can deter further exploitation or neglect of the ghetto. Even though municipal services may be limited and inadequate, they can insure that those resources are distributed equitably. Edward Kerr, the black eventually appointed police director in Newark, can influence police policy with regard to the ghetto.

It is clear that no genuinely thoroughgoing structural or economic changes can be brought about with a base of power only in city government. Nor is it clear that the black political potential can go much beyond the control of a certain number of city governments.

Andrew Kopkind has pointed to one possibility whereby a formal system might become more than a vehicle for half-way measures and halting steps: "Those who are working in the streets need to have a new coalition behind them to absorb the inevitable calls for repression . . . the urgent business now is for imaginations freed from the old myths to see what kind of society might be reconstructed that would have no need for imperialism and no cause for revolt."[41]

In Chapter 12, the last chapter, attention is given to the question of coalitions. Is a coalition embracing liberal and radical intellectuals, women, gays, and even the white working class a possibility? Many analysts see this kind of coalition, particularly including the white working class, as necessary to bring about progressive change in our society.

The Los Angeles Case

Although black municipal authority is likely only in cities with a substantial black population, in 1973 Thomas Bradley was elected mayor of Los Angeles, a city in which the black population is about 18 percent. The Bradley campaign is interesting and worthy of at least brief discussion. The following observations can be made about it.

In contrast to Gibson in Newark and Hatcher in Gary, Bradley had to avoid a vocabulary at all suggestive of black power. In terms of the kind of theater discussed in Chapter 2, with regard to the civil rights movement, he was a black actor playing to a largely white audience. Given the negative connotations of black power for many whites, Bradley had to present himself as a man not essentially different from most whites, except for being darker. The theater of Hatcher and Gibson was different. They played to a largely black audience and presented themselves as black but able to cope with the white world.

Related to this is the question of coalition politics. Bradley could not win without receiving a substantial proportion of the nonblack vote. His advisors assumed in the unsuccessful 1969 campaign that blacks and Mexicans, as "third world people," formed a natural coalition. They overlooked hostility between the groups over the division of funds from the war on poverty and long-standing black suspicion that Mexicans regarded themselves as better than blacks. Consequently, Bradley received only a third of the Mexican vote. He did somewhat better among Jews, traditionally liberal in their voting, but fell far short among other whites. In an interview I conducted with Bradley at the 1972 Democratic Convention, he spoke of extensive efforts to make himself better known among nonblack voters.

Bradley was aided immensely by the existence of a nonpartisan system. In a partisan system, he would never have been nominated, party leaders undoubtedly being certain that no black could win in a city like Los Angeles.

In his personal background and presentation of self, Bradley does not threaten white sensibilities. He is an expoliceman who worked his way through law school and served for years on the city council. This profile contrasted very favorably with that of the white incumbent, a man given to alternately playing clown and ogre, whose act increasingly resembled a daytime television rerun of an old situation comedy, but with the white actor losing legitimacy with the white audience.

In short, while the Bradley campaign is interesting, Newark and Gary are more typical of the cities in which blacks will assume municipal office. They present a more typical set of problems that will in the course of time more nearly determine the future of blacks in the United States.

REFERENCES

1. Jewel L. Prestage, "Black Politics and the Kerner Report: Concerns and Directions," in *American Politics and Public Policy* (Michael P. Smith, ed., New York: Random House, 1973), p. 277.

2. G. James Fleming, "The Negro in American Politics: The Past," in *The American Negro Reference Book* (John P. Davis, ed., Englewood Cliffs, N.J.: Prentice-Hall, 1965), p. 247.

3. John Hope Franklin, *From Slavery to Freedom* (New York, Alfred A. Knopf, 1947), p. 446.

4. Fleming, *op. cit.*, pp. 427–428.

5. *The Negro Handbook*, compiled by the editors of *Ebony* (Chicago: Johnson Publishing Company, 1966), pp. 273-275.

6. Harold Baron, et al., "Black Powerlessness in Chicago," *Transaction*, 6, No. 1 (November, 1968), pp. 27-34.

7. James Q. Wilson, *Negro Politics* (New York: The Free Press, 1960), p. 24.

8. Florence Murray, ed., *The Negro Handbook* (New York: The Macmillan Company, 1949), p. 236.

9. See John R. Howard, "Blacks Without Power," in *Where It's At: Radical Perspectives in Sociology* (New York: Harper and Row, 1970), for a systematic comparison of cities with high black representation in the councils of local government and those with low representation. One type was just as likely as the other to experience a riot.

10. These cities are New Orleans, Richmond, Baltimore, Jacksonville, Gary, Cleveland, St. Louis, Detroit, Philadelphia, Oakland, and Chicago. See *Report of the National Commission on Civil Disorders* (Washington, D. C.: Government Printing Office, 1968), p. 216.

11. Harold Baron, "Notes on the Political Economy of Racism," in *Government in the American Economy* (Robert Carson, Jerry Ingles, and Douglas McLaud, eds., Lexington, Mass.: D. C. Heath and Company, 1973), p. 412.

12. *Loc. cit.*

13. *Ibid.*, p. 416.

14. In 1972, there were 48 black mayors in the country, most in small communities.

15. Edward Greer, "The Liberation of Gary," *Transaction*, 8, No. 3 (January, 1971), pp. 33-34.

16. *Ibid.*, p. 34.

17. *Loc. cit.*

18. *Ibid.*, p. 35.

19. *Ibid.*, p. 34.

20. Ron Porambo, *No Cause for Indictment: An Autopsy of Newark* (New York: Holt, Rinehart and Winston, 1971), p. 345.

21. Fred Barbaro, "Political Brokers," *Transaction*, 9, No. 10 (September/October, 1972), pp. 45–46.

22. Greer, *op. cit.*, p. 34.

23. Porambo, *op. cit.*, p. 330.

24. Barbaro, *op. cit.*, p. 46.

25. *Loc. cit.*

26. Greer, *op. cit.*, p. 35.

27. Porambo, *op. cit.*, p. 341.

28. Joseph Conforti, "Newark: Ghetto or City?" *Transaction*, 9, No. 10 (September/October, 1972), p. 29.

29. Clark Taylor, "Newark Parasitic Suburbs," *Transaction*, 9, No. 10 (September/October, 1972), p. 36.

30. *Ibid.*, p. 35.

31. *Operating Budget: City of Newark, New Jersey*, p. 10.

32. *Ibid.*, pp. 38–39.

33. Raymond S. Franklin and Solomon Resnik, *The Political Economy of Racism* (New York: Holt, Rinehart, and Winston, 1973), p. 214.

34. Taylor, *op. cit.*, p. 38.

35. *Ibid.*, p. 37.

36. Greer, *op. cit.*, pp. 33–34.

37. Taylor, *op. cit.*, p. 39.

38. *Loc. cit.*

39. William Tabb, *The Political Economy of the Black Ghetto* (New York: W. W. Norton, 1970), p. 118.

40. Greer, *op. cit.*, p. 37.

41. Andrew Kopkind, "Soul Power," *The New York Review of Books*, 9, No. 3 (1967), p. 6.

4

THE OTHER MINORITIES:

Mexicans, Indians, and Puerto Ricans

ETHNIC STRATIFICATION SYSTEMS

Stratification is the practice of ranking categories of people in a hierarchy that yields unequal access to goods, services, pleasure, and power. In many societies these inequalities are rationalized by belief systems according to which the dispossessed have brought their problems on themselves through idleness or lack of innate ability. All societies stratify their members. In the United States, race and ethnicity are two of the dimensions along which people are ranked.

Most of the literature on racial and ethnic relations in the United States deals with blacks or European immigrant groups. Until recently there was considerably less on American Indians, Mexican Americans, and Puerto Ricans. Indians have received more attention from social scientists than the other two groups, but most of this literature is ethnographic or historical; it has not treated Indians as a minority group. The rise of militant protest movements among the three groups has sparked interest in them; thus, in 1972, over 15 books on Mexican Americans appeared, some new, some updated versions of work published years earlier.

The absence of sustained protest from these three groups partially accounts for their receiving less attention than blacks. Why have these groups not mounted a nationwide campaign equivalent to the black civil rights movement?

American Indians, Mexican Americans, and Puerto Ricans have a status distinct from that of blacks. They are not as visible. They are concentrated geographically, and, therefore, prejudice against them has not been as pervasive as antiblack prejudice.

Their status in the United States has been analogous to that of blacks in Brazil and Puerto Rico. There has been a good deal of confused discussion in the literature over the nature of prejudice in Latin America. It has been recognized, on the one hand, that the obsessive malevolence which has characterized attitudes toward blacks in the United States does not find a counterpart in Latin America but, on the other hand, that Latin Americans are not free of color prejudice. Blacks cluster at the lower end of the class ladder, and strong barriers exist to collective mobility. They are objects of class hostility and color prejudice. If a black is mobile in social class terms, however, he is put into an exemption category and becomes "white" for many social purposes. Shibutani and Kwan have observed that "In Brazil . . . darkness is still reminiscent of slave origins, but it can be compensated for by other qualities. Although darker people are still concentrated in the lower classes . . . many persons of unmistakable African ancestry are classified as Blanco and are so treated by their associates. One popular expression is that 'a rich Negro is a white man, and a poor white man is a Negro.'"[1]

Somewhat the same is true in the United States with regard to American Indians, Mexican Americans, and Puerto Ricans. Most are poor and are the objects of class hostility. The structure of opportunities does not afford mobility to any significant percentage of each group, but, where a member of any of the three exhibits the style and manner of the dominant group, he may escape the indignities otherwise visited upon members of his group. His ethnic background is not perceived as relevant by the dominant group, and he becomes, for all intents and purposes, part of the dominant group. Educationally and occupationally mobile members of these three groups can lose themselves in the dominant white group, an option not open to mobile blacks.

The position of blacks in the United States has been more like that of a caste than has the position of Indians, Mexicans, or Puerto Ricans. Caste domination occurs when the barriers between the dominant group and the minority are regarded as impermeable. Caste has been defined by the sociologist Joseph Himes as a "type of social organization composed of ranked, mutually exclusive units between which virtually no social mobility is permitted."[2] Historically, blacks have experienced rigid social exclusion, ruthless exploitation, and political powerlessness, all supported by law, sentiment, and the knout.

One of the key factors differentiating blacks from Indians, Puerto Ricans, and Mexican Americans is the assumed indelible character of black ancestry. In popular thinking, black ancestry constitutes an indelible genetic stain. Any person with known black ancestry is thought of as black, however "white" he may be phenotypically, whereas an individual with, say, equally slight Indian ancestry is not thought of as an "Indian." The concept of "passing" is based on the assumption that an individual who is phenotypically white but has remote black ancestry is black. On the other hand, a person with equally remote Indian or Mexican ancestry would not be regarded as "passing,"—that is, he would not be regarded as hiding his *true* identity.

The dominant group perceives a much greater degree of difference, a greater amount of distance, between itself and blacks than between itself and the other three groups. There have been three consequences of this perception:

1. Although all three groups have, like blacks, experienced persistent and widespread poverty, they have, until recently, been reluctant to identify themselves with blacks in a common cause, perhaps feeling that this identification would align them with a lower-status group.

2. None of the three have engaged in sustained protest. All have intermittently protested bad treatment, but none have mounted a sustained effort comparable to the black civil rights movement. Again, a belief that they were better than, and better off than, blacks has undoubtedly played a role.

3. Since educationally and occupationally mobile members of these groups could "lose themselves" in the dominant group, the pool from which leadership could be drawn has been smaller than among blacks.

A number of factors have combined, then, to forestall the development of militant protest among American Indians, Mexican Americans, and Puerto Ricans.

In the discussion which follows, attention is given to the social and historical context out of which the contemporary protest movement of these groups has finally developed.

MEXICAN AMERICANS

The Road To Huelga

In 1971, there were just over 5,000,000 persons of Mexican descent in the United States. Occupationally, they were clustered toward the lower end of the scale. Less than 5 percent of the males had professional or technical jobs, and more than 34 percent were laborers, farm workers, or service workers. Their median annual family income was about 70 percent of white family income. In 1971, 28 percent of Mexican Americans were in households in which the annual income was below the census bureau's poverty line. Less than half the adult males between the ages of 25 and 44 had completed high school.

About 80 percent are found in urban areas. Indices of residential segregation in southwestern and western cities reveal that Mexican Americans are less segregated than blacks but that they nevertheless cluster in distinct communities.

Some Mexican Americans in the Southwest are descendants of people who lived in the area before it was acquired by the United States; the bulk, however, are descendants of Mexicans who migrated to this country in the 20th century.

Mexican Americans have high visibility and a distinct social status only in parts of the country. Over much of the country their ethnic identity has low visibility. In the Southwest, where they concentrate in large numbers, they have long had the status of a minority group. Historically, in that region they have as a group been subjected to racial discrimination and economic exploitation. Manual Gamio in his study of Mexican immigration discussed the ambiguity of their status in the 1920's:

The darkest skinned Mexican experiences almost the same restriction as a Negro, while a person of medium dark skin can enter a second-class restaurant. A Mexican of light brown skin as a rule will not be admitted to a high-class hotel, while a white, cultured Mexican will be freely admitted to the same hotel, especially if he speaks English fluently.[3]

Paul Taylor, of the University of California, referring to the same period, quoted a waitress who articulated even finer distinctions. "We serve Mexicans at the fountain but not at the tables. We have got to make some distinction between them and the white people. The Negroes we serve only cones."

Segregation of Mexican Americans in the public school system was practiced until the end of World War II. School codes in California permitted the segregation of "Indian children or children of Chinese, Japanese, or Mongolian descent." Nothing was said about Mexican-American children, but they were segregated anyway. A case involving Mexican-American children foreshadowed the *Brown* vs. *Board of Education* Supreme Court ruling against segregation of black children. In a decision handed down on March 21, 1945, Judge Paul J. McCormick ruled that segregation of Mexican-American children found no sanction under California law and that it violated the "equal protection" clause of the Fourteenth Amendment.

Discrimination extended to employment. Carey McWilliams in *North From Mexico* contended in 1949 that:

The biggest factor regarding the assimilation of the Mexican immigrant . . . has been the pattern of his employment. . . . It is not the individual who has been employed but the group. . . . The jobs for which Mexicans were employed en masse had certain basic characteristics; they were undesirable by location (such as section-hand jobs on the desert sections of rail lines, or unskilled labor in desert mines and cement plants); they were often dead-end types of employment, and the employment was often seasonal or casual.[4]

Hostility toward Mexican Americans has persisted. Many Anglos express support for egalitarianism in the abstract, but when asked about specifics their responses indicate prejudice. Data gathered by the sociologist Alphonse Pinkney in Bakersfield, California, early in the 1960's indicated only 6 percent of Anglo respondents expressing dislike of Mexicans. They displayed considerable hostility, however, when asked about specifics such as integrated housing, joint membership in clubs, and equal employment opportunities. They were least opposed to nondiscriminatory employment and most opposed to mixed housing, with only 38 percent agreeing that Mexicans "should have the right to live with other Americans."[5]

Discrimination is often subtle. Theodore Parsons in a 1966 Stanford University doctoral thesis cited examples drawn from 40 days of observing classes in a San Joaquin Valley elementary school with 58 percent Mexican-American enrollment. One teacher explained why he asked an Anglo boy to lead five Mexican Americans in orderly file out of the room by saying, "His father owns one of the big farms in the area and one day he will have to know how to handle Mexicans." Another teacher explained the practice of calling on Anglo pupils to help Mexicans recite by stating, "It draws them [the Anglos] out and gives them a feeling of importance."

Several factors account for the persistence of the Mexican American's problems.

The Conquered Provinces

McWilliams has observed about Mexican Americans that:

> they are more like the typical minority in Europe than like the typical European minority in the United States. Mexicans were annexed by conquest along with the territory they occupied. . . . About the closest parallel that can be found in this hemisphere for the Mexican minority is that of the French Canadians in Quebec. . . . Like the Mexicans, the French Canadians were "here first" . . . . The parallel would be closer, of course, if the Province of Quebec were part of the United States. Then New Mexico could be regarded as the Quebec of the Mexicano.[6]

Over a period of a few years, Mexico lost an enormous amount of territory to the United States as a consequence of military defeat. The treaty of Guadalupe Hidalgo, executed on February 2, 1848, ceded to the United States all Mexican territory north of the Rio Grande. This included California, Arizona, New Mexico, and other territories. Ironically, the gold that Spanish adventurers from Cortes to Coronado to Onate had sought was discovered in California nine days before the treaty was signed, unbeknown to its signers. The Gadsden Purchase of 1853 added additional Mexican territory. Most of the Mexicans living in the ceded territories chose to remain and accept American citizenship.

While guaranteed rights of citizenship by the treaty, Mexicans quickly became the victims of Anglo animosity. They were, of course, not simply a conquered people, but a conquered people who differed in culture, religion, and ethnicity from their conquerers. The early 1840's had seen the rise of the anti-Catholic Native American Party in the United States. Some of this anti-Popery found expression in the war against Mexico, from 1846 to 1848. The Mexicans living in the ceded territories were, if not nonwhite, at least less white than their conquerers. Many were of mixed Indian ancestry.

Mexicans, in short, were different in enough ways to make it easy for Anglos to rationalize the depredations visited upon them. Once established, systems of oppression have a tendency to become self-perpetrating since one group always benefits psychologically and materially from the depressed status and restricted opportunities of another.

Mexicans fell victims early and inevitably to Anglo lust for their land. Under the treaty, Mexicans who remained in the ceded territory were guaranteed "free enjoyment of their liberty and property." In California, however, Mexican-owned land was systematically expropriated through a combination of force and chicanery. There were large ranches on the sites of what are now some of the major cities in the state: Oakland, San Diego, Los Angeles. Anglo squatters appropriated the land owned by the Peraltas, the Berreyesas, and other prominent Mexican families. Some families fought back with arms, and most became entangled in legal battles that dragged on for years, ending with the original owners landless and destitute.

The subordinate status of the Hispanos and of later Mexican immigrants found expression in the vitality of certain stereotypes. Race prejudice was circulated as scientific dogma in the early decades of the century; R. L. Adams of the University of California, in his 1921 text, *Farm Management*, stated that Mexicans were "childish, lazy and unambitious." He argued that as farm laborers they should be segregated from the Japanese who were "tricky" and that both should be kept separate from Negroes who were "notorious prevaricators . . . constantly annexing to themselves such minor things as chickens, lines from harnesses, axes and shovels." Simmons, writing in 1961, indicated that the south Texas stereotype of Mexicans pictured them as improvident, undependable, childlike, and indolent. They were also believed to be dirty, drunken, and criminally inclined.

Mexican Americans have had their opportunities curtailed and their civil liberties circumscribed. Most have accommodated themselves to subordinate status; however, there has been intermittent protest. This protest will now be examined in terms of the historical context out of which "La Causa" has grown.

From Banditry to La Causa

The first overt reaction of the Hispanos to Anglo incursions was banditry. Throughout the nineteenth century Mexican bandits roamed California preying on Anglos, rustling their cattle, and robbing their banks.

Banditry is an individual response to social dislocation and may enrich the individual, but does little to improve a group's status.

Organized Mexican-American protest has been centered largely, though not entirely, among agricultural workers. The roots of the Chicano movement lie in the fields.

Immigration of Mexicans in substantial numbers began in the first decade of this century, and many of the immigrants were farm laborers. Mexican labor had been used before World War I, but during the war the big influx began. Mexicans in groups of 1,500 to 2,500 were brought into the Imperial Valley by truck from San Felipe and Guaymas. During the 1920's, Mexicans were the largest single population group among the 200,000 agricultural workers in California. The Pacific Rural Express indicated that between 1924 and 1930 an average of 58,000 Mexicans a year were brought into the state to work in the fields.

As early as 1903, Mexican and Japanese sugar-beet workers went on strike in Ventura, California. In 1922, Mexican-American field hands sought to establish a union of grape pickers at Fresno. In November, 1927, a Confederation of Mexican Labor Unions was organized in Los Angeles, and in April of 1928 efforts were made to organize cantaloupe pickers in the Imperial Valley. The growers reacted quickly. Mass arrests were made, deportations took place, and scabs were brought in from Texas and Oklahoma. The strikes were broken.[7]

Two years later, 5,000 Mexican-American agricultural workers struck. After a temporary settlement, growers again counterattacked successfully with mass arrests. In June of 1933, 7,000 Mexican workers struck in Los Angeles County, walking out of berry, onion, and celery fields in the longest strike the state had seen until then. In the fall of 1933, the militant Cannery and Agricultural Workers Union called a series of strikes to organize the largely Mexican-American field hands in the southern San Joaquin Valley.

Not all the protest occurred in California. Mexican-American farm laborers struck in Arizona, Idaho, Washington, and Colorado. A 50-car caravan of workers toured the lower Rio Grande Valley in 1933 in protests against anti-union activity. In 1934, 6,000 pecan shellers struck in San Antonio against piece rates of two and three cents a pound.

Mexican-American protest is not new, but "La Causa" is. In the fall of 1965, a bitter strike broke out in the grape vineyards surrounding the little central California town of Delano. The strike was led by former agricultural worker and community organizer Cesar Chavez and his National Farm Workers' Association (NFWA). The strikers focused on bread and butter issues, the average annual income of Mexican-American farm laborers being $1,378. Unlike previous protest efforts, however, the strike seemed to infuse the population with a spirit of militancy. Eventually "Huelga," the strike, became "La Causa," a crusade to assert the dignity of the Mexican-American population.

Earlier efforts to organize had met with limited success. The AFL-CIO set up the Agricultural Workers Organizing Committee in the 1950's. Partly because its leadership was Anglo and had little grasp of Mexican culture, AWOC never solidly established itself with Mexican workers. Also, there were certain standard problems in organizing farm workers. Galarza has listed these:

> Farm wages are so low that the monthly union dues seem a heavy tax on the workers. There are long periods of unemployment when union obligations can be met only at considerable sacrifice. A trade union of farm workers must face and meet assaults on its security ranging from local irritation, through state legislative attacks, and up to international maneuvers to swamp local living and working standards.[8]

The Community Service Organization made the most important attempt to organize the urban Mexican community. CSO was the inspiration of Saul Alinsky, a professional in the business of organizing the powerless. Alinsky set forth his philosophy in Reveille for Radicals, indicating that a "people's organization" had to be established to insure that the interests of nonelites are represented in the councils of power. CSO undertook voter registration campaigns among Mexicans. "Through the CSO, the Mexican Americans began to take action, first on such bread and butter items as better sewage disposal and new sidewalks, and then through the ballot box. . . ." Early in the 1960's, Cesar Chavez, who had become General Director of CSO, put forth a proposal to organize farm laborers. The urban-oriented CSO found this approach too parochial and voted the proposal down at its 1962 convention, whereupon Chavez quit the organization, moved to Delano, California, and set about organizing.

At least three factors account for the unprecedented impact of the Chavez movement. First, the termination of the bracero program stabilized the labor force in the fields and denied growers a prime source of scab labor. In 1942, the Mexican and American governments entered into agreements allowing the recruitment of "braceros" or Mexican nationals as farm workers, their tenure in the United States being for the duration of their employment. Galarza has commented that "these agreements were originally signed as a wartime measure, but they were continued under the insistent pressure of the agricultural employers' association who were looking for a counterpoise to the wage demands of Mexican workers long resident in this country."[9] The end of the bracero program in 1964 removed from the hands of growers an important instrument for breaking strikes.

Second, the black protest movement had both generated conscious-ness of the possibility of reform and created a corps of young activists who supplied important know-how and manpower for poor people attempting to organize on a mass basis. Available in 1965 were thousands of young whites, veterans of Mississippi and the civil rights movement. This corp of veterans proved invaluable in the early days of the strike.

Third, leadership of "La Huelga" was Mexican-American. Earlier organizations such as Citizens for Farm Labor were made up almost entirely of Anglos, and, although they had spoken on behalf of the Mexican-American population, they had no roots in that community.

A combination of circumstances, then, created the conditions under which an effective protest movement could come into existence.

La Huelga

The strike began largely by accident. In the spring of 1965, Filipino and Mexican-American workers in the Coachello Valley south of Delano had gone out on strike for higher pay. After ten days they went back to work for $1.40 an hour, a raise of 20 to 30 cents an hour over their previous wage. Drifting north to Delano with the crops, they were reluctant to take lower wages than they had received in Coachello. On September 8, a strike was called. Chavez later commented, "That morning of September 8, a strike was the farthest thing from my mind . . . . The first I heard of it was when people came to me and said the Filipinos had gone out. They were mad that the Filipinos weren't work-ing and the Mexicans were. All I could think of was 'Oh God, we're not ready for a strike.' "[10]

AWOC was supporting the strike of the Filipinos and sought the aid of the NFWA with whom it had never been on good terms. Feeling that the credibility of his organization would be severely impaired if he did not support the strike, Chavez decided to go along. On Monday, September 10, with less than $100 in its strike treasury, the NFWA joined AWOC on the picket lines. Since a majority of the strikers were now Mexican, leadership passed into Chavez' hands.

Chavez moved immediately to enlist the support of civil rights people and the liberal clergy. This maneuver served both to make the struggle more than a localized affair known only to people living in the area and to give strikers access to the desperately needed resources to keep a strike going. The trade union movement contributed money, but it was not nearly enough. By the summer of 1966, the telephone bill of the NFWA was running $1,600 a month and gasoline was costing $4,000. The organization absorbed all of the expenses including rent, food, and car payments of the families on permanent picket duty. There was need for food to sustain strikers and their families, the weekly quantities amounting to 200 pounds of tortilla flour, 100 pounds of dry red beans, 100 pounds of pinto beans, 200 pounds of sugar, 200 pounds of potatoes, 50 pounds of coffee, two cases of canned fruits and vegetables, and enough powdered milk for 450 children.

The young people who went to Delano proved invaluable in organizing the support of the liberal and radical communities in California and eventually across the nation. Predictably, the local community was hostile to the strike and the strikers. There were reflex comments about "communists" and "outside agitators." Nevertheless, impressive support from outside the community helped to sustain the strike.

The situation was complicated. There were more than 30 growers in that area, some independent operators, others connected with national enterprises such as Schenley and DiGiorgio, which markets S & W and Tree Sweet canned food and fruit products.

Ultimately, any strike is a test of strength. Ironically, the weak, struggling NFWA, making its way with donated biscuits and amateur organizers, found the largest and most powerful of its opponents to be the most vulnerable. As national enterprises, Schenley and DiGiorgio were susceptible to a national protest movement. Moreover, having dealings with a number of unions, they were probably less prone than more parochial growers to see unions as evil incarnate. It is impossible to judge whether they were better able to settle financially; claims and counterclaims about the economic effects of agricultural worker unionization have never been satisfactorily evaluated.

The boycott was launched with an élan born of having little else to throw into the fray. Chavez indicated his reason for singling out

Schenley. "It was a simple decision. In the first place, booze is easier to boycott. And then it is usually the man who goes to the liquor store and he's more sympathetic to labor as a rule than his wife."

John Gregory Dunne recounted the launching of the crusade.

> *From an atlas, Chavez picked thirteen major cities across the United States as boycott centers, and then organized a boycott staff, all under twenty-five, from workers to volunteers who had impressed him on the picket line. They left Delano penniless and hitchhiked or rode the rails to the various cities where they were to set up shop. Chavez gave the boycott staff no money, both out of necessity and to prove a theory. He reasoned that if a person could not get his hands on enough money to maintain himself on a subsistence level, then he would be of little use raising money for the boycott and setting up an organization.[11]*

The boycott staff contacted liberal clergy, radicals, union leaders, and others in each city likely to listen and lend help. In New York, the Transport Workers Union assisted in printing and distributing leaflets to subway riders. A Boston Grape Party was staged in Boston, marchers winding through the city with crates of Delano grapes, which were then dumped in the harbor.

Schenley settled on April 6, 1966, seven months after the strike had begun. The circumstances attending the decision are still not clear. Some claim fear of an effective boycott, while others suggest an unfounded fear of a bartender's boycott of Schenley products.

The struggle against DiGiorgio proved more complicated. Unlike Schenley, the DiGiorgio firm had been in the agriculture business a long time and was as practiced at breaking strikes as it was at merchandising its food and fruit products. In 1939, 1947, and 1960, it had defeated attempts by its workers to organize. The national attention given the grape strike and the wide base of support accorded the strikers this time, however, faced the corporate giant with a much more demanding situation.

The already muddy situation became more confused when the Teamsters' Union began to evince interest in organizing farm laborers. The teamsters' interest was partially a consequence of an internal struggle for power among possible successors to James Hoffa, Teamsters' Union president who had received a jail sentence. DiGiorgio was interested in doing business with the Teamsters, possibly in the belief that a better deal could be made with them. A summer of bitter conflict culminated in an NFWA victory of 530 to 331 over the Teamsters in an election to determine which union would represent field workers. The Teamsters won the shed workers' vote 94 to 43.

Further negotiations finally brought a specific settlement. The contract provided for a union shop, a minimum wage of $1.65 an hour, a guarantee of four hours "reporting and standby" pay if no work was available, and a week's paid vacation for those employed more than 1,600 hours a year. The minimum wage was to be raised to $1.70 an hour in 1968 with two weeks' paid vacation for workers who had been with DiGiorgio for three years.

These victories in the first year of the struggle helped transform La Huelga into La Causa. A dispute over the wages of agricultural workers was generalized into a movement to redefine the status of an entire group.

The Brown Power Movement

Mechanization on the farm has decreased the need for agricultural workers. The long-range impact of the farm workers' revolt will probably lie in the cities rather than in the fields. Mechanization in Hawaii, for example, reduced the work force in island sugar from 35,000 in 1945 to 10,500 in 1966. The United Farm Workers' Organizing Committee (the successor to the NFWA) claimed 17,000 members in California and the Southwest in 1967. Most of the Mexican population, however, lives in the city.

Today there are many faces in the brown power movement. Reies Tijerina espouses a nationalist renaissance among Mexicans in New Mexico. "Corky" Gonzalez in Denver has addressed a different set of problems. And in California, Chavez continues the fight, with many growers still resisting unionization. Mexicans have joined in demands on California campuses for "third world" and ethnic studies programs.

Each spokesman has a somewhat different constituency, reflecting the diversity within the Mexican-American population. The demands posed by Tijerina and the *Alianza Federal de Mercedes* are those of a people whose roots go back centuries in the area in which they claim to have been victims of injustice. Chavez' approach reflects a constituency which is migrant, uneducated, and historically defenseless against the power of the growers.

Reies Lopez Tijerina and the *Alianza* first came to public attention when, on June 5, 1967, they attacked the Tierra Amarilla Courthouse, released 11 of their members being held prisoner, and for an hour and a half controlled the village. They claimed legal right to millions of acres in central and northern New Mexico and proclaimed the founding of the Republic of Rio Chama. The followers of Tijerina had roots in New Mexico back to the 17th century. Under the *Recapilación de Leyes de las Reinos de Indios* (Compilation of Laws of the Kingdom of the

Indies) millions of acres of "common lands" had been ceded by the King of Spain to his subjects resident in the Southwest. These rights were respected by the government of Mexico when it ruled the area from 1821 to 1848, and the United States, when it signed the treaty of Guadalupe, pledged itself to respect property rights recognized under Mexican rule. Thus, argued the *Alianzas*, millions of acres in the Southwest were legally theirs.

The *Alianza* was formed in 1963 to press for reclamation of this land. Between 1950 and 1960, the Anglo population expanded by 59.1 percent and the Mexican population by 8.1 percent, changing a situation in which the two populations had been roughly equal. In that decade, the job situation of Mexicans in New Mexico had also deteriorated. In 1950, Mexican males had a lower rate of unemployment than males in California, Colorado, and Arizona. By the end of the decade, their unemployment rate was higher. One response among Mexican Americans to their declining situation was the *Alianza*, with its demand for the formation of a separate Spanish state.[12]

In urban areas, the brown power movement has taken a number of forms. Some of the gangs in East Los Angeles developed a political sense and began to call themselves "Brown Berets." Intellectuals developed journals such as *Atzlan* and *El Grito*.

The movement takes many forms, reflecting the different circumstances in which Mexican Americans find themselves. Its future shape and form will depend on the impact it makes on those circumstances.

PUERTO RICANS

From Gang Warfare to Political Protest

The Puerto Rican experience is different from that of Mexican Americans and American Indians.

The United States acquired Puerto Rico at the turn of the century as a by-product of the Spanish-American War. Cuba was the major preoccupation in the conflict, but with the bloodless seizure of Puerto Rico, the nation found itself in possession of a pleasant Caribbean Island about the size of Connecticut with a population of nearly 1,000,000. During World War I, American citizenship was conferred on the island's people.

The effects of continental control on the islanders were varied. In the first three decades of this century, the death rate was reduced by half, the birth rate rose, and the population doubled. On the other hand, the island was virtually turned into a sugar plantation. Within four decades, the sugar industry accounted for 40 percent of employment and 60 percent of exports. Profits, however, accrued to 8,000 entrepreneurs, and the island was known as "Uncle Sam's sweatshop." A host of statistics defined the deprivation of the population as compared with that of the mainland. By 1930, the infant mortality rate was twice that in the continental United States. Afflictions such as hookworm were common, particularly in the rural areas.

Migration patterns have fluctuated with economic changes on the island and on the mainland. Sporadic but unsuccessful attempts were made very early to recruit Puerto Rican farm laborers. In 1900, 5,000 laborers were brought to Hawaii to work in the sugar cane fields, and another 1,500 were recruited to Arizona in 1926 to work in the cotton fields. Whatever the reason, these attempts were not successful, and New York City became the center of Puerto Rican immigration. There had been a tiny Puerto Rican community in the city as early as 1838, a Spanish Benevolent Society having been formed for their compatriots who were in need. The city had "500 persons of Puerto Rican birth in 1910, 7,000 in 1920, 45,000 in 1930."

Two factors combined to promote immigration to New York City: first, the degree of "racial" discrimination encountered in the city was less than that experienced in other parts of the country; and second, the 1924 Immigration Act shut off the influx of workers from Europe and created a demand for new sources of labor on the part of the needle trades. As early as 1919, 130 Puerto Ricans were sent to Brooklyn by the Island Immigration Bureau to work in a cottage factory. Between 1921 and 1930, immigration from the island increased substantially. The migrants were mostly young, mostly urban, and more skilled than non-immigrants. For the most part, family groups came.

During the worst years of the depression, more people returned to the island than came to the continent. Following World War II, migration increased sharply, averaging 50,000 a year in the first decade after the war. According to the anthropologist Elena Padilla:

> over a period of years statisticians observed a mathematical correlation of .82 between net migration from Puerto Rico and national income in the United States. This high correlation has linked Puerto Rican migration out of the island with favorable business and employment conditions in the United States. In turn, throughout periods of economic recession in the United States, many Puerto Ricans have returned to the island.[13]

By 1960, there were 613,000 first- and second-generation Puerto Ricans in the city, and by 1970 the number was close to 1,000,000.

West Side Story

In the late 1950's, the musical *West Side Story* marked the coming of age of Puerto Ricans as a minority group. Their status was sufficiently "real" to be the key plot element in a popular entertainment.

The "West Side" of *West Side Story* referred to the area of Manhattan bounded north and south by 130th Street and 96th Street and east and west by the East River and Central Park. It is otherwise known as "Spanish Harlem," "El Barrio," or "Island in the City."

The area was dominated by Italians through the end of World War II. By 1950, 30 percent of its population was Puerto Rican. Puerto Ricans have spread out to the other boroughs with the concentration in the Bronx being sufficiently high as to be instrumental in the election of a Puerto Rican, Herman Badillo, as borough president.

El Barrio is a classic American slum. Puerto Ricans are at the bottom of the economic ladder among the city's ethnic groups. In the late 1960's, whites on the average earned nearly $8,000 a year, nonwhite families (principally black) earned nearly $5,000, while Puerto Rican families made just under $4,000.

In other respects, Puerto Ricans were in more straitened circumstances than blacks. Herbert Bienstock, regional director of the Bureau of Labor Statistics, has indicated that 36.9 percent of Puerto Rican workers in East Harlem in 1968 were unemployed or underemployed. The rate for blacks was lower. In Brooklyn's Bedford-Stuyvesant section, the unemployment rate was 29.7 percent among Puerto Ricans and 27.6 percent among blacks. The Puerto Rican unemployment rate was 12 percent in Harlem while 8 percent of blacks were unemployed.

"About half of all private dwellings in East Harlem are dilapidated. Almost one in three is overcrowded." Tuberculosis rates and venereal disease rates are high. One pregnant woman in three gets no prenatal care and the infant mortality rate is 37 per 1,000 live births as compared to a city average of 26 per 1,000 live births. While 38 percent of blacks and 64 percent of the whites in East Harlem owned their own homes in 1960, few Puerto Ricans did. One in three of East Harlem's Puerto Ricans lives in high-rise public housing developments called "projects," of which there are nine in East Harlem.

East Harlem's schools are slum schools. Patricia Sexton, who did a pioneering study of social class and education in Detroit, commented in 1965: "In recent years 57 percent of East Harlem's school teachers had permanent licenses, 25 percent were substitutes, 18 percent had probationary licenses. In junior high 44 percent had permanent licenses and 43 percent were substitutes. Many licensed teachers in junior high taught subjects they were not licensed to teach. Many with only elementary licenses were teaching in junior highs."[14]

The longer East Harlem children stay in school, the more their reading and I.Q. scores decline. Sexton has indicated that,

> *In the third grade, students in one district scored 2.8 on a reading test compared with the city average of 3.5. By the eighth grade, the East Harlem students were two full years below grade level. . . . By the eighth grade their I.Q. score was 83.2, compared with 103.4 for the city. In the third grade it had been 91.2, compared with 98.8 for the city. . . . In the junior high schools, 12 percent of students were reading above grade level, 8 percent on grade level, 10 percent one year below grade level, and 70 percent more than one year below grade level.[15]*

Most of the Puerto Ricans who are graduated from high school receive a general diploma, 8 percent a vocational degree, and 1.2 percent an academic diploma facilitating entrance to college.

Statistically, the problems of Spanish Harlem and black Harlem are very similar. There are differences, however, with regard to style of life and cultural outlook. Puerto Ricans brought with them to the mainland a nominal Catholicism, a strong belief in a double standard of behavior for the sexes, and a pattern of extended family organization.

The Puerto Ricans came seeking a better life. For many, the reality is El Barrio. Puerto Rican experiences have been similar in certain respects to those of other immigrant groups, but certain factors, which will now be examined, have prevented their assimilation.

The Making of a Minority Group

In some ways, the history of Puerto Rican immigrants parallels that of other groups. The West European Jew who settled in the United States prior to the great wave of immigration of East European Jews tended to look with disfavor on the newcomers, feeling that their behavior and appearance lent credibility to the antisemitic stereotype. Similarly, the small number of Puerto Ricans living in New York prior to mass immigration to the mainland felt themselves not to be victimized by prejudice and were critical of the migrants. Brown has commented:

> *Since the immigration of Puerto Ricans became a reality in 1928, conditions have changed in New York. Those who came here twenty years ago have seen a marked change in the attitude of the continental. An old resident of a Puerto Rican barrio, among those*

expressing this view, said that twenty years ago, one could say with
pride: "I am a Spaniard or Puerto Rican and the people would be
courteous to you. It is a very different situation now."[16]

Probably the key factor inhibiting Puerto Rican assimilation is
color. Some unknown percentage of the population is discernibly nonwhite. Glazer and Moynihan, among others, have compared Puerto
Ricans and the Italian immigrants who came to the country at the
turn of the century, speculating on the likelihood of a similar adaptation
for Puerto Ricans. The complicating factor is color. The Italians were
white, and some portion of the Puerto Rican population is not.

Puerto Rican attitudes towards color have been more complicated
and less negative than those of Anglos, and this has made their adaptation more difficult. From the Puerto Rican perspective, mainland
attitudes about race are simpleminded and malevolent. The Puerto
Rican lexicon on color is much richer than that found on the mainland.
An individual regarded as a "Negro" by an Anglo might be termed
triguero, indio, grifo, hispano, or *negro* by a Puerto Rican. An individual
designated "white" by an Anglo might be referred to as *hispano, grifo,*
triguero, or white by a Puerto Rican. The terminology reflects very fine
discriminations in terms of skin color, physiognomy, and hair texture.
On the level of interaction:

> *As in the United States . . . two major radical groups are recognized*
> *socially; they are white and Negro. But the recognition of these two*
> *groups does not result in the formation of two distinct subgroups*
> *of caste-like separation as it does in the United States. . . . Much*
> *social interaction takes place and many interpersonal relations of*
> *an intimate and warm nature occur among individuals regardless of*
> *whether or not they have Negro ancestry and whether they look Ne-*
> *groid or white, though there is a stated preference for being white.[17]*

Color differences among Puerto Ricans sometimes cut across
families, complicating the process of assimilation and raising the possibility of a mobile white group and a nonmobile black group. Language
is another barrier to assimilation and a cause of discrimination. More
conventional discrimination by trade unions and landlords has also
served to lock Puerto Ricans into low-paying jobs and restrict them to
decaying sections of the city.

Puerto Rican Power

The black power movement set off an upheaval among the numerous outcast and outsider groups in the United States. In the wake of

that movement has come the "red power" and "brown power" movements, the women's liberation movement, the gay liberation movement, and, not surprisingly, a protest movement among Puerto Ricans. If the most oppressed group could rise up, then surely other oppressed groups could rise up as well.

In mobilizing themselves, Puerto Ricans had to face the fundamental issue of color differences within the group. A number of observers have indicated that light-skinned Puerto Ricans attempt to move into the mainstream and lose themselves, while darker-skinned Puerto Ricans seek to differentiate themselves from blacks by, among other things, speaking Spanish in public.

It is not at all clear how Puerto Ricans have resolved this problem; there have been a number of instances, however, of common action by blacks and Puerto Ricans. Specifically, a black and Puerto Rican student coalition in Newark, New Jersey, addressed itself to the task of using the numerical majority of blacks and Puerto Ricans in the city to gain control of the machinery of city government; and black and Puerto Rican students united at City College of New York during the academic year 1968–1969 to push a common set of demands, among them that proficiency in the Spanish language be a requirement for people being trained to teach in the city's school system, in which so many of the students are Puerto Rican.

The Puerto Rican movement addresses itself to many of the same issues that agitate blacks: poor schools, bad housing, and widespread poverty. Like blacks, browns, and reds, they have demanded control over institutions affecting the Puerto Rican community and the passage of legislation designed to deal with problems of poverty.

Puerto Ricans have engaged both in the politics of the ballot box and in the politics of the street. Among the organizations which took to the streets to dramatize Puerto Rican demands was the Young Lords. They played an important role in involving more Puerto Ricans in politics.

The Young Lords

The Young Lords represent the transition among the urban, Puerto Rican young from gang activity to political protest. Rather than engaging in typical urban gang behavior—petty theft, drunkenness, sporadic violence—they directed their attention to political issues.

According to Rafael Viera, their one-time "Chief Medical Cadre," the Lords were formed in Chicago in 1965 as a street gang. Some time in the late 1960's, according to Viera, this group, under the influence of its president, Cha Cha Jiminez, became politically oriented. The change in orientation was inspired, in part, by the example of the Blackstone Rangers, a black gang which had become active in antipoverty programs. According to Viera, a group of young New York Puerto Rican college students, in contact with the politically aware Chicago group, borrowed its name. This group then set about attempting to make itself known at the grass roots level and to establish grass roots support. Out of this attempt grew the famous "garbage offensive," whose purpose was to dramatize the failure of the city's sanitation department to serve the Puerto Rican community.

For three consecutive Sundays, members of the Lords swept streets in Spanish Harlem, put the refuse in garbage cans, and set the cans out for the city's garbage trucks. But the trucks never came. This led to a series of street demonstrations, ending in a confrontation with the police that brought the Lords to public attention.[18]

The Lords also undertook a campaign against lead poisoning. Ghetto children often eat chips of the paint peeling from the walls of tenements. The lead content of this paint can cause brain damage. The Lords organized medical personnel to go from door to door in Spanish Harlem examining the urine of children for traces of lead poisoning.

Although using a rhetoric full of the hyperbole of "revolution," the Young Lords basically sought to make the various agencies of government, particularly at the municipal level, more responsive to the needs of the Puerto Rican community. Billing itself as a "Revolutionary Political Party," the Lords called for the overthrow of capitalism and for solidarity with the oppressed people of the world. They sought, however, to improve the delivery of public services to the Puerto Rican community and to facilitate the development of more effective pressure groups among Puerto Ricans.

In the nature of things the contest was uneven. The Lords were essentially a voluntary organization confronting a massive municipal bureaucracy. The ability of this bureaucracy to weather the indignation of local groups is very great. Thus, the Lords could not deliver, and they gradually faded from public view. Their activity, however, plus the continual increase in the size of the Puerto Rican community in the city, contributed to the first serious attempt by a minority group member to win city hall.

Puerto Rican Politics

Puerto Rican electoral politics in New York City centers mostly around the figure of Congressman Herman Badillo. Badillo, a white Puerto Rican, could probably have "lost himself" in the white population had he chosen to deemphasize his Puerto Rican ancestry. As a self-identified Puerto Rican, however, he became a member of a minority group and, when he ran for mayor, was seen as both the candidate of nonwhites and the nonwhite candidate.

In the 1973 contest in which Badillo ran, any candidate obtaining 40 percent of the vote in the primary became the nominee of the Democratic Party; otherwise, there was to be a runoff election between the two candidates getting the largest number of votes. Badillo's chances of obtaining enough votes to win the primary or enter a runoff were not rated as very good on the grounds that his basic constituency, low-income Puerto Ricans, have a low rate of voter turnout, particularly in primaries. In addition, his black support was seen as uncertain, because of possible hostility between blacks and Puerto Ricans.

In the primary election itself, Badillo finished second, thereby entering the runoff. Voter turnout in Puerto Rican areas was very high, indicating a willingness on the part of low-income persons with low levels of education to come to the polls if there is a candidate with whom they can identify or who speaks to their needs. Badillo also received heavy black support, suggesting that coalitions of the dispossessed do sometimes occur.

In the runoff, he lost almost two to one, although he received 75 percent of the black vote and over 90 percent of the Puerto Rican vote. Between the primary and the runoff, he was unable to expand beyond his basic Puerto Rican–black constituency, since the city's other ethnic groups—Italians, Jews, and Irish—came together to throw their support almost solidly behind the other candidate.

The Badillo campaign suggests a political awakening among Puerto Ricans, although they lack the numbers to win major municipal offices at the polls. As their numbers increase and the number of blacks increases, however, the likelihood of greater influence over public policy at the municipal level also grows.

AMERICAN INDIANS: GOODBYE TO TONTO

It is the fate of American Indians to exist in the national consciousness mainly as figures in a myth of the American past. Black writer James Baldwin's observation that "nobody knows my name" applies equally to Indians. Ralph Ellison's "invisible man" is the Indian as well as the black man. His mythical essence is more than his contemporary existence.

In the American psyche, Indians have existed to provide a human challenge to whites as they marched across the continent. Their resistance provided the stuff of myths of conquest and glory. Winthrop Jordan, the historian, commented in *White Over Black* on the symbolic meaning of the Indian in American experience in the 18th and 19th centuries: "Confronting the Indian in America was a testing experience, common to all the colonies. Conquering the Indian symbolized and personified the conquest of the American difficulties, the surmounting of the wilderness. To push back the Indian was to prove the worth of one's own mission, to make straight in the desert a highway of civilization."[19]

For many Americans there is something faintly anachronistic about contemporary Indians. One looks at them as figures out of the past, as relics of a more heroic age. Put somewhat differently, their existence has been hard to grasp. It is only recently that they have begun to make their special presence known.

American Indians Today

Just how many Indians there are in the United States is unclear. The 1960 census places the figure at just over 500,000 but Vine Deloria, former executive director of the National Congress of American Indians, estimates the number at closer to 1,000,000. There is also disagreement as to the number of Indians on reservations. The 1970 census reported 243,312, while Deloria, and Robert Sherrill in his work on the Pine Ridge Sioux, speak of close to 400,000.[20] Disagreements about the total number are partly a consequence of problems of definition. What degree of Indian ancestry makes one an Indian? Unfortunately, there are no data that allow us to differentiate clearly, among persons of mixed ancestry, between those who identify themselves as Indian and those who do not.

Whatever the disagreement about numbers, all parties are in accord that Indians have the sad distinction of being the most depressed of America's racial and ethnic groups. Sherrill has observed that "No minority group in this country is as poor as the 380,000 or so Indians who live on reservations. The average family income for Indians is said to be about $1,500, but the average on-reservation income is much lower. Unemployment ranges from 45 percent to 98 percent, the latter being the winter rate on some of the Dakota reservations."[21] The Bureau of Indian Affairs estimates that 71 percent of reservation Indians live in inadequate housing. The infant mortality rate is two to three times that of the rest of the population. Records compiled by the University of Colorado School of Medicine indicated a rate of 88.2 deaths per 1,000 live births among the Utes in 1960. Sherill described the large Pine Ridge reservation visited by the late Robert Kennedy: "In housing, employment and life style, the 10,000 to 12,000 Sioux . . . on the Pine Ridge Reservation are still untouched by the benevolence of Washington. A few families are living in abandoned automobiles. Some families live in tents, some in abandoned chicken coops. . . . At least 75 percent of the dwellings on this reservation have no plumbing."[22] The life expectancy of a reservation Indian is 46 years, considerably less than that of both whites and blacks.

Indians are most heavily concentrated in the Southwest, with over 100,000 living in Arizona and New Mexico. Another 64,000 live in Oklahoma. Numerous smaller communities and tribes are found in California, Oregon, and Washington, and in the north-central states of North Dakota, Minnesota, Wisconsin, and Michigan. Other groups are found in New York, North Carolina, Rhode Island, and other states.

The essence of the Indians' problem is that they lack the power to act in their own behalf. Their powerlessness derives in part from lack of numbers and in part from their unique legal status. Indians are citizens, the Indian Citizens Act of 1924 having conferred full constitutional rights on all Indians who were not then citizens. Their collective tribal rights are also defined by certain treaties, however, and they are subject, in certain respects, to the Bureau of Indian Affairs. The Bureau of Indian Affairs acts within a framework of powers defined by Congress, and Congress has from time to time enacted legislation which has been devastating to Indian interests.

While Indians are citizens, they are also dealt with, insofar as tribal lands and tribal rights are concerned, as members of a conquered nation whose rights can be expanded, contracted, or otherwise modified as the conqueror sees fit.

Recent years have witnessed a rise in Indian militancy. Vine Deloria, a Standing Rock Sioux, articulated the Indian's position in *Custer Died for Your Sins*.[23] In locales with large Indian populations, there are bumper stickers bearing testimony to the new spirit: "Indians Discovered America," "Indian Power," "Custer Had It Coming." The fairly complicated situation and protest of the Indian is made easier to grasp by placing it in historical context.

The Changing Status of American Indians

As it has for blacks, the majority society has, from time to time, asked itself what to do with, about, or to American Indians. Farb has observed that "Two contrasting images of the Indian—as Noble Red Man and as Blood Thirsty Savage—have prevailed in the minds of whites in the past five hundred years, and feelings have tended to shift back and forth between the two."[24] In recent decades, Indians have been either ignored or viewed as the special concern of people given to exotic causes; the country and western singer Johnny Cash, for example, is known to have a "thing" about convicts and Indians.

No national policy on Indians existed before the end of the 18th century; prior to that time no white American nation existed, and neither did Indians exist as a political or social collectivity. Just as European colonial power imposed a collective national identity on disparate African peoples, so the collective identity of Indians derives from their common experience of defeat and mistreatment at the hands of Euro-Americans.

A turning point of Indian policy, an event which defined the status of Indians in the new nation, occurred with the expropriation of the Cherokees' land. Indians faced the problem of how to adapt to the penetration of Europeans. A few chose to fight; others, seeking advantage over rivals, entered into temporary alliances with the newcomers, assuming that the coming of Europeans would entail no fundamental change in their traditional way of life. As the reality of European domination became clearer, the Cherokee chose to adopt the ways of the conqueror.

About 1790 the Cherokees decided to modify their traditional culture. They established churches, schools, and well-cultivated farms. Farb writes:

> In 1826 a Cherokee reported to the Presbyterian Church that his people already possessed 22,000 cattle, 7,600 houses, 46,000 swine, 2,500 sheep, 762 looms, 1,488 spinning wheels, 2,948 plows, 10 saw mills, 31 grist mills, 62 blacksmith shops, and 18 schools. In one of the Cherokee districts alone there were some 1,000 volumes "of good books." In 1821 . . . a Cherokee named Sequoya perfected a method of syllabary notation in which English letters stood for Cherokee syllables; by 1828 the Cherokee were already publishing their own newspaper. At about the same time they adopted a written constitution providing for an executive, a bicameral legislature, a supreme court, and a code of laws.[25]

To what extent would white society accommodate itself to Indians who were "just like everyone else"? The answer was, "Not at all." The Cherokee were unable to save themselves even by adopting what, from the majority perspective, should have been viewed as exemplary values. White demands for Indian land created pressure for their removal. The Cherokee were simply one of a number of tribes to be moved west of the Mississippi. On December 19, 1829, the Georgia state legislature passed an act appropriating a large area of the Cherokee nation. Georgia only reflected the mood in Washington. Farb indicates that:

> . . . President Jackson had been reared on the frontier and he was utterly insensitive to the treatment of the Indians. He denounced

as an "absurdity" and a "farce" that the United States should bother even to negotiate treaties with Indians as if they were independent nations with a right to their lands. He was completely in sympathy with the policy of removal of Indians to new lands west of the Mississippi. He exerted his influence to make Congress give legal sanction to what in our time, under the Nuremberg Laws, would be branded genocide. Dutifully Congress passed the Removal Act of 1830, which gave the President the right to extirpate all Indians who had managed to survive east of the Mississippi River.[26]

Some tribes chose to fight. The Seminoles of Florida resisted from 1835 to 1842, costing the United States the lives of some 1,500 troops and $20,000,000.

Many of the Iroquois sought sanctuary in Canada, and the Oneida and the Seneca were moved westward, although fragments of Iroquois tribes managed to remain behind in western New York. The Sac and Fox made a desperate stand in Illinois . . . but ultimately their survivors were forced to move as were the Ottawa, Potawatomic, Wyandot, Shawnee, Kickapoo, Winnebago, Delaware, Peoria, Miami and others who are remembered now only in the name of some town, lake, county or state, or as a footnote in the annals of a local history society.[27]

The Cherokee appealed to Washington but eventually were uprooted and forced westward over the 1,000-mile "trail of tears." An estimate made at the time stated that 4,000 died en route.

The fate of the Cherokee and other tribes forced west reflected a policy of confining Indians to tracts of land on the western plains. But white migration inevitably created pressure for more and more expropriation of reservation lands.

Greed for Indian lands, and a sympathy for Indians expressed as the desire to encourage their assimilation, came together to produce the Dawes Act of 1887. It marks the beginning of the modern era in the history of relations between Indians and the larger society. Indians are still suffering from its tragic consequences.

The period immediately preceding passage of the Dawes Act marked the last stand of the Indians. It is the period celebrated in innumerable cowboy movies. The Sioux rose in 1876, the Nez Perce in 1877, the Cheyenne in 1878, and the Apache in the 1880's, until Geronimo with 36 survivors finally surrendered to General Crook. A way of life had disappeared, and what was to replace it was not clear. White land hunger was unabated, and a movement started among some people sympathetic to the Indian "to give the remnant of Indian populations the dignity of private property . . . the plan was widely promoted in the halls of Congress, in the press and in the meetings of religious societies." Senator Henry L. Dawes, the Act's sponsor, hoped it might salvage something for the Indians. Unfortunately, it had loopholes which also made it attractive to those coveting Indian territory.

The Dawes Act authorized the President to parcel out tribal lands to individual Indians, each adult to receive 160 acres and each child, 80 acres. The argument was that, if given his own plot of land, the Indian could become an industrious farmer. Whatever acreage was left over was to be declared "surplus" and offered for sale to whites, the proceeds presumably to be spent by the Department of the Interior for the benefit of the Indians.

Some tribes resisted allotment, and the Creeks, Choctaws, Chickasaws, Cherokees, Seminoles, and several others were exempted. The Act failed to break up tribes or convert Indians into farmers; instead, it resulted in the impoverishment of much of the Indian population. Between 1887 and 1932, approximately 90 million acres out of 138 million initially held by Indians passed to white ownership. Vine Deloria observed:

> The effects of individualizing the tribal estate was the creation of extreme poverty on many of the reservations. Individual Indians, unaccustomed to viewing land as a commodity, were easily swindled out of their allotments.
>
> Indians who sold their land did not merge into white society and disappear. They simply moved onto their relatives' land and remained within the tribal society. Thus, the land base was rapidly diminishing while the population continued to remain constant and, in some cases, grew spectacularly.[38]

The rapid decline of Indians was finally halted with the passage in 1934 of the Wheeler-Howard Act, better known as the Indian Reorganization Act. This legislation grew out of investigations of Indian conditions in 1926. The Indian Reorganization Act tacitly acknowledged that assimilation was still far off. It ended the allotment policy, encouraged the reformation of tribal government, improved social services on tribal lands, and restored freedom of religion for Indians. The Act sought to let the Indian use his own culture.

Government policy has ever been inconsistent, however, and the early 1950's brought another attempt to enforce assimilation and new hardship to certain tribes. The principal piece of legislation was a resolution declaring the intent of Congress to terminate federal relations with the tribes at the earliest possible time. The legislation was spurred by cries that the reservations were havens for the irresponsible and a burden to the taxpayer.

Termination proved to be a disaster for those tribes which felt its impact. First, it lent itself to several interpretations. It could mean the transfer to the federal government of certain services performed by the Bureau of Indian Affairs, the B.I.A. Division of Health, for example, giving way to the United States Public Health Service. It could mean the transfer of Indian students to public schools. It could mean the extension of the criminal and civil laws of the state to the reservation, thereby depriving tribes of substantial powers of local government.

In its most grievous form, it entailed the appropriation of Indian assets. Four bands of Paiutes were the first whose relations with the B.I.A. were terminated, and their experiences augured ill for those Indians to whom the law was to be applied. The Shivwits, Koosharem, Indian Peaks, and Kanosh bands of the Paiutes held approximately 46,000 acres of land. They were terminated in 1957, and a year or so later, after their already desperate circumstances had become even worse, they were asked why they had agreed to termination in the first place. A Kanosh man indicated that, at the time of the hearing, they had not understood what was happening. The low educational level of the bands and their general poverty testified to the validity of his assertion. Upon termination, Paiute land was transferred from the Bureau of Indian Affairs to trustees of the Walker Bank and Trust Company in Salt Lake City, 160 miles away. Aberle and Brophy recount:

> *The Paiutes had difficulty getting transportation to the bank and then communicating with the trust officer. An Indian Peaks man said that they finally collected enough money for gasoline to go to Salt Lake City, where they saw the trustee, but they could not understand his remarks and after a few minutes were shown out of his office. They tried unsuccessfully to get advice from an attorney appointed by the bank and paid with Paiute money. Later the attorney wrote the Indian Peaks official that he would have samples of valuable minerals found on tribal land tested. But, the Paiute continued, we do not know one stone from another.*[29]

Basically, the Paiutes were cast forth and told to survive. They had neither the resources nor the experience. Sending their children to public school entailed a $15-a-year activity fee per child and one dollar a week for school lunch, expenses they could not meet. They could not pay doctor or hospital bills. The very circumstances of their old life denied the possibility of easy survival under the new system;

lacking birth certificates and social security numbers because they had not been needed, they had difficulty obtaining social services after certain forms of B.I.A. assistance were withdrawn.

Termination had the same unhappy consequences for the relatively well-off Menominee as it had for the already impoverished Paiutes. The Menominees owned a forest in Wisconsin and operated a sawmill to provide employment for tribal members. Deloria described the effects of termination:

> *Termination of Federal Supervision meant an immediate tax bill of 55 percent on the sawmill. To meet this, the sawmill had to be automated, thus throwing a substantial number of Indians out of work and onto the unemployment rolls. To meet the rising unemployment situation, the only industry, the sawmill, had to be taxed by the county. There was an immediate spiral downward in the capital structure of the tribe so that in years since the termination bill was passed, it has had to receive some $10 million in special state and Federal aid. The end is not yet in sight.[30]*

Rising Indian protest brought an end to actual termination during the Kennedy and Johnson years, although it still, presumably, remains the intent of Congress. The War On Poverty brought a variety of new programs to Indian tribes and, in many instances, involved Indians in decision-making capacities with regard to the kinds of programs a reservation would have and how they were to be run. Indians are now attempting to formulate a set of goals for their people; they are attempting both to define themselves as Indians and to work out a coherent and effective set of strategies for acquiring sufficient political power to act on their own behalf.

Indian Power: What It Means

With the end of the plains wars between the last independent Indian tribes and the United States army, a different kind of "Indian problem" faced the nation. It was no longer a matter of seizing and holding Indian lands but rather of working out a policy toward a conquered people. Those favoring termination of the reservations, whether under the Dawes Act or, several decades later, under the House resolution, assumed, implicitly, that there would be no Indian problem if there were no Indians. Legislation to force assimilation had the consequences, however, of eroding the resources of those Indians who remained on the reservations without providing assistance to those pushed out from under the domain of the B.I.A. In other words, it imposed upon

Indians the worst of both worlds. Thus, Indians today are the nation's most depressed ethnic group.

Ironically, federal policies intended to eradicate the "Indian problem" helped to create the social base of the contemporary Indian protest movement. In the years following World War II and the Korean War, "In the hope that the Indian youth would leave the tribal reservations at last and enter the 'mainstream,' the government made education the top priority in Indian affairs."[81] Steiner indicates that, "Within ten years —1950 to 1960—the number of Indian high school students increased from 24,000 to 57,000. In that decade the Indian youth attending college for one year or more went up from 6,500 to 17,000."[82]

Among Indians in college, there was a high dropout rate, but, significantly, Indians with high academic aptitude were as likely to drop out as Indians with moderate academic aptitude. College introduced Indians to a broader cultural world than they had experienced on the reservation but also forced many to confront the question of whether they wanted to "pass" into the white world or retain an Indian identity. In essence, the federal policy afforded to them the chance to be "white," provided they would stop being Indian.

It was from among this group, more broadly acquainted with the larger world than reservation Indians and more closely acquainted with the struggles of other minority groups, that the leadership of the contemporary Indian movement came. Included were Vine Deloria, Herbert Blatchford, founding director of the National Indian Youth Council, Mel Thom, and many others.

For the most part, Indian protest has involved symbolic actions. An example was the two-year occupation of Alcatraz Island.

When the federal penitentiary on the island in San Francisco Bay was abandoned by the government, there was a good deal of discussion over what to do with it. Before an official decision could be made, about 80 Indians, on November 20, 1969, occupied the island. The action struck a responsive chord among Indians, and groups from all over the United States journeyed to Alcatraz. The action was symbolic and meant both to provide an example of Indian unity and to draw public attention to Indian grievances against federal policy.

Perhaps because they are relatively few in number and, unlike blacks, are below the threshold of public attention, Indians have had to resort to "dramatic actions" to present their case.

An increasing number of Indians are demanding "Indian Power." The program associated with Indian power is twofold. First, Indians resolve the dilemma of dual citizenship by wanting the best of both worlds. They desire to retain reservations as bases from which to develop. By developing the reservations in whatever terms seem to make economic sense, they seek some degree of economic independence and it is hoped, even affluence. They are motivated to retain their land, for symbolic and instrumental reasons. Symbolically, it is all that is left to them of a continent they once owned. Instrumentally, without the land their resources are nil, and they become like the dust of the plains, blown here and there with no place of their own.

They seek, however, to change the terms under which they have held the land. They have been treated as wards in both legal fact and administrative reality. The Great White Father has assumed that his Indian children were incompetent in running their own affairs. Indians desire all the services they can get from the federal government, but they also want to make their own decisions with regard to how these services and resources can best be used in the interests of the Indian community.

Anglos might question the propriety of this approach: "They want to have their cake and eat it too." The unspoken Indian response is, "You made us what we are today—poor, untutored, dependent—you should help us become something else."

Second, Indians desire to retain their identity as Indians. Retention of tribal lands seems to be both a strategic matter relating to an enhanced standard of living and an affirmation of Indian identity. In a sense, this is more important than the economic issue. Indians were defeated by Europeans, not only militarily and politically, but also psychologically. The negative self-image of blacks, extirpated by the black power movement, has its analogue in the shattered ego of Indians— "drunken redskins," "bloodthirsty savages," "gifted makers of beads and trinkets"—expunged by the Indian power movement. It is not a law of nature that Tonto must ride in the Lone Ranger's shadow. Implicitly, the supporters of termination deny the value of Indian culture and the validity of the contemporary Indian's historically derived and probably unique perspective. They deny that the communalism expressed in the tribal holding of land is worth retaining. For an Indian, to support this view is to agree that he has fulfilled his historical purpose and is no longer "needed." The implicit, and probably growing, cultural nationalism of the Indian power movement asserts the value of Indian culture and seeks the survival of Indians as an identifiable people.

REFERENCES

1. Tomatsu Shibutani and Kian Kwan, *Ethnic Stratification: A Comparative Approach* (New York: The Macmillan Company, 1965), p. 551.

2. Joseph Himes, *The Study of Sociology: An Introduction* (Glenview, Ill.: Scott, Foresman, and Company, 1968), p. 483.

3. Manual Gamio, *Mexican Immigration to the United States* (Chicago: University of Chicago Press, 1930), p. 123.

4. Carey McWilliams, *North From Mexico* (Philadelphia: J. B. Lippincott, 1949), p. 215.

5. Alphonse Pinkney "Prejudice Toward Mexican and Negro Americans: A Comparison," in *Mexican Americans in the United States* (John H. Burma, ed., Cambridge, Mass.: Schenkman Publishing Co., 1970), p. 78.

6. McWilliams, *op. cit.*, p. 207.

7. *Ibid.*, p. 130.

8. Ernesto Galarza, "The Mexican American: A National Concern," in *Race Prejudice and Discrimination* (Arnold Rose, ed., New York: Alfred Knopf, 1951), pp. 64–65.

9. *Ibid.*, p. 58.

10. John Gregory Dunne, *Delano: The Story of the California Grape Strike* (New York: Farrar, Straus & Giroux, 1967), p. 79.

11. *Ibid.*, pp. 128–129.

12. Joseph L. Love, "La Raza: Mexican Americans in Rebellion," in Burma, *op. cit.*, p. 58.

13. Elena Padilla, *Up From Puerto Rico* (New York: Columbia University Press, 1958), p. 23.

14. Patricia Sexton, *Spanish Harlem: Anatomy of Poverty* (New York: Harper and Row, 1965), p. 55.

15. *Loc. cit.*

16. Warren Brown, "The Puerto Rican in New York City," in Rose, *op. cit.*, p. 92.

17. Padilla, *op. cit.*, p. 72.

18. Philip S. Foner, *The Black Panthers Speak* (Philadelphia: J. B. Lippincott, 1970), pp. 229–239.

19. Winthrop Jordan, *White Over Black: American Attitudes Toward the Negro 1550-1812* (Baltimore: Penguin Books, Inc., 1968), pp. 90–91.

20. Robert Sherrill, "Red Man's Heritage: The Lagoon of Excrement," *The Nation* (Nov. 10, 1969), pp. 500–503.

21. *Ibid.*, p. 501.

22. *Ibid.*, p. 502.

23. Vine Deloria, Jr., *Custer Died For Your Sins* (New York: Avon Books, 1970).

24. Peter Farb, *Man's Rise To Civilization as Shown by the Indians of North America From Primeval Times to the Coming of the Industrial State* (New York: E. P. Dutton, 1968), pp. 295–296.

25. *Ibid.*, p. 302.

26. *Ibid.*, pp. 300–301.

27. *Ibid.*, p. 301.

28. Vine Deloria, "The War Between the Redskins and the Feds," *New York Times Sunday Magazine* (December 7, 1969), pp. 92 and 94.

29. William Brophy and Sophie Aberle, *The Indian: America's Unfinished Business* (Norman, Oklahoma: University of Oklahoma Press, 1966), p. 195.

30. Deloria, *op. cit.*, p. 96.

31. Stan Steiner, *The New Indians* (New York: Dell Publishing Company, 1969), p. 31.

32. *Loc. cit.*

MOVEMENTS FOR SEXUAL LIBERATION

5

THE TRANSFORMATION OF STIGMA:

An Analysis of the Gay Liberation Movement

Homosexuality has been among the most stigmatized forms of social deviance in the United States.[1] At the same time, as the sociologist Edward Sagarin observed, "No group so large in number, so completely stigmatized, and placed into so disadvantaged a position remained so long unorganized in this organizational society."[2]

The enormous stigma attached to homosexuality probably accounts, in part, for the relative slowness of a homosexual political movement to develop. The immediate costs to individual homosexuals in terms of loss of employment, family disgrace, and the like outweighed any long-term benefits a gay movement might realize in terms of improved public attitudes towards gays.

In the late 1960's, a gay liberation movement did develop, and over a period of a few years a flourishing gay subculture surfaced in the major cities of the country. In New York, several movie houses showed only gay films, gay theater flourished off-Broadway, a number of gay newspapers and magazines were found on newsstands, there were gay radio programs, and an annual gay parade. A gay newspaper called *Come Out*[3] appeared, and several underground papers carried gay liberation supplements. Protest groups such as the Gay Liberation Front and the Gay Activists Alliance were formed, and student homophile organizations were organized at a number of major schools. New York City police officials acknowledged, "We can't take gay people for granted anymore, we can't assume they're placid and won't rebel."[4]

Initially it was the purpose of this chapter to account for the rise of the gay liberation movement in theoretical terms. It became obvious almost immediately, however, that the world of gay political activism was much more complex than was at first believed and that a good deal of attention should be devoted to describing it accurately.

It became necessary to differentiate the actual movement from the media movement. With gays, as with women's liberationists and black militants, the media movement may bear only a distant relationship to the real movement. For example, late in 1969 two newspapers, *Gay* and *Gay Power*, appeared on the newsstands and were viewed by many as heralds of gay liberation. In reality, both were subsidiaries of what might be termed "hard-core heterosexual" publications and exploited the market for homosexual pornography. *Gay* was sponsored by the publishers of a girlie newspaper called *Screw*, and *Gay Power* by the publishers of a similar sheet called *Kiss*. While making bows to the ideology of gay liberation, both sought their major market among those interested in nude frontal photographs of men. Rather than being manifestations of the gay movement, as many took them to be, they were money-making ventures sponsored by heterosexuals.[5]

It was a major task, then, to identify and define the limits of this complex and partially hidden movement.

In the first section of this chapter we will examine the circumstances attending the rise of politically active homosexual organizations. Primary attention will be given to the difference between the Mattachine Society and the gay liberation movement. The objective will be to differentiate the gay liberation movement empirically and conceptually from previous homosexual political movements. In the second section of this chapter, a tentative theoretical formulation is advanced to account for the gay liberation movement.

SOCIAL AND POLITICAL MOVEMENTS AMONG HOMOSEXUALS

The first known organization of homosexuals in the United States was founded by four people in Chicago in 1925. Known as the Society for Human Rights, it flickered briefly, then sputtered out.

The next effort came in New York City 20 years later with the Quaker Emergency Committee, an agency which counseled homosexuals arrested in public places. A dispute between the Quakers and one of their professionals, the psychiatrist George W. Henry, led to Henry's withdrawing to set up his own organization, the George W. Henry Foundation.

Among the early groups having a lineal connection with the Mattachine Society, the first successful and most enduring gay political group, was the Veterans' Benevolent Association. Founded in New York City in 1945 by recently discharged veterans, it had a membership of about 75 and was primarily concerned with social life and recreation rather than with the legal and social disabilities visited upon homosexuals. In other words, it was expressive rather than instrumental. Significantly, it feared publicity. Members were particularly hostile to homosexuals who were overtly effeminate, and the organization dissolved in 1954 because of its inability to resolve disputes between those who were critical of any departure from a masculine image and those who believed there should be room for all types. Like some members of other minorities, many members of the Veterans' Benevolent Association believed that their problems as a minority group could be explained in large part by the scandalous behavior of a small number of people in the group. In the same way, there has been resentment of lower-class blacks by some middle-class blacks, the former being viewed as loud, vulgar, razor-wielding, semiliterate embodiments of the white stereotype. And many of the Jewish residents in the country in the late 19th century were resentful of the recently arrived East European Jews whose appearance and behavior, they believed, lent support to antisemitic stereotypes. The Veterans' Benevolent Association, like later homosexual political organizations, had to decide whether to be "respectable" and keep out the "flaming queen" or to be inclusive and fight for the queen's right to be a queen. They were unable to resolve this issue, and it destroyed them.

In the period between the birth and death of the Veterans' Benevolent Association the Mattachine Society, the most enduring of the homosexual political groups, came into existence.

The Mattachine was founded in 1950. To understand homosexual politics and the relationship of the contemporary Mattachine Society to gay liberation, it will be useful to discuss the circumstances out of which the Mattachine developed.

The high degree of stigma attached to homosexuality affected the development of homosexual organizations in several ways. It meant, first, that every homosexual was likely to make an intense effort to keep his sexual preference secret. As a result, it was difficult for homosexuals to identify one another. Second, the stigma had the consequence of confining most homosexual contacts to fleeting encounters in public rest rooms and parks. The lack of sustained interaction in these encounters inhibited the formation of extensive, stable, informal networks. It also prevented the development of a shared "counter ideology," a belief system which would have provided homosexuals with a set of rationalizations and justifications for their sexual preference. Third, in the absence of a group-derived counter ideology, many homosexuals internalized prevailing "straight" definitions of their behavior, coming to view it as "sick," "criminal," and "degenerate" and consequently experienced profound feelings of guilt.

The contemporary gay has a powerful counter ideology which supplies him with justifications and rationalizations for being gay. But in the period immediately following World War II, gays had no such counter ideology and thus internalized the sentiment expressed by one of the homosexuals in the play *Boys in the Band*: "Show me a happy homosexual and I'll show you a gay corpse."

Until the development of the gay liberation movement, "straights" were not as predisposed to speak out for homosexuals as they were for other minority groups. It has often been the case with minority groups that members of higher-status groups initiate organization and militant protest. Whites were instrumental in organizing the N.A.A.C.P. and the Congress of Racial Equality. A high-status person is less likely to be vulnerable to reprisals and more likely to have contacts with the powerful and influential. Public abhorrence of homosexuality reduced the operation of this factor in promoting the political organization of homosexuals. Homosexuality is what might be termed a "contagious stigma," a form of stigma in which the advocate of tolerance is seen as speaking from self-interested motives. Certain forms of deviance have an element of contagion in them, while others do not. To be a fervent and vocal champion of equal rights in Mississippi would be deviant, but it would not be contagious deviance. It might make one a "nigger lover" but, in the view of the redneck, it would not make one a "nigger." On the other hand, until recently, to have championed the rights of homosexuals would have raised suspicions in the public mind that the advocate was himself gay.[6] To speak out in favor of a system with regard to heroin addiction, in which the addict is offered his required dosage under the auspices of a physician, does not raise suspicions that one is an addict looking for an easy fix, but in some communities, to champion civil liberties for avowed communists has raised suspicions in many minds that one is a "red."

Where contagion is present, the probability that high-status non-deviants will take the lead in organizing a stigmatized group is less than it is where contagion is not present.

The contribution of straights to the political organization of homosexuals was indirect. In 1948, the Kinsey report, *Sexual Behavior in the Human Male*, appeared. It dealt broadly with sexual behavior and attitudes and drew fire from blue-stockings all over the country. The discussion of homosexuality would have been regarded as outrageous if published separately, but in the context of a work which many found generally offensive it was not singled out for special attention except by homosexuals, and they were stunned by it. The report indicated that homosexuality was much more widespread than anyone had believed. From their data, Kinsey and his associates stated that 37 percent of the white male population had had at least some overt homosexual experience to the point of orgasm between adolescence and old age; 18 percent of those having had such an experience, had at least as much homosexual as heterosexual experience for at least three years, 8 percent were exclusively homosexual for at least three years, and half of these individuals, or 4 percent, were exclusively homosexual.[7] Sagarin suggests that the

Kinsey report had a catalytic effect. "Shortly after the Kinsey volume appeared, there arose in many cities a number of discussion groups of homosexuals. They came on the scene spontaneously, usually with no connection with each other."[8]

Out of meetings in Los Angeles came the Mattachine Society. There had been previous attempts to organize in the Los Angeles area; in 1948, a Bachelors-for-Wallace organization had supported Henry Wallace, the presidential candidate on the Progressive Party ticket. But the founding of the Mattachine marked the first successful effort at gay political organization. It was founded in 1950, and the name commemorated the fools and jesters of legend who "spoke the truth in the face of stern authority." In the context of its time it was radical, but the seeds of subsequent conflict with the gay liberation movement were present from the beginning. Like the Veterans' Benevolent Association, the Mattachine was concerned with image and sought to dissuade members from any behavior which, they believed, would confirm public stereotypes about "limp-wristed faggots." Some women's liberation groups face a similar issue today when meeting charges that their members are lesbians. Should they try to induce members to avoid in their manner or appearance anything which would lend credence to these allegations or should they admit to their ranks women who are in fact lesbians? Believing themselves to be functioning in an extremely hostile environment, the Mattachine chose to be circumspect. Its stand was almost apologetic. The membership pledge adopted in 1951 stated: "While it is my conviction that homosexuality in our society is no virtue, but rather a handicap, I believe I can live a well-oriented and socially productive life." In another section of the pledge, the member "swore to unswervingly guard the anonymity of all members of the Mattachine Society, of sponsoring organizations and affiliates."[9]

The Mattachine began, however, to formulate an ideology which has come in a more dramatic form to be espoused by the gay liberation movement. The ideology which evolved bears a striking resemblance to that of other beleaguered minorities. Functioning to explain and justify the deviance of the organization's members, it had three components. These might be termed the higher morality argument, the normal man argument, and the great man argument.

The higher morality aspect of the ideology suggested that the inclination toward homosexuality is widespread but only certain people have the courage to acknowledge their homosexuality. By not becoming "closet queens" (homosexuals who hide their homosexuality), they manifest a higher form of morality. The normal man argument suggested that the homosexual is just like everyone else except for his sexual preference. It stressed that homosexuals are found in all walks of life and in all occupations, even those considered very "masculine." The position was similar to that voiced by the civil rights movement for a considerable period of time, that blacks are just like everyone else save for the color of their skin. The Mattachine even spoke of integration with heterosexuals. The third dimension in the ideology identified great men who were homosexual and, at least implicitly, attributed their greatness to their homosexuality. In the ranks one finds Walt Whitman, Tschaikovsky, Christopher Marlowe, Hans Christian Andersen, Michelangelo, Proust, Andre Gide, General Kitchner, Verlaine, and Rimbaud.

Minority group ideologies function to suggest to the members of a group that they have nothing to be ashamed of, that they are "just like everyone else except for one little thing," and that they should even be proud of that "one little thing" since it has produced great men. An extension of this development would be a demand for "gay studies programs."[10]

Factionalism wracked the Mattachine as it seems to have wracked all homosexual organizations and soon a number of fissures appeared. Members who wanted to put out a popular magazine broke away to form *One*, the name coming from a Thomas Carlyle quotation, "A mystic bond of brotherhood makes all men one." Mattachine societies were organized in a number of cities, and there were attempts at a national structure, which collapsed after a decade in a welter of recriminations over alleged high-handedness on the part of the president and charges of misuse of funds. Various local chapters became autonomous and functioned beside other homosexual organizations which came into existence.

The Gay Liberation Movement

Until the rise of the gay liberation movement, the factions were not qualitatively different from one another. By the late 1960's, in the United States and Canada, there were many agencies, voluntary associations, publications' centers, and local social clubs which, taken together, constituted the homosexual movement."[11] Throughout the 1960's, there were sporadic, isolated instances of gay protest. In 1963, several gays picketed the Whitehall Induction Center in New York City in protest against the violation of the confidentiality of draft records of homosexuals. In 1966, a handful of homosexuals undertook a "sip-in" at a series of bars in protest against New York State Liquor Authority regulations prohibiting service to homosexuals. But these were the actions of militant individuals rather than the manifestations of a movement.

A series of dramatic events at the end of the decade marked the rise of the gay liberation movement. In April, 1969, a group called Homosexuals Intransigent was formed at City College of New York. The distinctive characteristic of Homosexuals Intransigent—and a decisive factor in the development of a gay liberation movement—was that it encouraged its members to acknowledge their homosexuality publicly. The organization insisted that voting members not conceal their homosexuality but allowed gays not yet at this stage to participate as nonvoting members. They insisted that gays come out of the closet, that they acknowledge unashamedly, both to themselves and others, the fact of being homosexual.

The second event was the Stonewall "riot," which has come to be commemorated by an annual gay parade. To understand the significance of the Stonewall riot, it is necessary to examine the patterns of social life among gays.

Gay social life is organized around certain public places. These public places fall into two categories: those which are manifestly public, and those which are *de jure* public but *de facto* gay. Put somewhat differently, there is public turf and there is gay turf (or what some gays refer to as "gay ghettoes"). Public turf includes such places as train and subway rest rooms, secluded spots at parks and beaches, and the balconies and rest rooms of certain theaters. These are places where transient contacts are made for fellatio, mutual masturbation, and, sometimes, sodomy. Places of this kind also pose the greatest danger. Arrest data indicate that most homosexuals are picked up on public turf. The chances of being arrested in a private dwelling, hotel room, or on gay turf are considerably smaller.[12] Gay bars and the public baths heavily frequented by gays constitute gay turf. The baths offer the opportunity to cruise (walk around looking for a sex partner) and, in the rooms, the opportunity to engage in sexual acts in relative privacy. The bars allow for cruising, conviviality, and, in some places, sexual acts. In every large city, there are a number of gay bars, New York alone having more than 80, most located in the gay ghettoes of Greenwich Village and midtown Manhattan.

Since there are a limited number of places where open contacts can be made, the gay ghetto is important to gays. With regard to communities of deviants, Goffman has observed that "Social deviants . . . are temporarily tolerated . . . providing they are restricted within the ecological boundaries of their community. Like ethnic and racial ghettoes these communities constitute a haven of self-defense and a place where the individual deviant can openly take the line that he is at least as good as anyone else."[13] For these reasons, police incursions on gay turf represent fairly serious threats. Nevertheless, the raids take place.

The Stonewall was a gay bar on Christopher Street in New York. In their raid, the police, much to their surprise, met open resistance as the Stonewall's patrons pushed them back into the street. A crowd gathered, police reinforcements were called in, and street fighting started. Members of the gay liberation front commented on the event, saying "It was not the . . . bar as such, which was being defended. Rather, it was the idea of defending just one place, even in a gay ghetto, where people could meet without harassment and intimidation."

The organization of Homosexuals Intransigent and the Stonewall riot were turning points in the gay movement. They represented two essential elements differentiating the gay liberation movement from previous political efforts of homosexuals: open declaration of identity, and tactical militance.

The gay liberation movement differs from earlier gay movements in three ways. In addition to the two factors already cited, a counter ideology developed which repudiated the strongly negative ideology of straight society.

HOMOSEXUALS, SELF-IDENTITY, AND THE GAY LIBERATION MOVEMENT
The Mattachine was founded as a secret society. The concern with anonymity extended even to members wanting to be protected from each other. When a doctoral dissertation on a Mattachine chapter was undertaken, the student had to ensure some of his respondents who were on the mailing list that he would not reveal their identity to other members of the chapter.

The problem of identity is a constant in biographies of homosexuals.[14] During the period of adolescence, many persons who later become homosexual begin to sense that their sexual preferences depart from the norm. Because homosexuality was highly stigmatized, few gays could openly discuss being gay. The public perceived homosexuality as sickness or perversion. Inevitably, many homosexuals were influenced by this perception and had to face the choice between accepting it, thereby defining themselves as evil or perverted, and rejecting it but without social or intellectual support for the rejection. Many gays accepted the definition, viewed themselves as "sick," and sought psychiatric care in order to be "cured" of their homosexuality.

In raising questions of identity, gays have also raised the issue of the roles they play vis-à-vis each other. Many older gays assumed either the "femme" or "butch" roles; that is, they were either very feminine or very masculine.[15] In other words, their conception of interpersonal relations mirrored that of heterosexuals. Now, partly because of changes in heterosexual definitions of sex roles and partly because of homosexual debate about roles, identity, and authenticity, gays are also moving away from being limited to the femme/butch alternatives.

The gay liberation movement confronted the problem of identity and insisted that gays come out of the closet. Interviews conducted by the author have indicated that a good deal of time at campus homophile meetings is devoted to consciousness-raising that, in effect, means making manifest to oneself that one is gay and not hiding it from others.

Charles L., leader of a campus homophile group, has indicated: "There are a lot of people who are really gay but try to hide it from themselves. They either deny it absolutely or they call themselves bisexual. At these meetings a person can come out of the closet. They can come to deal with themselves." Charles is black, and he was asked which took precedence in his identity, being black or being gay.

> *I was active in the civil rights movement in the 1960's and I worked out the black thing then. I hid from people that I was gay, none of the people I was close to in the movement knew it. I would say that now the most important thing is being gay. What happens to me now and the people that I move with are more determined by my being gay than by my being black.*

This student homophile group also undertook a series of talks in the dorms to educate other students.

There are publics and publics, however, and while they had been able to make their identity known to friends and to the kinds of secondary groups encountered in dorms, only three of 17 of these college students had informed their parents of their homosexuality. Sally L., a lesbian, enlarged on the difficulty:

> *My mother has it all mapped out for me. I'm 20 now and she figures in five years I'll be married and have two kids. She's looking forward to having grandchildren. I had high hopes of getting off the hook when my older brother got married, but he got a divorce and is bitter now about marriage.*

"Are you going to tell her?"

> *No, I can't. I'm my mother's daughter and she expects certain things of me. I'll just live my life. They don't live here anyway and they don't have to know. They'll be disappointed that I don't get married and they'll keep talking about it—about finding a man. But I doubt they'll ever catch on.*

Gerald G. was handling the matter differently:

> *They won't let themselves think it and I won't tell them right out. I'm trying to ease them into it. At some time they're going to figure*

*out that these guys I bring home aren't just school chums. I'm plan-
ning to take them to see Boys in the Band just so they can see that
being gay is not that much of an underground thing. [This surprised me and I even viewed it as a tactical error as Boys in the Band
has been attacked in the gay press as a vicious and bitchy put-down
on gay life. I raised the point with Gerald, and he indicated that
he thought they would benefit simply from seeing that homosexuality was sufficiently aboveboard to be the subject of a popular
play and movie.] Anyway, I think their favorite relative, my uncle,
is gay. He was married some years ago—but got a divorce and for
the last 15 years or so has been living with a so-called roommate.
They would just not let themselves think about it, though.*

He picked up a theme which many of the student homophile members
voiced in one way or another: "Even if they knew, they would not
admit it to themselves. They would just not talk about it. They would
not acknowledge it. They would know, but it would be a nonfact."
Charles had told his mother, and the reaction had been predictable:

*I told her when I went home over the spring vacation and she be-
came hysterical. She's a nurse and began to tell me all these stories
about homosexuals being brought into the hospital all beat up.
I'm supposed to go home this weekend and she's got an appointment
for me with a psychiatrist. From her point of view I'm sick and
that's it. There is nothing else she will listen to or understand.*

The meaning of "making it public", then, must include the idea
that there are several publics, some tougher than others.

TACTICAL MILITANCE   Gay liberation groups are generally more militant in their tactics than many Mattachine chapters, employing different
means to accomplish the same ends. Both the Mattachine Society of New
York and gay liberation groups are desirous of legislation outlawing job
discrimination against gays, but they differ in their approaches. D. L., of
the Mattachine, enlarged on the matter in an interview with the author:

*They [the gay liberation front] want C. W. [a member of the city
council] to introduce a bill, and, of course, she'll just be a laughing
stock if it comes out of the blue. As a matter of fact, I can hear
some of our wittier councilmen referring to it as "blue" legislation
only to have some other wag reply, "No, this isn't a blue law, it's a
pink law." What I'm trying to do is get ten or so councilmen together in a room and talk about it so that when it comes up they'll
know about it and the whole thing will go smoothly.*

Tactical disagreements between Mattachine and gay liberation about gay bars are more complicated. Following a police raid at a bar called the Snakepit, resulting in the arrest of a large number of patrons, one of whom was severely injured attempting to escape, demonstrations were organized by liberationists. D. L. of the Mattachine dissented, however:

> What they [gay liberation] are doing is unwise. They are trying to get B [Chief Inspector of the morals squad]. B does a reasonable job for a cop. He raided a bar the night before the Snakepit raid and nothing happened. When they come into one of these places that are going after hours, technically all that they can do is take in the bartender and the owner and that's all that B does. He lost his head at the Snakepit. He's got to pull off some of these raids; otherwise the people above him are going to begin asking him what the hell he does with his time. What the gay liberation people don't know is that the narcotics squad is all hot to get into the gay scene. So far they haven't because it's B's territory. But if the gay activists make it so hot for him that he's pulled out by higher-ups, then the narco squad will move in, and if they come in the scene is different. Today half the guys in a bar may have a joint in their pockets or some pills, and the narcs can legitimately pull them all in.

In its own way, D. L.'s Mattachine group was supporting the chief inspector.

The Development of a Counter-Ideology

With the development of the gay liberation movement, a gay counter ideology began to take shape. The counter ideology functioned to refute certain mainstream ideas with regard to homosexuality and to provide positive intellectual supports for maintaining a gay identity.

Psychology, psychoanalysis, and psychiatry have been major targets in the gay counter ideology. Psychoanalysts such as Bieber take for granted that homosexuality is an illness. Bieber, a major spokesman on the topic, has declared that "fear of heterosexuality underlies homosexuality . . . fear of disease or injury to the genitals . . . associated with fear and aversion to female genitalia."[16] Barbara Gittings, founder of the New York chapter of the Daughters of Bilitis, articulated one of the tenets of the counter ideology: "The best thing psychiatrists could do for homosexuals would be to stop churning out literature about homosexuality as a psychiatric "problem" for the homosexual and start challenging the problem where it really is—in the bigotry of society."[17]

A second tenet of the ideology goes beyond the contention that gays should not be subject to violations of their civil rights when they assert the right to develop uniquely gay patterns of social relations. In other words, some gays have moved beyond condemning such things as job discrimination against homosexuals to declaring that homosexuals should have the legal right to get married and to adopt children.

Some gay liberation groups have evolved an ideology which attempts to equate homosexuals with other minority groups, seeing them all as victims of an oppressive system. Opposition to gay liberation is viewed as part of a system that is broadly oppressive.[18]

There is no single gay counter ideology; rather, there is a variety of propositions subscribed to in varying number and intensity by different gays and gay groups. They constitute a more elaborate intellectual armor than gays had available to them before the rise of the gay liberation movement. Gay activists often denigrate the Mattachine by comparing it to the N.A.A.C.P., meaning to imply that it is monolithic and conservative. But it is misleading to speak of Mattachine as analogous to the N.A.A.C.P. The N.A.A.C.P. has a national office that sets broad limits within which the local chapters may act. There is a certain kind of organizational and therefore ideological coherence. The N.A.A.C.P. national office can and has disciplined locals which took certain ideological positions or engaged in certain kinds of actions. By contrast, the Mattachine has no national structure. Each chapter assumes whatever character its circumstances and membership happen to yield. Thus, while the New York Mattachine is in a bitter struggle with gay liberation groups, Mattachine Midwest, operating out of Chicago, is to the left of many New York gay liberation groups.

Gay liberation is itself a many-splendored thing, ranging from hard-line Marxists in the big cities through campus gays in the hinterlands, concerned mainly with consciousness-raising and social activities and only dimly aware of the factionalism and ideological debates which characterize the urban scene.

Gays: Male/Female

Gay liberation movements include lesbians as well as male homosexuals. Lesbians had for some time been organized in the Daughters of Bilitis. This organization was founded in San Francisco in October, 1955, by Phylis Lyon and Del Clark, who felt there should be a place other than bars where lesbians could meet each other. Like the Mattachine Society, it served primarily to provide conviviality and a bit of education for its members. As the women's movement and the male gay movement developed the Daughters of Bilitis developed a more critical perspective.

Male homosexuals were criticized as "sexist." Lyons and Martin indicated that the Daughters of Bilitis experienced steady growth because "male-oriented gay groups wanted them as secretaries, coffee makers, and hostesses. Had we been in their organizations . . . I think we would have had to fight tooth and toenail to get into any policy-making position."[19]

Women's liberation groups were urged to speak out on the problems of lesbians. It was pointed out that lesbians, in supporting themselves, experience discrimination as women in the job market and on the job.

The Los Angeles chapter of the National Organization of Women was persuaded to put forth a strong statement on behalf of lesbians:

No other woman suffers more abuse and discrimination for the right to be her own person than the lesbian . . . [she] is doubly oppressed both as a woman and as a homosexual . . . because she defines herself independently of men, the lesbian is considered unnatural, not quite a woman . . . as though the essence of womanhood were to be identified with men.[20]

The lesbian struggle, then, has been threefold: with the straight world on the issue of its hostility to lesbianism; with the straight world on the issue of sexism; and with male gays on the issue of sexism.

TOWARD A THEORY OF GAY LIBERATION

The process by which the gay liberation movement has developed may shed light on two interesting questions: (1) How does a radical perspective emerge? and (2) What factors allow individuals to undertake militant protest once they have acquired a radical perspective?

As regards the development of a radical perspective, gays, like women's liberation activists and other militants, cite the example of the black movement. The black movement had a spill-over effect. Through its style and dynamism, it inspired other protest movements.

But how was this influence brought to bear? To answer this question, we need to examine what might be termed the "synergistic element in deviance." Cities have bohemian quarters, places where the community tolerates types of people and kinds of behavior it would otherwise not sanction. In addition, even where social pressure does not segregate deviants geographically, they develop in-group networks.

Greenwich Village in New York is not only a center of the gay world but a gathering place for deviants of many sorts. A wide variety of nonconformists—pacifists, worker-priests, philosophical anarchists, religious mystics, etc., congregate in the area. They form a community of dissenters. There is an extensive literature on the manner in which the community reacts to deviants but none on how deviants affect each other. It would appear, however, that a generalized radical or noncon-formist perspective develops, that some general sense of the lack of legitimacy of the social system and its institutions grows, and that each dissenter, whether anarchist or pacifist, counter culture communard or unreconstructed Stalinist, gay liberationist or black activist, receives reinforcement for his particular kind of deviance by being exposed to a general culture of dissent. While there is great ideological diversity in this community of dissenters, there is agreement on the lack of legiti-macy of existing institutions.

Insofar, then, as the straight community isolates gays ecologically, and insofar as the gay ghetto is a segment of a larger bohemian ghetto, gays are exposed to a subculture which is likely both to engender a certain broad estrangement from the normative and institutional sys-tem and to reinforce the gays' commitment to being gay.

Deviants are isolated in their own communities to prevent them from contaminating the rest of society and to facilitate social control over them. An ironic consequence, however, is that a kind of subculture may develop which provides stronger psychological and ideological supports for deviance than might otherwise be available.

A militant perspective does not necessarily result in militant action. Not all gays are equally likely to undertake militant protest. To dif-ferentiate those who do from those who do not, we may invoke the concept of centrality. Centrality may be defined as the extent to which the deviant's needs are satisfied within the deviant community or, al-ternatively, the extent to which he is independent of the straight com-munity in the satisfaction of his needs.

It might seem that those individuals who are most deviant are those most likely to be subject to society's sanctions. In fact, it may be the case that those individuals who are most deviant are less likely to be sanctioned by the society than individuals who participate more periph-erally in a deviant subculture. As regards gays, it was indicated that there are individuals who participate marginally in the gay world by making sexual contacts in places which I have labelled "public turf" while publicly maintaining straight social ties. They may even be married. They may be contrasted with the career gay whose friends are gay, who moves in a gay social world, and who may even have a job in which his sexual proclivities are known and not resented.

Obviously, society can bring to bear much more severe sanctions on the pseudostraight than it can on the unrepentant gay. It can strip the pseudostraight of his job, his friends, and even his spouse. The career gay is more centrally located within gay culture and is therefore less vulnerable to social sanction, hostility, and pressure, and more available for militant protest. The pseudostraight may have internalized a nonconformist perspective as a result of marginal participation in bohemian subculture, but he is not socially available to act on his perspective. His ties to the straight world make him more vulnerable than the career gay who, according to the values of the straight world, is a more reprehensible character.

It is suggested, then, that the ecological characteristics of deviance, the promotion of communities of deviants by straight society, has the effect of facilitating the development of a generalized radical perspective on the part of participants in that community. When the deviant not only participates in the subculture but has few of the kind of ties to straight society which would make him vulnerable to reprisals, he is available for militant protest.[21]

Movements which have any degree of initial success have spin-off effects. Thus, having come into existence and having slain some dragons, gay liberation began to attract persons quite different from those who gave it birth. Into the movement came nonideological gay college students, hard-line Marxists who happened to be gay, and a variety of others.

The transformation of gay stigma has to be understood partly in terms of the history of the gay movement itself and partly in terms of certain broader social trends. The center no longer holds in the society. There is a black movement, a chicano movement, and from the Indians a "red power" movement. There is a women's liberation and the new left and a high school underground movement. It is clear that the gays were swept up in a radical movement which they had not initiated and that the fate of gay liberation hinges on the fate of that radical movement in general.

REFERENCES

1. J. L. Simmons, "Public Stereotypes of Deviants," *Social Problems*, 13, 1965, pp. 223–232.

2. Edward S. Sagarin, *Odd Man In* (Chicago: Quadrangle Books, 1970), p. 79.

3. Gays, like members of other underground subcultures, have an "in-group" vocabulary, a set of terms and references which are not wholly meaningful to those

not familiar with the subculture—"rough trade," "cruising," "meat rack," and so on. Sociologists who have studied gay subcultures sometimes have to translate these terms; see, for example, Laud Humphreys, *Tearoom Trade* (Chicago: Aldine Publishing Company, 1970). The title of the gay liberation newspaper *Come Out* is addressed to "closet queens," i.e., homosexuals who are afraid to admit their homosexuality, and implores them to "come out of the closet."

4. Jonathan Black, "The Boys in the Snake Pit: Games Straights Play" *The Village Voice*, 15, No. 12 (March 20-26, 1970), p. 61.

5. Lige Clark and Jack Nichols suggested *Gay* to the publishers of *Screw*. Both are long-time activists in the gay movement, but the initial support for *Gay* came from *Screw*.

6. Until recently, few male sociologists did research on homosexuality, probably out of fear of being labelled gay. The increase in public sophistication can be seen on many fronts. For example, with regard to mainstream films a number of actors have portrayed homosexuals in the last ten years, including Marlon Brando in *Reflections in a Golden Eye*, Rod Steiger in *The Sergeant*, Rex Harrison and Richard Burton in *Staircase*, and Peter Finch in *Sunday, Bloody Sunday*. In each instance, though, reference was made by the advertising men to the fact that "of course, they are flaming heterosexuals." If they had played alcoholics, there would have been no need felt on the part of their managers and agents to quiet speculation by suggesting that "they are, of course, teetotalers."

7. Alfred Kinsey, et al., *Sexual Behavior in the Human Male* (Philadelphia: W. B. Saunders Co., 1948), pp. 650–656.

8. Sagarin, *op. cit.*, pp. 83–84.

9. Members of the New York Mattachine were finding it difficult to write a history of the organization given the fact that members had been reluctant to reveal identities and background information about themselves even to each other in the period before the gay liberation movement developed.

10. Dick Leitsch of the Mattachine Society indicated in an interview that there are at least two contemplated attempts to institute gay studies programs, one at an Eastern school, the other at a Midwestern school.

11. Some homophile groups were the following: The Knights of the Clock, the Hollywood Assistance League, the Society for Individual Rights, and, on the lesbian side, the Daughters of Bilitis.

12. Homosexuality per se is not illegal but certain acts such as sodomy and fellatio are prohibited by many states. Often the laws are vaguely worded, referring to "outrageous conduct," "lewd and lascivious behavior," "outrages to public decency," and the like. Vagrancy laws are also used against homosexuals. Milton Hoffman, in *The Gay World* (New York: Basic Books, 1968), cites data (pp. 85–88) indicating that most homosexual arrests occur on what I have referred to as public turf, gay turf being relatively safe.

13. Erving Goffman, *Stigma: Notes on the Management of Spoiled Identity* (Englewood Cliffs, New Jersey: Prentice-Hall, 1963), p. 145.

14. *The Gay Crusaders*, edited by Kay Tobin and Randy Wicker (New York: Coronet Communications, Inc., N.Y., 1972), provides interesting biographical data on 15 homosexuals. An interview conducted by the author with Dick Leitsch of the Mattachine Society also provided biographical data.

15. See, for example, interviews with Lige Clark, Jack Nichols, Phylis Lyon, and Ed Martin in Tobin and Wicker, *op. cit.*

16. Irving Bieber, *Homosexuality: A Psychoanalytic Study of Male Homosexuals* (New York: Random House, 1962), p. 303.

17. Tobin and Wicker, *op. cit.*, p. 231.

18. *Gay Liberation,* (New York: Red Butterfly Press), p. 11.

19. Tobin and Wicker, *op. cit.,* p. 52.

20. *Ibid.,* p. 58.

21. Data presented by Leznoff and Westley on 40 homosexuals inferentially support this kind of reasoning. They differentiated between "secret" and "overt" gays. Of these 15 overt gays, nine were artists or otherwise had positions which made them less vulnerable to straights, while 13 of the 25 secret gays were professionals, two were craftsmen, and nine others had clerical or sales jobs. Inferentially, the secret gays were more vulnerable and perhaps that is why they were secret. See Maurice Leznoff and William Westley, "The Homosexual Community," *Social Problems,* 3, No. 4 (1956), pp. 257–263.

6

THE WOMEN'S LIBERATION MOVEMENT

In 1920, two milestones were passed in the modern history of American women. The Nineteenth Amendment was ratified, giving women the vote, and plans were formulated for the first Miss America contest. These events marked the closing of one era and the beginning of another. The passage of the Nineteenth Amendment represented the successful culmination of a struggle which had lasted 72 years. The birth of the Miss America contest, following closely in the wake of the suffrage amendment, reflected the limited character of that success. Indeed, protest against the Miss America contest almost half a century later was to bring the new feminist movement to public attention.

Some historians have suggested that the seeds of the flawed victory of the first feminist movement lay in the emphasis on the vote. In the 70-year struggle for the ballot, a variety of women and women's groups had been active, and there were vast differences among them. Victoria Woodhull and Sarah Norton advocated free love, while other feminists counseled sexual continence. Elizabeth Cady Stanton questioned the institution of marriage itself, while other women active in the movement advocated laws regulating the conditions and hours under which women worked in order that they would have more time for domestic duties, thereby strengthening the family and the institution of marriage. Carey Thomas was an elitist who became President of Bryn Mawr College, while Florence Kelley was a socialist who complained that suffragists were primarily concerned with the problems of middle-class women.[1] Among the few issues on which women and women's groups across this broad spectrum could agree was the importance of obtaining the vote.

Thus, in time, the women's movement came to be identified with women's suffrage. Once the ballot was obtained there was the inevitable euphoria followed by apathy, despite the fact that the place of women in society had in no fundamental way been altered.

The situation of women remained the same after they received the vote. Discrimination continued in the education of women. Data going back to 1870 indicate that more females than males finished high school each year, while far fewer females than males went on to college.[2] This was true throughout the 19th century and continued to be true. In 1919-1920, the year of the Nineteenth Amendment, 14 percent of female high school graduates went on to college, and in 1930-31, 14 percent went on; for men the figures were 40 percent and 27 percent.

Women continued to be excluded from certain occupational areas. Pay differentials continued to exist for men and women doing the same work. Woman's place continued to be defined as subordinate to man's.

The group protesting the Miss America contest nearly a half century after the passage of the Nineteenth Amendment described what they believed to be the contest's symbolic meaning: "Miss America represents what women are supposed to be: unoffensive, bland, apolitical . . . since its inception in 1921, the Pageant has not had one black finalist . . . there has never been a Puerto Rican, Alaskan, Hawaiian or Mexican-America winner."[3]

In a sense, the new feminist movement has taken up the unfinished agenda of the earlier movement. The sentiments and demands of 19th-century feminists echo in the voices of 20th-century activists. By systematically comparing the two movements, it may be possible to discern the social basis of the feminist movement and to make certain projections with regard to the second feminist movement.

There are striking similarities in the way the two movements developed. In both the 19th and 20th centuries the development of the movement followed a rapid increase in the number of women who were both educated and involved in the world of work outside the home. This is the group from which both movements sprang. In each era, involvement in other progressive movements schooled women in the pragmatics of politics and helped them to formulate an ideology regarding their own rightful place in society.

The 19th-century women's movement developed between 1840 and 1860; the Seneca Falls meeting of July 19 and 20, 1848, is regarded by historians as the point at which collective discontent was translated into an organizational effort to improve the status of women.

The two decades which preceded the Seneca Falls meeting saw an expansion of the number of educated women involved in work outside the home. In such work, they encountered aspects of sexual stratification that otherwise might have been foreign to their experience —lower pay for the same work, job discrimination, and slower rates of promotion despite superior qualifications and better work performance. Since most of these women were working because of financial need, either supporting themselves or making a significant contribution to family income, these disabilities were more than trivial.

Sexual stratification in a family is less likely to be clearly perceived than sexual stratification in an institution or organization. Relations within a family are defined in highly personalized terms. The behavior of relatives is explained on the basis of personal biography. There is a tendency to say "that's the way _____ is." In the office or on the factory floor, the boss and the worker are not part of a kin group. Therefore, the boss's behavior is more likely to be seen as endemic to bosses or to males than as a personal idiosyncrasy.

In addition, negative feelings generated by circumstances outside the home are more likely to be acted upon. The female in a work setting may be able to acknowledge hostile feelings in herself toward her situation and toward those who sustain and perpetuate it more easily than she would be able to acknowledge hostile feelings toward mother, father, and siblings.

Involvement in the world of work, then, increases the potential for a critical consciousness. When combined with such involvement, education increases that potential further. First, educated women involved in the world of work found that they had made the same investment in time, energy, and intellect in their schooling as men but without commensurate payoff. Second—and more important—education provided women with the conceptual apparatus to understand their situation. Sheer deprivation was not enough. They needed to be able to conceptualize it in terms of the operation of a social system rather than simply as "fate" or "bad luck."

In the early 19th century, education for women was hardly known. As the historian Eleanor Flexner has indicated, "By 1812, despite the dissemination of a few fertilizing ideas, education for women had made little progress. It was still limited to the well-to-do few, and consisted largely of such pursuits as embroidery, painting, French, singing and playing the harpsichord."[4]

The spread of education for women in the United States was an aspect of the growth of an industrial and commercial system. The demand for a factory labor force with at least minimal literacy grew, as did the demand for workers sufficiently literate to perform clerical and secretarial tasks. These factors contributed to the slow development of a school system and a demand for teachers. In addition, the steady trickle of immigration, which swelled to a torrent by the end of the century, generated pressure for at least enough schooling for immigrants and their children as to render them fit for work requiring minimal literacy. Finally, a bourgeois class was coming into existence—the daughters of merchants and ministers and politicians. Women of this class were not expected to go into factories, but it was socially acceptable for them to be trained to teach the children of people who did.

In the 1830's, then, the strong resistance to formal education for females began to erode. Teaching was one of the few professions open to women, and by 1837 Emma Willard, who had founded the Troy

Female Seminary, had organized the Willard Association for the Mutual Improvement of Female Teachers. The colleges of the time did not admit women; therefore the salaries paid to women teachers were less than those paid to men, who were often college graduates. Thus, sex differences in pay for teachers was instituted from the beginning.

In 1833, Oberlin College in Ohio became the first institution of higher education in the United States to open its doors to all comers, including women. On the assumption that women could not absorb the same material as men, they were at first offered a diluted program. Among the first women to take a regular program at Oberlin were Lucy Stone and Antoinette Brown, both of whom later became noted feminists. In 1837, Mt. Holyoke opened as a women's institution with a curriculum that began to approximate that of men's colleges. Botany, chemistry, astronomy, geology, algebra, and logic were taught, and the prevailing belief that female minds could not assimilate the same material as male minds was challenged. (Significantly, the new institutions for the education of women were often supported financially by the contributions of businessmen and public officials. The town council of Troy, New York, voted to raise $400 for the building which housed the Troy Female Seminary, the first endowed institution for the education of girls in the United States.)

As a result of these developments, there was an extraordinary expansion in the number of educated women in the United States who were also working women. These women began to experience sexism outside the home but, having acquired more education than was the norm for women and having already made certain advances in a "man's world," they had the ability to articulate their grievances.

Students of the feminist movement have alluded to these factors. O'Neill, in a review of the biographies of ten prominent 19th-century feminists, indicated that, "Seven of the ten were college graduates, indicating what a disproportionate contribution a handful of educated women made to the cause."[5] Rossi expressed it somewhat differently: "The hardcore of activists in past suffrage and feminist movements were women without marital and family ties, ex-wives, non-wives, childless wives, whose need to support themselves triggered concern for equal rights to vote, to work, and to advance in their work."[6]

It was not unusual for women in the 19th century to work, but most did brutalizing, arduous labor in factories and mines, working 14 and 16 hours a day. The sheer drain on their energy, as well as their lack of education, decreased their ability to articulate grievances in terms of social class or sex. There were also a few women who had education before the spread of schools for women, but they were not involved in the world outside the home in ways which would have led them to develop a critical feminist perspective. They were gentlewomen whose domain was the home and whose responsibilities embraced managing the home.

A somewhat similar though not identical process attended the development of the second feminist movement. After the long hiatus that followed the passage of the Nineteenth Amendment, a series of demographic changes began to occur which dramatically increased the number of women who had education, who worked, and who began to encounter sexism outside the home.

Although only a small percentage of American women are college graduates, the second feminist movement has been largely confined to college-educated women. In the period immediately before the development of the movement, this class expanded very rapidly and under conditions conducive to the development of a critical perspective.

From 1950 onward, there has been a steady increase in the percentage of women who work and at the same time a very rapid expansion of the number of educated women. During this period, however, the distribution of women occupationally showed interesting trends. The percentage of women in professional and technical positions increased very slowly, while the percentage in jobs as managers or officials of various sorts actually decreased between 1960 and 1968. The most rapid expansion occurred in clerical positions. In other words, beginning in 1950, more and more educated women were coming into the job market, where they were being channelled into lower-paying, less responsible jobs. In 1950, there were 1,560,392 males in institutions of higher education and 720,906 females. By 1960, this had become 2,256,877 males and 1,211,296 females, and by 1970, 4,478,000 males and 3,134,000 females.[7] There was, then, approximately a 130 percent increase in enrollment for men and a 230 percent increase for women. The female population with higher degrees expanded rapidly, there being almost a sixfold increase between 1950 and 1969 in the number of females who received their Ph.D.[8] During the same period, the number of women with M. A.s increased more than fourfold, from 17,000 to 72,000.[9] But this better-educated female population found themselves, more so than males with equivalent or worse credentials, being forced into clerical jobs.

Colleges and universities, centers of protest for peace, civil rights, and youth, saw considerably more women become faculty members between 1960 and 1966 than in the 20-year period between 1940 and 1960.[10] But here also a rapidly expanding, highly educated work force encountered discrimination and sexism, for women faculty members fared worse than men with similar qualifications as regards rank, salary, and promotion.[11]

Demographic changes alone, however, were not sufficient to create a movement. They created a mobilizable stratum in the female population, but at least two other conditions were required for mobilization to occur.

In both the 19th and 20th centuries, women from the new class were involved in other progressive and radical movements. This involvement taught them how to carry on a political struggle. Moreover, certain contradictions in the otherwise liberal and radical ideologies of these movements led some of the women to formulate ideologies bearing more directly on the role, status, rights, and needs of women.

In both the old feminist movement and the new, women gained an apprenticeship from prior involvement in radical movements of the time. The historian Eleanor Flexner has observed that "It was in the abolition movement that women first learned to organize, to hold public meetings, to conduct petition campaigns. As abolitionists they won the right to speak in public and began to evolve a philosophy of their place in society and their basic rights."[12]

Similarly, many of the women attracted to the new feminist movement had had some experience with, or exposure to, the black movement, the peace movement, or the new left. Given the "service" ideology attending the traditional role of women, it is perhaps understandable that in both periods they should become active on behalf of others.

At the same time, certain contradictions in the progressive movements of both periods contributed to the development of a critical feminist perspective. Although many of the women active in the 19th-century feminist movement were active abolitionists, not all abolitionists were supporters of feminism. Women engaged in the struggle for black freedom sometimes found themselves subject to inferior treatment on grounds of sex. Thus, Elizabeth Cady Stanton and Lucretia Mott, both active abolitionists, attended the World Anti-Slavery Convention in London in 1840 but were excluded from the proceedings because they were female. As a result, they were thrown together in an alliance which led to the Seneca Falls meetings of July 19 and 20, 1848, from which came the first American feminist movement. Robin Morgan, editor of *Sisterhood is Powerful,* observed that:

> The current woman's movement was begun largely though not completely, by women who had been active in the civil rights movement, in the anti-war movement, in student movements, and in the left generally . . . . Thinking we were involved in the struggle to build a new society, it was a slowly dawning and depressing realization that we were doing the same roles in the Movement as out of it: typing . . . making coffee . . . being accessories to the men.[13]

Efforts by women to have the question of their role in progressive and radical organizations placed on the agenda of meetings were often voted down. In 1964, Ruby Robinson, an activist in the Student Movement Coordinating Committee, wrote a paper on the role of women in the organization, but the question raised in her paper never received serious attention. In 1966, attempts to pursuade SDS to adopt a resolution on women's liberation were met with ridicule.

The hippie movement, in some ways the most radical of the dissenting movements, may be taken as an example of the contradictions in the "new culture." The hippie movement flourished in a context of social ferment and upheaval. Hippies, along with other radicals, offered a trenchant critique of American society; yet, with regard to women, they mirrored many of the traits of traditional society. In this way, the hippie movement, like the radical movement in general, became one of the seedbeds of the women's liberation movement. All of the radical movements of the 1960's called for a redefinition of social roles: blacks would no longer shuffle; students would no longer grovel; the male would no longer have to define his manhood as a readiness to kill for his country. None of the radical movements went so far, though, as to pose a new and different role for women. Indeed, some of the most radical voices spoke in reactionary terms when the conversation turned to women. Stokely Carmichael, for example, is reputed to have responded to a charge of male domination in the Student Nonviolent Coordinating Committee by stating that "the role of women in SNCC is prone and silent."

The hippie movement represented an incomplete revolution as regards sex roles. It eroded differences in dress and decoration of the body, and it sanctioned more flexible codes of sexual conduct than were found in traditional society, but it retained substantial elements of that society's definition of the female role. The movement asked women to bear the risks of deviance but withheld some of the rewards.

Straights* attached great importance to those symbols and signs differentiating males from females and thus reacted with hostility to hippie liberalization of dress codes. "Why, I couldn't tell whether it was a boy or a girl" was a common remark in the early days of the hippie movement and presumably carried devastating impact in straight society. The changes to which the straight was reacting entailed a greater expansion of the male role than of the female role. Before the rise of the hippie movement, males had had fewer options in dress and styles than females. Either long or short hair was appropriate for women but only short hair for men. Women wore slacks or trousers and had

*Ordinary citizens, nonhippies.

available a wide range of personal adornments; whereas, for males, dress tended to be formal except on specified occasions. The hippie movement promoted a "feminization" of the kind of self presented in everyday life by males. Men now wore long hair and bright colors, and there was a convergence of male and female styles as represented by unisex clothes. The change represented a combination of aesthetics and repudiation of the drill-sergeant, butch-haircut conception of maleness.

Although they defined the public image of the hippie movement, dress and style were less important than social organization and the assignment of roles. The roles of men and women in the movement could not be inferred from their unisexual presentation of self.

The hippie movement did repudiate certain elements of the traditional female role. Neither chastity nor permanent attachment to a single man was prized. Both males and females lived serially with a variety of partners. On the other hand, with whomever she happened to be living, the female was expected to play a subordinate role. Cooking and tending the children were primarily within her sphere. Even within the framework of a revolutionary idea and a heroic effort, the definition of sex roles was conventional. Women did "women's work" while men did "men's work."

Many hippie women contributed financially to their households through such marginal pursuits as panhandling or selling underground newspapers or by holding such straight jobs as waitress or secretary. But they worked more from economic necessity than from any notion of female liberation. They were comparable to working-class housewives who make a vital contribution to family income by clerking in supermarkets or slinging hash while still playing a highly traditional sex role in the home.

Women, then, were paranymphs to radical movements, and possibly the growing incongruence between movement rhetoric and the reality of their own circumstances generated some of the discontent which helped fuel women's liberation.

If there are striking similarities in the way that the first and second feminist movements developed, there are also important differences. As regards issues, many of the 19th-century feminists were also temperance advocates; others advocated "free love," a cause which no longer stirs sentiment or excites passion; some opposed contraceptives on the grounds that their use would encourage male lust. The major difference, however, is that the second movement does not have a single coalescing issue like that which came to dominate the first feminist movement. Contemporary feminists have nothing equivalent to the fight for the ballot.

There has been considerable consensus among women on a broad range of issues, including abortion law reform, an end to discrimination in employment, and passage of the Equal Rights Amendment. But other issues have had a divisive effect on the movement. The relationship between issues and the structure of the women's movement will be explored at greater length in the next section.

The struggle for suffrage allowed otherwise quite different feminists to paper over their disagreements, but it also distorted the analytic perspective of the movement and drained its energy once the ballot was won. The absence of a single unifying issue may have one of two very different effects. It is notoriously difficult to sustain involvement in voluntary organizations. There are relatively few people sufficiently motivated to give over their time to voluntary organizations for very long. A single dramatic issue may help sustain that enthusiasm and energy (say, the fight for passage of the Equal Rights Amendment). On the other hand, the absence of a single issue may in the long run allow a movement, even with a small following, to develop a surer analysis of its own situation.

The second feminist movement is characterized by a situation in which a "thousand flowers bloom."[14] In the next section of this chapter, the major ideological and organizational characteristics of that movement are analyzed.

CONSENSUS AND DISSENSION IN THE WOMEN'S MOVEMENT

This section focuses on the social organization of the contemporary women's liberation movement.

According to Acker and Howard, it is characteristic of contemporary feminism that:

> . . . *there is no single leadership which can speak for, direct or regulate the movement. . . . [The movement is made up of] many small units which proliferate and reform, independent of any central direction. . . . In the women's movement, this form of organization is not only the consequence of the process of movement development, it is also a central tenet of movement ideology. Supposed leaders are largely the creation of the press; identifiable units are usually leaderless and highly egalitarian; many women who identify themselves as being feminists belong to no group or only sporadically participate in group activities. The ideology which supports this type of organization contends that women must not recreate in*

their own groups the forms of structured oppression of the male-dominated, bureaucratic world. No one person or group can lead or dictate policy because women will not be liberated until they individually assume control of and responsibility for their own destiny.[15]

There are few enduring groups like the National Organization for Women and many shifting and transient groups like the Red Stockings and Bread and Roses.

The issues articulated by the movement have been numerous: sex-role stereotyping in raising children, the right of abortion on demand, the need for day-care centers, the need to do away with stereotyped sex role-playing in male-female relations, and the need to abolish discrimination in employment.

It is unlikely that all issues raised by the movement are equally important to all feminists. While feminists have sex identity in common, they differ in regard to age, level of education, marital status, and employment status. The loose structure of the movement is probably partly a function of the differences among feminists; different clusters of feminists have different central concerns.

Because of differences among feminists, certain issues are highly divisive. Courses of action or policy stands advocated by one group of feminists may seem foolish or threatening to others. On the other hand, the common sex identity of feminists and their shared experiences do lead to a high consensus on certain issues.

There is, then, a kind of tension in the movement. On the one hand, there is a strain organizationally toward fragmentation into particularistic groups representing the interests of homogeneous subpopulations of feminists. On the other hand, there is a concern with issues which transcend differences. The first strain creates tensions within the movement; the second creates a sense of common identity and purpose. We will now examine some issues of both kinds.

Marriage or, more broadly, the character of the female relationship to men, is one of the key divisive issues in the movement. The tension arises out of the different kinds of relationships that women have with men as they become involved emotionally and socially with the movement. Put somewhat differently, the way in which the question of relations with men is phrased by each feminist probably depends on the place from which she is starting.

For some the question is, "Should I have any interpersonal relations with men at all?" For others, it is, "Should I live with the guy?" For yet others, it becomes, "Should I get married," or, "Should I change the terms of the marriage?" The phrasing of the question depends in part on whether the woman is younger or older, married or single.

The constituencies of different feminist groups are partly a function of the questions to which the group addresses itself. Women within the movement have to make different kinds of choices, and they are drawn to organizations that phrase choice alternatives that seem meaningful in terms of the realities of their own lives.

The Feminists, a group based in New York City, opposes marriage altogether, saying to feminists: "We can't destroy the inequities between men and women until we destroy marriage. We must free ourselves and marriage is the place to begin."[16] This answer is not likely to be acceptable to those feminists already married and not condemnatory of marriage as such.[17] Indeed, it might even be threatening to them insofar as it implies that women who continue to have close relations with men are truckling with the enemy. It represents a meaningful option only for some younger feminists.

Acker and Howard, in a study of feminists at two universities, one on the east coast and one on the west coast, found that many saw their father as supportive of their achievements and aspirations and reported support from the males with whom they were then involved.[18] The position advanced by the Feminists states the alternatives in terms that many women find too stark and too inconsistent with their own experience. For the women interviewed by Acker and Howard the question was not "males or no males" but males within what system of interaction.

Married women within the movement have tended to address themselves to the issue of less oppressive patterns of interaction within marriage. For both younger women not unhappily married and older married women of the generation that Betty Friedan wrote about in *The Feminine Mystique*, that has been the more important issue. These are not the women likely to be found in the Feminists or the Radical Lesbians, nor were the latter likely to be in their groups.

Betty Friedan, founder of NOW, the National Organization for Women, has commented on the tension between these two segments of the movement: "Those who preached the man-hating sex/class warfare threatened to take over New York NOW, and National NOW, and drive out the women who wanted equality, but who also wanted to keep on loving their husbands and children."[19]

Her comments reflect some of the differences among feminists with regard to relations with men:

I thought it was a joke at first—those strangely humorless papers about clitoral orgasms that would liberate women from sexual dependence on a man's penis . . . then I realized, as Simone de Beauvoir once wrote, that these women were merely acting out

> sexually their rebellion and resentment at being "underneath" in society generally, being dependent on men for their personal definition. But their resentment was being manipulated now into an orgy of sex hatred that would vitiate the power they now had to change conditions they resented.[20]

Married women with children form an identifiable subpopulation among feminists. Their experiences and concerns are not identical with those of the unmarried or never-married feminists, and consequently they focus on a different dimension of change. Various proposals for altering the forms of interaction within marriage have spoken to the needs of this population.

One of the approaches which has drawn attention is the "marriage contract." This is a "contract" negotiated between the couple and focusing on problem areas such as the expectation that the wife will have major responsibility for the housework despite also holding a job outside the home. A contract might specify a division of labor with regard to such matters as transportation of the children to school and to friends' homes. It might state that on weekends the wife will take full responsibility for the children one day and the husband the other. The essential thrust of the contract is to make the division of labor explicit, particularly with regard to housework and child care. It defines for the husband a larger role and set of responsibilities in those areas than he ordinarily carries.[21] The contract is seen as relevant even where the wife does not work outside the home. Housework is seen as having several important symbolic and substantive meanings. Some argue that the housewife as cook, chauffeur, babysitter, maid, etc., makes a significant but unrecognized contribution to the financial status of the family and therefore should receive a salary. Others condemn housework as such, arguing that it is repetitive, mentally numbing labor which erodes the energy, intellect, and imagination of women. They repudiate the idea that there is any such thing as satisfying housework and call for women to find more of themselves by working outside the home. They warn women, however, not to be trapped into doing the housework despite working outside the home.

The marriage contract represents in a dramatic form the concerns of a certain constituency of feminists. For this constituency, the misogamist position of the Feminists or similar organizations is not wholly meaningful.

The concept of "open marriage" poses a more fluid approach to the issue of redefining sex roles in paired, heterosexual relationships than does the marriage contract. It posits *commitment of the partners to each other's growth, perceptions of the need for one's partner, enlargement of self, and a posture that relationships can be renegotiated as conditions change. Values embody mutual trust, realistic expectations, living fully and intimately in the present, recognizing the need for privacy, and open companionship. Open and honest communication is the dominant process.*

To effect an open marriage along these lines may require a radical departure from the husband-wife role set of the "closed" or traditional marriage.[22]

The difference between couples drawn to the marriage contract and those drawn to open marriage or similar approaches to interpersonal relations may be one of temperament. The essential point is that background differences among feminists sensitize subgroups to different and even contradictory positions on certain key issues.

In contrast to the issue of relations with men, the other key issue in the movement, women's place in the world of work, tends to have an integrative effect. As was indicated previously, high levels of education and involvement in the world of work seem to be two of the factors associated with the development of a critical feminist perspective. There is also an association between level of education and work outside the home. The higher her level of education, the more likely a woman is to be working full-time outside the home. In 1968, only 24 percent of women with an eighth-grade education were in the labor force full-time, 47 percent of women high school graduates worked outside the home full-time, 54 percent of college graduates, and 71 percent of women with graduate training, rising to 81 percent for those over 40.[23]

Hence, while the 45-year-old feminist married 20 years and the 24-year-old unmarried feminist might hold irreconcilable positions on the matter of relations with men, they can and do come together on the basis of common experience with sexism in the occupational sphere.

Protest over employment discrimination has an integrative potential because: (1) the definition of the problem is relatively clear; (2) the proposed solutions are consistent with the interests of all feminists irrespective of differences among them; and (3) the essential goal is in conformity with certain larger national values, thus legitimatizing that aspect of the movement in the popular mind.

There is universal agreement among feminists that the issue in employment is sexism, and a major part of the feminist literature is devoted to documenting this charge. The argument as advanced by feminists breaks down into two components: that women have less opportunity to acquire the kind of education which has career potential and that, when they do, they are discriminated against in employment, salary, and promotion. The literature of the movement has introduced feminists to the evidence on these matters. It has helped create a common perspective on a matter of central concern and has laid the basis for shared political identity on the part of a group whose premises might otherwise be irreconcilable.

The literature has helped amplify a world view. Some of the particulars of that world view are as follows:

> *It is generally assumed that with increased skills and increased education the income differentials between women and men disappear. Yet an examination of some highly skilled professions shows the contrary.* Chemical and Engineering News *did a study of chemists' salaries in the Fall of 1968, which showed that, with seniority held constant, women with Ph.D.'s made less than men with only B.A.'s.*[24]

The women's literature also indicates that

> *The general belief, used to justify the lower pay given to women, is that theirs is a luxury income, which supplements that of their husbands. Yet 35% of all women of marriageable age are not married and study after study has shown that most women, married or not, work out of economic necessity.*[25]

> *Women with doctorates are less likely to be teaching advanced courses [in college]. Women hold lower rank than men with comparable qualifications in all kinds of institutions.*[26]

Discrimination in the areas of education and employment provides powerful integrative issues for the movement. They give the movement a shape, and a certain coherence, and provide a common focus of concern for women whose interests otherwise might be in conflict.

There are at least two additional areas of high consensus within the movement: sex differences in socialization, and the need for passage of the Equal Rights Amendment. Until the Supreme Court decision broadening legal access to abortion, the fight for abortion law reform also had integrative consequences for the movement.

There is unanimity within the movement on the importance of socialization. Girls learn to be "girlish." It is recognized within the movement that no system of oppression rests wholly on force; most of the time those at the bottom accept the legitimacy of their position. It is not that husbands consciously force wives to be domestic drones, but that the weight of her upbringing leads the female to feel guilty if she does not assume the housewife-helpmate role. A number of persons within the movement point to socialization as the ultimate key to a society free of role-playing along sexual lines. They argue that the little girl has no chance to discover her full potential socially, emotionally, or intellectually nor, for that matter, does the boy. Both are precipitated along paths which their parents, as surrogates for society, view as "normal" or "natural."

One of the objectives of the movement, then, is to see an increasing number of children raised in an "unnatural" manner, in a manner free of sex-role constraints. There is the hope or assumption that the unnatural may, eventually, become the natural. This kind of goal does not lend itself to a legislative focus. One cannot legislate the manner in which people raise their children. Changes in socialization practices remain a goal, an aspiration, an area in which people in the movement seek to "transform by example." They can raise their own children free of sex-role stereotypes and hope that their example will be sufficiently impressive to persuade others to the same course.

The fight for passage of the Equal Rights Amendment has mobilized women of otherwise diverse interests, according to Betty Friedan.[27]

Among the many issues confronting the women's movement are some which tend to divide the movement and others which provide an integrative potential. Feminists themselves are a diverse group and this is reflected in the disagreements over issues and tactics. Their important common characteristics, however, help give a certain unity and coherence to the movement.

THE SOCIAL ORGANIZATION OF THE WOMEN'S MOVEMENT

Organizationally, the women's movement may be contrasted with the black movement of the 1960's.

In the black movement, there was a small number of major organizations and a number of "leaders," most of whom had an explicit organizational base. The organizations included the N.A.A.C.P., C.O.R.E., SNCC, and SCLC (and in the late 1960's the Black Panthers), and the leaders included James Farmer, Martin Luther King, Jr., Stokely Carmichael, H. "Rap" Brown, Malcolm X, Hughey Newton, and Bobby Seale.

In contrast, there are relatively few national organizations in the women's movement, and many of the "leaders" are actually celebrities with no clear organizational base. The National Organization for Women, which had chapters in 30 cities in 1970 and 3,000 members, is the major body, and Betty Friedan is its founder.[28] Kate Millett, Germaine Greer, Gloria Steinem, and several other prominent feminists are really literati with no organizational base. They are literary people who function as inspirational leaders, defining issues, articulating problems, providing a highly visible "female presence" on public occasions (TV talk shows, college lectures, etc.), offering a defense of the movement and an exposition of its goals.

In the black movement, local organizations functioned as branches of national bodies, but, as Acker and Howard have indicated, the typical group in the women's movement is small and autonomous.

The women's movement is characterized by two kinds of groups, those which are instrumental in character and those which rest on fictive kinship, i.e., the notion that all women are sisters.

Instrumental groups are concerned with clear-cut issues and address themselves to the tangible, measurable interests of their constituents. Women's caucuses in professional associations are a major example. By the early 1970's, women's caucuses had been formed in the professional associations of sociologists, political scientists, anthropologists, and a number of other groups. These caucuses turned the spotlight of anger on the many faces of sexist discrimination in academia. They clearly documented the existence of sexism in each of the professions. Women were hired at less pay, promoted less rapidly, and terminated more quickly than men. The caucuses provided a mechanism whereby women could develop both analytic and political skills for confronting sexism at the instructional level in academia.

On the other hand, there are a large number of more expressively oriented groups, many characterized by what might be termed "fictive kin" ties. In this category, one may place many consciousness-raising groups and some of the "women's centers."

Whereas the instrumentally-oriented groups are organized in a conventional manner, the more expressive groups attempt to function without hierarchy. They explicitly repudiate the notion of centering leadership in one person or in a few persons.

The theory of the leaderless group is important to many feminists. They argue that women are taught to be subordinate, to be passive, to be followers. They insist that an essential element in the personal liberation of women is the development of the capacity to act, to make decisions, to shape events, rather than simply being molded by them. It would be self-defeating, they point out, if women's groups simply mirrored other groups and had a hierarchal structure in which the majority of women were followers. The only way women can learn not to be passive and dependent is to be in situations in which their dependency is not built into the structure. Consequently, women's groups must repudiate the principle of individual leadership in the interest of maintaining a structure in which all women can feel free to act and can learn not to lapse into a passive or subordinate role.

Many consciousness-raising groups are devoted to encouraging women to express their latent hostilities and grievances. The groups also function to help them redefine their personal history. Women can come to understand that the whole weight of cultural tradition and male bigotry pressured them along the path into the kitchen rather than the laboratory. They can come to see that this weight put them in the typing pool rather than behind the executive's desk.

It is an open question, however, how long a consciousness-raising group can last without involving its members in instrumental tasks. For how long a period can meetings be devoted to the venting of personal feelings and discussions of individual biography? Eventually, both the fund of personal information and the collective capacity for indignation diminish. It can be hypothesized, although the data are not available, that, unless a consciousness-raising group turns to pragmatic political protest, it quickly disintegrates. A counter hypothesis might suggest that the sheer expressive nature of the group provides a safety valve for women who otherwise might not have a channel for venting their feelings and that, indeed, the non-instrumental nature of the group makes it a good mechanism for engaging in public forms of protest with relatively little risk.

THE FUTURE OF THE WOMEN'S MOVEMENT

Some of the theorists within the movement have given thought to what society would look like "if women win."

Gloria Steinem focused on equal rights:

Women do not want to exchange places with men . . . . this is not our goal. But we want to change the economic system to one more based on merit. . . . There will be free access to good jobs . . . and decent pay for the hard ones women have been performing all along, including housework.

With women as half the country's elected representatives and a woman President once in a while, the country's machismo problems would be greatly reduced.

In this country, come utopia, men and women won't reverse roles; they will be free to choose according to individual talents and preferences.

The most radical goal of the movement is egalitarianism.[29]

Kate Millett's formulation is somewhat different:

A *sexual revolution would require, perhaps, first of all, an end of traditional sex inhibitions and taboos, particularly those that most threaten patriarchal, monogamous marriage. Homosexuality, "illegitimacy," adolescent, pre-extra-marital sexuality. The negative aura with which sexual activities has generally been surrounded would necessarily be eliminated, together with the double standard and prostitution. The goal of revolution would be a permissive single standard of sexual freedom, and one uncorrupted by the crass and exploitative economic bases of traditional sexual alliances.*

A *relevant event here would be the re-examination of the traits categorized as "masculine" and "feminine," with a reassessment of their human desirability. The violence encouraged as virile, the excessive passivity defined as feminine proving useless in either sex; the efficiency and intellectuality of the "masculine" temperament, the tenderness and consideration associated with the "feminine" recommending themselves as appropriate to both sexes.*[30]

The fate of these goals hinges partly on the future of the women's movement, and the future of the women's movement hinges partly on demography and partly politics. Politics alone is not enough. To be effective, politics must be exercised in a favorable social climate. For example, colonized people always resisted imperialism, but imperialism did not collapse until the cost of maintaining colonies went beyond what the mother countries could or would pay. Neither is demography alone enough, without politics. The sheer fact of a greater number of female college graduates who work outside the home does not yield more women in the movement; it merely means that the pool of women from among whom feminists are typically recruited expands.

Three demographic factors will increase the proportion of women who are mobilizable for the liberation movement. First, the proportion of the female population with higher education will continue to rise; second, the proportion of women working outside the home will also continue to rise; and, third, the birth rate among married women will stabilize and an increasing number of married women will have no children at all. These three factors are interrelated. The women's liberation movement has been middle-class in its social base. It has attracted women having certain characteristics, and the proportion of women in the population with those characteristics is increasing.

Between 1958-59 and 1968-69 the ratio of females to males earning the Bachelor's or first professional degree rose from 1:2 to 3:4, and projections through 1978-79 suggest that nearly as many women as men will be receiving college degrees (494,000 to 562,000).[81] As was previously indicated, the proportion of the female population involved in work outside the home has also risen steadily, and it is the more educated women who are likely to be involved in such work. In other words, if one examines the profile of contemporary feminists, demographic data suggest that the proportion of women showing that profile is on the increase. The social base from which feminists come is expanding.

Politically, the women's movement has had certain proximate, highly instrumental goals, such as doing away with discrimination, and other, less proximate but nevertheless important, goals, such as changing the broader cultural definitions of "male" and "female."

It is a question of whether the attainment of some of the more tangible and immediate objectives will erode the energy and enthusiasm needed to pursue longer-range, less tangible, but equally fundamental, goals. The consequence of proximate successes may be to decrease the momentum of the movement. Women agitating for better career opportunities undoubtedly have serious career interests. Those women appointed to more responsible positions in academia, business, or government will therefore pursue those career interests. This is not to say that there will be a loss of interest in the women's movement on the part of these women or a decrease in commitment to its ultimate goals; it is only to say that the terms of the relationship to the movement will change. Few women will be able to compete against stiff competition in academia, law, medicine, publishing, or engineering and devote equal time to movement activities.

In summary, then, demographic trends indicate that the percentage of the female population having the characteristics of feminists will continue to expand. At the same time, certain proximate ends of the movement are being realized. The opportunities for highly educated women with career aspirations appear to be improving. As women move into responsible careers, the demands of adequate performance will probably alter the terms of their involvement with the movement.

It is not clear that the movement will or can make an impact on certain fundamental aspects of sexism, such as the relative indifference of the great mass of women, the derogation of women in advertising (a phenomenon that seems trivial but is actually very important because it bombards the public with the notion that a woman's proper role is that of housewife and overseer of the family as a consumption unit), and the perpetuation of sex role differences in socialization (as reflected in any toy store at Christmas time, etc.).

There are signs, however, that even some working-class women are forming consciousness-raising groups. But, again, the issues to which they address themselves reflect concerns differing vastly from those of young, college-educated, career-oriented women. A common complaint among working-class women who have formed their own consciousness-raising groups is that, after they become "fat and forty," their husbands lose sexual interest in them. In a sense, they seek to extend the period during which they are viewed as sex objects by their husbands.[32]

Thus far, the social base of the movement has been middle-class. It could expand to include a significant number of women whose husbands are working-class if inflationary pressures force larger numbers of such women into the job market. If, as a result, a large number of working-class women become sensitive to the broad issues raised by the movement, genuinely revolutionary changes in American mores and behavior might occur.

REFERENCES

1. Among the better histories of the first feminist movement are Eleanor Flexner's *Century of Struggle: The Woman's Rights Movement in the United States* (Cambridge, Massachusetts: Harvard University Press, 1959) and William O'Neill's *Everyone Was Brave: The Rise and Fall of Feminism In America* (Chicago: Quadrangle Books, 1969).

2. Alvin Renetzsky and Jon S. Greene, eds., *Standard Educational Almanac: 1971*, (Los Angeles: Academic Media, 1971) pp. 75 and 103.

3. "No More Miss America" in *Sisterhood Is Powerful*, Robin Morgan, ed., (New York: Random House, 1970), pp. 521–524.

4. Flexner, *op. cit.*, p. 23.

5. O'Neill, *op. cit.*, p. 140.

6. Alice Rossi, "Sex Equality: The Beginnings of Ideology," in *Toward a Sociology of Women* (Constantina Safilios-Rothschild, ed., Lexington, Massachusetts: Xerox College Publishing, 1972), p. 349.

7. Renetzsky and Greene, *op. cit.*, p. 111.

8. *Ibid.*, pp. 103 and 120.

9. *Loc. cit.* There is misinformation in the popular women's liberation literature with regard to trends in education for women. In *Sisterhood Is Powerful*, it is stated that "the number of women awarded Master's degrees is lower today [1969] than in 1930" Morgan, *op. cit.*, p. 561. This is not even remotely true: in 1920, 1,294 women received the Master's degree (2,985 men); in 1969, 72,225 women received the Master's (121,531 men). In the opening essay in that book, "You've Come a Long Way, Baby," Connie Brown and Jane Seitz state that "more women received Ph.D.'s in 1930 than ever before—or since." (*Ibid.*, p. 26). That is only partially true: 353 women received the Ph.D. in 1930, but 407 in 1932, 430 in 1938, 939 in 1957, and 3,436 in 1969. The dates indicate a tremendous acceleration from the late 1950's on in terms of the production of women Ph.D.s, the point made here.

10. Renetzsky and Greene, *op. cit.*, p. 101.

11. *Discrimination Against Women: Hearings Before the Special Subcommittee on Education of the Committee on Education and Labor,* House of Representatives, 96th Congress, Parts 1 and 2 (Washington, D.C.: U.S. Government Printing Office, 1971).

12. Flexner, *op. cit.,* p. 41.

13. Morgan, *op. cit.,* p. XX.

14. Among the organizations which have appeared since 1966 are the following: Red Stockings, WITCH, the Feminists, the Radical Feminists, the National Organization for Women, Bread and Roses, Women of the American Revolution, the Radical Lesbians, and SCUM (the Society for Cutting up Men).

15. Mary D. Howard and Joan Acker, "On Becoming a Feminist." Paper presented to the American Sociological Association, New Orleans, 1972, pp. 10–11.

16. Morgan, *op. cit.,* p. 537.

17. Perhaps the most extreme articulation of this position came from Valerie Solanis in the manifesto of SCUM: "It is now technically possible to reproduce without the aid of males (or, for that matter, females) and to produce only females. We must begin immediately to do so. The male is only a biological accident: The Y (male) gene is an incomplete X (female) gene, that is, has an incomplete set of chromosomes. In other words, the male is an incomplete female, a walking abortion aborted at the gene state ... " (Morgan, *op. cit.,* p. 514).

18. Howard and Acker, *op. cit.,* p. 20.

19. Betty Friedan, "Up From the Kitchen Floor," *The New York Times Magazine* (March 4, 1973), pp. 32–33.

20. *Ibid.,* p. 34.

21. Susan Edmiston, "How to Write Your Own Marriage Contract," *Ms* (Spring, 1972), pp. 67–72.

22. Nina O'Neill and George O'Neill, "Open Marriage: A Synergic Model," *The Family Coordinator: Journal of Education, Counseling and Services,* 21, No. 4 (October, 1972), pp. 403–409.

23. Marvin B. Sussman and Betty E. Cogswell, "The Meaning of Variant and Experimental Marriage Styles and Family Forms in the 1970's," *The Family Coordinator: Journal of Education, Counseling and Services,* 21, No. 4 (October, 1972), pp. 380–381.

24. Joreen, "The 51 Percent Minority: A Statistical Essay," in Morgan, *op. cit.,* p. 38.

25. *Ibid.,* p. 39.

26. *Discrimination Against Women, op. cit.,* Part 1, p. 312.

27. Friedan, *op. cit.,* pp. 30–34, 37.

28. *op. cit.,* p. 34.

29. Gloria Steinem, "What It Would Be Like If Women Win," in *Liberation Now: Writings From The Women's Liberation Movement* (Deborah Babcox and Madeline Balkin, eds. (New York: Dell, 1971), pp. 55–56, 61.

30. Kate Millett, *Sexual Politics* (New York: Doubleday and Company, 1970), p. 62.

31. Renetzsky and Greene, *op. cit.,* p. 150.

32. Susan Jacoby "What Do I Do For The Next 20 Years?" *The New York Times Magazine* (June 17, 1973), pp. 10, 39–43, 49.

THE
YOUTH
MOVEMENT

7

OF YOUTH AND YOUTH MOVEMENTS

The social category we call "youth" is a relatively recent cultural development, as indeed is the category we call "childhood." The Romans of the pre-Christian era did not clearly differentiate between infancy, childhood, adolescence, and young adulthood. "In medieval society," according to Phillipe Aries in *Centuries of Childhood*, "the idea of childhood did not exist."[1] Rather, children, especially among the poor, participated in the adult world as soon as they were beyond infancy. Historically, in English civil law, an adult was "a male infant who has attained the age of fourteen; [and] a female infant who has attained the age of twelve."[2]

The social category "youth," as it is presently understood, emerged in relation to broad economic and social changes. "In agrarian societies," according to the sociologist Gerhard Lenski, "young people were largely integrated into the adult world and separated from one another, while in advanced industrial society, owing to the spread of public education, young people tend to be cut off from the more inclusive adult world and thrown into a narrower world made up almost exclusively of their age peers."[3]

In technologically advanced societies, certain long-term trends have both created the category "youth" in its contemporary sense and expanded its upper limit. The historical trend in industrial systems has been toward the requirement of ever higher levels of literacy and skill on the part of the work force. As Garth Mangum, former Executive Secretary of the National Commission on Technology, Automation and Economic Progress, has indicated, "Modern technology demands a generally higher level of educational attainment, not only for the mastery of specific skills, but also because a sound basic education is a necessity, as retraining is required at a later date."[4]

The ever-increasing sophistication required to function effectively in industrial economies has entailed longer and longer periods of training. In 1940, less than half the adult wage earners in the United States had a high school education. By 1960, most adults had graduated from high school and many were going to college. Between 1960 and 1970, the number of people in college more than doubled, and in states like California and New York, a substantial proportion of high school graduates went on to college. Enrollment in federally aided vocational programs rose from 205,000 in 1920 to almost 8,000,000 in 1969.[5]

One consequence of this change has been the extension of dependency among young people to longer and longer periods beyond puberty. Most people reach their physical, mental, and sexual peak between the ages of 17 and 19 and are then, in physiological terms, adults. Primitive societies confer adult status four or five years below the physiological transition period, industrial societies three or four years beyond it.

The extension of the upper limits of the category "youth" can be understood in economic and legal terms. It was partially a consequence of the need to train a work force capable of functioning effectively in an ever more demanding economy. The public high school, a relatively recent institution, came into existence in response to industrial and social needs. It was not until the late 19th century that high schools became common in most parts of the country. Robert Bremner, the historian, observed that "the worlds of commerce, industry, and even of the home were . . . increasingly demanding" and the high schools were viewed as necessary in preparing the young "for greater efficiency as workers of all kinds."[6] In addition, "the colleges and universities, responding to new directives and depth in the advance of organized knowledge, wanted their entering students to be better prepared to take up the tasks of learning and the professions."[7]

It can be doubted that the extension of life expectancy played a role in the development of the idea of youth. There is nothing in an increase in life expectancy which would necessarily confer adult status on an individual at a later age. The cultural formulation of the category "youth" would seem to be more directly related to requirements of additional years of schooling.

Simultaneous with the extension of their schooling was the gradual exclusion of the young from the job market. This exclusion was due partly to the pressure of the increasingly strong trade union movement and partly to the efforts of newly developing social welfare groups. In 1842, Massachusetts and Connecticut limited the working day for children under 12 to ten hours, while Pennsylvania and Rhode Island barred children under 12 from factory work.[8] In 1884, New York outlawed contract labor of reform school children. Significantly, in 1910, the Boy Scouts was founded.[9]

Youth as a social and cultural category evolved, then, over a long period of time. In Western industrial societies, as in non-Western agrarian societies, age categories do not necessarily relate to biological realities but derive from economic need and cultural preference.

In industrial societies, youth begins with puberty and extends through that time when one ceases to be dependent by entering the job market as a self-sufficient wage earner. Significantly, there are major social class differences in the length of the period called youth. "Youth movements" are largely a middle- and upper-class phenomenon because middle-class persons are likely to remain in the "youth" category much longer than lower-class and working-class people.

In many industrial democracies, working-class youth leave school at 15 or 16 to enter the job market. They do not "drop out"—they are simply not expected to go on. They take the relatively less sophisticated jobs requiring lower levels of skill and information. Working-class youth marry and assume family responsibilities earlier than middle- and upper-class youth.[10] In other words, they stop being "young" at an earlier age than those in the middle class.

Whereas the period of dependency of working-class people may extend three or four years beyond puberty, that of middle-class persons in American society is likely to extend anywhere from 10 to 15 years. Thus, the "youth" movement of the 1960's came to embrace graduate students in their middle and late twenties. There was at least an implicit attempt to establish an upper limit to youth with the coining of the slogan during Berkeley's Free Speech Movement turmoil: "Don't trust anyone over 30." Within a short period of time, however, some of the most prominent members of the movement passed that dividing line, carrying the upper limits of the category "youth" with them.

THE RELATIONSHIP BETWEEN ADULTS AND YOUTH

The relationship between youth and adults can be viewed as part of the stratification system. Historically, the status of youth has been associated with subordination and dependence. Aries, writing about medieval France, has indicated that "The idea of childhood was bound up with the idea of dependence: The words 'son', 'varlets', 'boys' were also words in the vocabulary of feudal subordination. One could leave childhood only by leaving the state of dependence, or at least the lowest degrees of dependence. That is why the words associated with childhood would endure to indicate . . . men of humble rank. . . . "[11] Historically, in English law, the phrase "younger children" referred not to chronological age but to dependency status. It included daughters older than the oldest son but who, by virtue of sex, were not entitled to settlements of land and thereby remained dependent.[12] In the United States the term "boy" was used to mark the subordinate status of black males. Irrespective of age, the black male was, in the lexicon of the white bigot, a "boy."

Subordinate status is the key dimension in the relationship between youth and adults. In recent years, a number of scholars have come to recognize the potential for conflict in this dimension. Lenski has observed that *of all the class struggles in modern societies, the most underrated may prove to be those between age classes, especially those between youth (in the sense of adolescents and young people) and adults . . . the basis for this struggle lies in the fact that the younger generation is subject to the authority of the older, while the older generation enjoys the lion's share of the rewards.*[13]

Traditionally, adults have entertained negative stereotypes about youth and subscribed to the view that youth have to be subjected to more than ordinary measures of social control. Edgar Z. Friedenberg, the sociologist, has drawn an analogy between the young and colonial peoples:

Adolescents are among the last social groups in the world to be given the full nineteenth-century colonial treatment. Our colonial administrators, at least the higher policy-making levels, are usually of the enlightened sort who decry the punitive expedition except as an instrument of last resort. They prefer to study the young with a view to understanding them, not for their own sake but in order to induce them to abandon their barbarism and assimilate the folkways of normal adult life. The model emissary to the world of youth is no longer the tough disciplinarian but the trained youth worker, who works like a psychoanalytically oriented anthropologist. Like the best of missionaries, he is sympathetic and understanding toward the people he is sent to work with, and aware and critical of the larger society he represents. But fundamentally he accepts it, and often does not really question its basic values or its right to send him to wean the young from savagery.[14]

Images of Youth

Some critics might dispute the observation that youth occupy a subordinate position in the stratification system, arguing that they are glorified in the society and that, indeed, there is even a "cult of youth." It is true, of course, that television advertisements suggest that it is a triumph for a 45-year-old woman to look like her 20-year-old daughter, and it is also true that the over-thirties of both sexes are bombarded with ads for skin creams, laxatives, breakfast cereals, wigs, wrinkle removers, cinch belts, exercise programs, hair dyes, and other products which purportedly will help them look and feel "young again."

It is probably the case, however, that the view of youth implicit in that perspective is equivalent to the view of blacks implicit in the plaintive cry, "Oh, to be a nigger on Saturday night." It is a perspective in which envy of a group is based on the assumption that they are irresponsible and carefree. In other words, the very elements which make the group seem attractive are also cited to justify its subordinate status. The capacity of "niggers" to have a good time on Saturday night is presumed to be associated with a general incapacity for serious pursuits; the association of the idea of youth with the "good times" is linked with the view that people who in fact happen to be young are not ready to play a serious role in serious affairs.

The glorification of youth, then, is probably an aspect of the subordination of youth.

Lateral and Vertical Deviance

Adult glorification of youth rests, then, in part, on the fact that adults see youth as a period when one has the energy for sin and no time for sorrow. Youth is seen as a time when one can live a life which is not "serious."

This view of youth accommodates a belief that the young have to be controlled and guided in the interests of developing in them the capacity and the will to become serious people engaged in serious pursuits. Youth, from this perspective, is regarded as a time when one is likely to do frivolous or foolish or dangerous things because one is not yet "mature." From this perspective, then, the young are seen as incipient transgressors, as incipient rule-breakers, as people resisting the adult effort to socialize them, to prepare them to play responsible roles in adult society.

In fact, the young habitually do a good deal of rule-breaking. Schools have never been very popular, dress codes have always been resisted, high school pregnancies do occur. It is for this reason that some observers have dismissed the contemporary youth movement as simply the traditional rebellion of the young against parental authority. The point of view taken in this chapter is that the contemporary youth movement differs in important ways from earlier movements such as that of the radical youth in the 1930's or the "lost generation" of the 1920's, two groups with whom contemporary youth have often been compared. To clarify this difference, it will help to identify two quite different types of transgressions in which subordinate groups in a stratification system may engage.

Vertical and *lateral* deviance occur where differentiations according to rank exist, such as officer-recruit, teacher-student, adult-child, boss-employee, or guard-convict. Inevitably, certain privileges and prerogatives attach to the superior ranks. Adults can smoke, consume alcoholic beverages, obtain drivers' licenses, sign contracts, and do a host of other things denied to children or teen-agers.

Vertical deviance occurs when persons in a subordinate rank attempt to enjoy the privileges and prerogatives of a superior rank. Thus, the ten-year-old who sneaks behind the garage to smoke is engaging in a form of vertical deviance, as is the 14-year-old who drives a car or the 16-year-old who bribes a 22-year-old to buy him a six-pack of beer. They are indulging themselves in ways deemed inappropriate to persons of their rank.

Lateral deviance occurs when persons in a subordinate rank develop their own standards and norms apart from and opposed to those of persons in a superior rank. Thus, the teen-ager who smokes pot rather than tobacco is engaging in lateral rather than vertical deviance, as is the 17-year-old girl who runs away to live in a commune rather than eloping with the boy next door. Lateral deviance occurs in a context in which the values of the nondeviant are rejected. The pot-smoking 17-year-old, wearing Benjamin Franklin eyeglasses and an earring, does not share his parents' definition of the good life. Whereas value consensus characterizes vertical deviance, lateral deviance involves value conflict.

Where vertical deviance occurs, power ultimately remains with the privileged. The rule-breaker wants what they have. They can control him by gradually extending prerogatives to him in return for conforming behavior. They have the power to offer conditional rewards and, in that way, can control and shape the deviant's behavior. The 16-year-old is told that he can take the car if he behaves himself at home. Where lateral deviance occurs, the possibility of conditional rewards to induce conformity disappears. The deviant does not want what the privileged have; therefore, they cannot control him by promising to let him "have a little taste." From the standpoint of the privileged, the situation becomes an extremely difficult one to handle. Value differences remove a powerful lever for inducing conformity.

Being unable to maintain control via conditional rewards, the parent, adult, or other representative of authority is forced to adopt more coercive tactics. These, of course, further estrange the deviant. What constitutes coercion varies with the situation, and can range all the way from locking a teen-age girl in her room to setting the police on anyone with long hair or "strange ideas." Lateral deviance has a built-in potential for polarization. To the extent that polarization takes place, the deviant becomes more committed to his deviance. The point of view taken here is that lateral rather than vertical deviance has tended to characterize the contemporary youth movement. The very notion of a counter culture implies the rejection of traditional values.

MIDDLE-CLASS "YOUTH MOVEMENTS" AND LOWER-CLASS "DELINQUENCY"

Many observers have remarked that the youth movement of the 1960's and 1970's has drawn its membership primarily from the middle class. It is probably the case that the differential relationship of lower-class and middle-class youth to the educational and industrial systems produces different forms of deviance.

The relationship of middle-class youth to the system has been one of prolonged periods of dependency in the category "student." By contrast, the problem of working-class youth is that of incipient obsolescence. Whereas middle-class youth are subjected to very long periods of training to prepare them to function in the economic system, lower-class youth experience abbreviated periods of training and may rapidly become marginal to the system.

Middle-class youth have traditionally reacted to their position by engaging in vertical deviance—thus, for example, the continual struggle of colleges and universities to enforce dormitory closing hours for 20-year-old girls (thereby, it was presumed, protecting them against the loss of their virginity) when more than half the girls of the same age, but not in college, were already married and starting families.

A good deal of the rule-breaking of middle-class youth has traditionally entailed indulging in the prerogatives of adult status—sex, liquor, etc.—while not being regarded culturally as occupying an adult status.

On the other hand, a good deal of the deviance of lower-class youth has related to having the responsibilities of adult status without the wherewithal to support it. Of every 1,000 pupils who started the fifth grade in the fall of 1961, 261 did not graduate in the spring of 1969.[15] Presumably, the bulk of that population, at least among the males, were seeking, without very good credentials, to secure a place for themselves in the job market. They were adults with many legal prerogatives of adults but without the wherewithal to enjoy the status: young men reluctant to marry their pregnant girl friends because they had no steady employment; they were found among the 8 percent of young men in New York who in 1969 could not meet the mental requirements for service in the military, and among the 12 percent in New Jersey, and the 24 percent in South Carolina.[16] The deviance of these young men is likely to take the form of petty thefts and minor hustles to secure access through illegal means to a life denied them by conventional channels.

The collective discontent of the middle-class young is likely to express itself in "youth movements," while that of lower-class youth is likely to take the form of gang delinquency and hooliganism. The aggregation of thousands of young people in colleges and universities facilitates the translation of individual grievances into collective demands. Very large numbers of people of similar background and with a similar status within the institution find themselves in a limited and defined space. Within that space, there are excellent channels for communication, including thoroughfares through which many have to pass, and malls set aside especially for public speaking. The very character of the institution places a premium on verbalization and exposition; thus, there are likely to be many people skilled at articulating collective sentiments. The conditions exist for mass movements ranging from panty raids to football "pep" rallies to "ban the bomb" demonstrations.

In addition, the dissent of the middle-class young is probably more likely to be taken seriously than that of lower-class young people, both because the middle-class young are better able to articulate their case than lower-class youth and because they are more likely, by virtue of social class, to be closer to opinion-makers and media people.

By contrast, there are no substantial aggregates of lower-class youth. A high school with 1,000 students is large; in 1968 the average was 751 nationally and 1,440 for the largest school districts.[17] On the other hand, a college with 5,000 students is small. Student life is much more rigidly controlled in high school and the opportunities for discontented collectivities to form are severely limited, as they are, of course, in reformatories, prison, and the military, other settings in which numbers of lower-class youth are to be found. Out of school, the lower-class boy finds himself in a neighborhood situation in which ethnic, religious, and racial cross pressures operate to restrict the size of the group within which he moves. His protest, then, is not likely to rise above the gang level.

Summary

It may be helpful to sum up the exposition to this point. The category "youth" is a cultural creation. It came into existence in Western societies primarily in response to the changing demands of industrial and commercial economies. The need for higher and higher levels of literacy on the part of the system extended the period of schooling. This longer period of schooling, together with pressure from trade unions and social welfare groups, gradually led to an extension of dependency among the young for longer periods after puberty. There are significant class differentials in the length of time that the individual remains in the youth category. In general, it is much longer for middle-class than for lower-class youth. Middle-class youth have traditionally chafed at the restrictions imposed upon them, but this discontent has, generally, expressed itself as vertical deviance. With the development of the counter culture, lateral deviance became the norm. The balance of this chapter focuses on the circumstances attending the rise of the counter culture.

THE COUNTER CULTURE

Recent observers of the social scene have seen youth as the vanguard of a new society. Though the cynic might dismiss such observations as modern versions of the biblical belief that "a child shall lead them," the fact remains that major changes in the social role of youth are occurring in contemporary American society, and youth have forced changes in American social structure and mores.

The counter culture posed alternatives to existing patterns of norms, values, and social organization. Theodore Roszak, in *The Making of a Counter Culture*, observed that "if the resistance of the counter culture (to mainstream culture) fails, I think there will be nothing in store for us but what anti-utopians like Huxley and Orwell have forecast.[18] There is no way of knowing whether this position is correct, but the fact that it was advanced by a first-rate scholar in a widely admired work suggests the impact of the counter culture on serious thinking.

In a certain sense, the counter culture defies definition, a circumstance which would please its more nonlinear adherents. In the literature, there has been little consensus on its nature. Some observers have focused on young professionals—lawyers, architects, teachers, etc.—who had chosen to place their professional skills at the service of "have-nots" rather than "haves."[19] Others identified the phenomenon with rock music enthusiasts, heavy drug users, and dropouts,[20] and yet others focused primarily on the new commune movement.[21]

One feels intuitively that all of these groups, despite their differences, should be considered part of the counter culture. Yet there would seem to be little disagreement that vast differences exist among these groups. Both the young, long-haired lawyer representing convicts and welfare recipients and the individual raising food organically on a rural commune are authentically part of the counter culture. What then of a definition? Perhaps the issue can be approached in the following manner.

The counter culture is not a coherent, self-contained entity; it is a collection of attitudes, values, and behavior. Analytically, however, two major emphases can be discerned, each of which has a historically identifiable derivation. One orientation can be labeled *expressive-affective* and is currently manifested in the commune movement; the other is *political* and is currently reflected in the rise of what might be termed "vocations for social change."

Basic to the expressive-affective perspective is the belief that the individual should be concerned with "getting his head together," and should be learning how to relate to others in an open and unafraid manner. On the level of pop culture, encounter groups and sensitivity sessions reflect this notion. Central to the expressive-affective view is the belief that the roles commonly made available by the society to the "normal" person are overly constricting. It is argued that the individual should break out of these roles—"mom," "dad," "son," "daughter," "student," "boss," "teacher"—in order to determine who he is, what he is, and what his capacities really are for feeling joy, pain, love, grief, happiness, and sorrow. Otherwise, he is like an actor condemned to play a lifetime role which taps only a meager part of his capabilities. He might get good "reviews," i.e., he is regarded as "responsible," but that is not enough. Unless the actor breaks out of his role, the unused talents, abilities and sensitivities eventually wither.

The immediate historical antecedents of this perspective are found among artists and writers of the "beat generation" of the 1950's, some of whom were influential in the counter culture in the 1960's. Allen Ginsberg's *Howl*,[22] Norman Mailer's *The White Negro*,[23] Jack Kerouac's *On the Road*,[24] and other works of that period dealt with the need to "break out" and the deleterious consequences of not doing so.

This perspective manifested itself in the expressive-affective aspects of the counter culture—leather and jewelry work, drug taking, and, ultimately, certain forms of communal living.

A basic assumption of the expressive-affective orientation is that true authenticity can be experienced only by relating to people in a manner not mediated by considerations of class, race, sex, or those other characteristics that "straight" society regards as important in establishing its hierarchies of prestige and social worth.

Radical politics, the other major emphasis in the counter culture, traces its lineage back through the various phases of radical political dissent in the United States. Its immediate antecedent was the "new left." C. Wright Mills, the prominent sociologist and social critic, first used this term in 1961 to identify the developing movement among the young intelligentsia which focused on the issue of peace, the need for nuclear arms control, and support of Fidel Castro and the Cuban Revolution.[25]

The political phase of the youth movement developed with the dramatic expansion of black protest in the 1960's. Thus, there were sit-ins, followed by freedom rides, followed by "freedom summer" in Mississippi. In the late 1960's, antiwar protest came to replace civil rights protest as the focal activity.

The core assumption of political youth is that political activism can yield significant dividends in progressive social change. Political activism may range all the way from support of the most acceptable mainstream candidate, through civil disorder, to violence.

Participants in these two segments of the counter culture are sometimes openly hostile to each other. Politics were repudiated in an interview that the author conducted with a young man living in a commune: "Everything political is being tried somewhere—China, Russia, Cuba, the United States. If politics could do it, surely it would have done it somewhere, some place. Wherever you look, people are being messed over. That indicates that politics can't change things. People have got to get themselves together first. Then they will change politics. Politics won't change them."

Youth: The Making of a Minority Group

Although it is difficult to frame a coherent theory of the sources of the counter culture, certain explanations for its genesis can be dismissed. The existing social science literature strongly calls into question the idea that those youth involved in protest are in revolt against the values and ideals of their parents. On the contrary, their dissent seems to be partly in the name of those values and ideals. Richard Flacks has observed that:

> *Several years ago, when some of us at the University of Chicago looked into the social backgrounds of the New Left students, we found . . . after interviewing their parents, that there was a substantial continuity between basic values and aspirations of the two generations. Both the activists and their parents were hostile to the self-denying, competitive, status-oriented individualism of bourgeois culture, and both sought a way of life that emphasized self-expression, humanism, openness to experience and community.*[26]

The psychologist Kenneth Keniston made a similar observation in his study of young radicals and their families:

> *Somehow these parents communicated, often without saying outright, that human behavior was to be judged primarily in terms of general ethical principles: that right conduct was to be deduced from general maxims concerning human kindness, honesty, decency, and responsibility; that what mattered most was the ability to act in conformity with principles.*[27]

The youth movement, then, cannot be explained (or explained away) in terms of the displacement onto the larger society of hostilities and frustrations developed within the family situation. An approach to an explanation might be found in exploring the currently popular analytic tactic of applying the "minority group" concept to populations other than blacks and other racial minorities.

There is a growing body of literature in which the concept of minority group is employed to understand the problems and status of women, youth, the aged, the physically handicapped, and various other categories of persons. This literature suggests that concepts and models originally developed in the study of racial and ethnic categories may have analytic utility when applied to populations not ordinarily thought of in minority group terms,[28] and, indeed, as was indicated earlier in this chapter, the status "youth" can be viewed as a subordinate position in the stratification system.

A certain amount of caution must be exercised in drawing the analogy between youth and groups more conventionally identified as minorities. Clearly, there are significant differences between youth on the one hand and, say, blacks or women on the other. Youth is a transitory status, whereas sexual or racial characteristics are fixed. And whereas all blacks are in varying degrees victimized by racism, and all women by sexism, only a small portion of youth are into the counter culture and, therefore, subject to the kinds of pressures to be described.

Nevertheless, those young people who have moved to communes or who have become involved in a serious way in various new left political activities ("Free Angela," "Free Bobby," "Free Huey," "Remember Attica," etc.) did experience some of the hostility conventionally visited upon obstreperous minority groups.

The available data suggest that many youthful adherents of the counter culture are from homes which were comfortable or even affluent. Paradoxically, then, individuals who were at one time members of a privileged group came to be, in some respects, members of a minority group. For that reason, understanding the sources of the counter culture entails understanding a process which might be referred to as "the niggerization of youth." Put somewhat differently, it involves understanding the process whereby the public moved from viewing youth as "good niggers" who knew "their places," and who were due a bit of indulgence for getting drunk on Saturday night (staging panty raids), to viewing them as "bad niggers" who did not know their places (demanding a voice in running schools, etc.).

The New Class

In the years following World War II, there developed in the

United States a class new to the country, and possibly without precedent historically. In those years, a young intelligentsia, comparatively large in number, came into existence. It was made up primarily of persons who had been raised in circumstances of comparative comfort. As Flacks noted:

> By 1960 . . . the development of the American intelligentsia as a class had come to this. Demographically, it had grown over several decades from small pockets of isolated, independent intellectuals to a substantial stratum of the population, including many in new white-collar vocations.[29]

The proportion of the population aged 18-21 in college more than doubled from the end of World War II to the early 1960's. In 1962-64, approximately 34 percent of all American youth aged 18-21 were enrolled in college. By 1965, over 75 percent of American youth were graduating from high school and over half this group were going on to college. By 1969, 60 percent of high school graduates nationally were going on to college.[30] As Havighurst and Neugarten have pointed out, "a much larger percentage of the youth of the United States attend college than any other country—at least twice as many as Canada or New Zealand and many times that of other countries."[31]

Thus, in the 1960's, there was emerging in the United States a stratum made up of substantial numbers of young people, raised in comfort, exposed in their formative years to ideals which their parents, products of the depression years and thereby constrained by concerns related to "making a living" and gaining economic security, had professed but been unable to pursue. They were the children of an older generation of liberal intellectuals, a generation which had centered its hopes for change in left and New Deal politics of the 1930's and 1940's and in the fight against Hitlerism. This older generation, remembering the hungry years of the depression, had been cowed into silence by the McCarthy movement of the early 1950's. Their children, however, were not in revolt against their values. Rather, they criticized their acquiescence to the status quo. Flacks has observed:

> In part, the disaffection of these youths is a direct consequence of the values and impulses their parents transmitted to them. The new generation had been raised in an atmosphere that encouraged autonomy and individuality. Implicitly and explicitly, it had been taught to be skeptical about the intrinsic value of money-making and status and to be skeptical about the claims of established authority . . . . they were young people for whom the established means of

social control was bound to be relatively ineffective (and here they were particularly different from the older generation). Growing up with economic security in families of fairly secure status, the normal incentives of the system—status and income—were of relatively minor importance, and indeed many of their parents encouraged them to feel that such incentives ought to be disdained.[32]

A unique class began to emerge in the country. It was relatively well educated, was not hag-ridden by fears of economic insecurity, and by and large espoused liberal and humanist values. Although a relatively privileged group from one perspective, adults were willing to grant them privilege only within certain limits. In a social sense, they were defined as "youth"—they were college students. They were, by definition, people who were still learning. They had not assumed responsibility. From the adult perspective, ultimately, they were not to be taken seriously.

The emergence of this class was not of itself sufficient, of course, to generate the counter culture. Corrosive confrontations with the forces of authority in three major and interrelated areas played a significant role in creating the degree of estrangement from mainstream norms that was necessary to the development of new life-styles. The civil rights movement, the Vietnam war, and reform of the university were the three major areas of conflict which engaged youth in the 1960's.

At first, youth criticism of society was mild and reformist. It took cognizance of the ills which afflicted the society—poverty, racism, expansionist tendencies internationally, etc.—but assumed that these were the mistakes of a system which was fundamentally healthy and progressive. For example, the Port Huron statement formulated by Students for a Democratic Society in June of 1962 was oriented toward political reform rather than revolution.

The youth movement of the early 1960's was based on the assumption that the society needed only a little prodding in order to attend to its ills. The "freedom riders," for example, undertook the violation of segregationist laws partly on the assumption that the public, once its attention was drawn to such laws, would demand their removal.

The assumption of the possibility of reform began to be questioned as liberals and other progressives (theoretically on the side of youth and other groups seeking change) began to compromise on certain issues and openly to resist change on others. This resistance was more crucial than the resistance of conservatives, and it probably led many youth to speculate on whether the evils of the society were endemic rather than incidental.

The Democratic convention of 1964 was a turning point. The party projected itself as "liberal" in establishing a contrast to the conservatism of Republican party nominee Barry Goldwater. Party leaders, however, allowed a segregationist Mississippi delegation to retain its seats despite a challenge from an integrated slate. Members of the integrated slate were able to demonstrate that they risked violent reprisals in coming to the convention at all and that the segregationist slate had used force and terror in keeping blacks away from polls. Tom Hayden, one of the founders of Students for a Democratic Society, has spoken of this episode as "an experience traumatic for that whole generation of activists."[33]

The University of California at Berkeley, long regarded as a progressive institution as well as one where excellence was the norm, witnessed the first massive student protest of the 1960's. A liberal governor, Edmund G. (Pat) Brown, and a set of administrative officers regarded as progressive, gave the order for the arrest of over 700 students sitting-in at Sproul Hall in a protest over whether fund-raising and other civil rights activities could be engaged in on campus.

The Vietnam war escalated in an administration staffed in large part by people who had come to Washington as "Kennedy liberals." These individuals championed the war against criticism from the left.

The strong resistance to change by many liberals and progressives in government and the university probably played a more important role in transforming the perspective of youth from reform to counter-culture alienation than did the recalcitrance of conservatives. The hesitation of liberals on the issues of justice for minorities, an end to the Vietnam war, and university reform suggested problems more deeply rooted than had been imagined in the idealistic days of the early 1960's.

Tom Hayden, in an autobiographical interview, described the process of disillusionment:

> At first you thought, well, the Southern system is some kind of historical vestige that somehow continued for the last 100 years without our noticing it. And now we're bringing the spotlight to it, it will fall away like a vestigial organ in any other healthy body, and instead we found out that the structure of power in the South was very much tied into the power structure in the whole U.S.[34]

The change from reform to counter culture began around 1966. Allen Ginsberg, the beat poet of the 1950's, was rediscovered. An audience materialized for ex-Harvard Professor Timothy Leary as he preached the gospel of LSD. Ken Kesey, author of *One Flew Over the Cuckoo's Nest*, became an underground culture hero because of his life-style rather than for his writing.

In short, young people were coming to assume the point of view that the old society could not be reformed. New life-styles began to be explored and soon the hippie was seen in the land. A counter culture—as distinct from a culture of political dissent—began to emerge. From that point on, the analogy of youth as a minority group became more and more appropriate. The "niggerization" of youthful dissenters began.

By the summer of 1968, a restaurant near Boulder, Colorado, was displaying a sign saying "Hippies Not Served Here." Large billboards in upstate New York carried slogans like "Keep America Clean: Take a Bath" and "Keep America Beautiful: Get a Haircut." *Newsweek* reported vigilante attacks on hippie neighborhoods in Cambridge, Massachusetts, following a verbal attack by the mayor. The Chief of Police in San Francisco was quoted in *The New York Times Magazine* in May, 1967, as saying that "Hippies are no asset to the community. These people do not have the reality of life. They are trying to escape. Nobody should let their young children take part in this thing." In Indiana, Police Chief Paul E. Genung was quoted as saying, "If we see a boy with long hair, we insult 'em. We shame 'em a little bit and they cut their hair."

There were mass police assaults on gatherings of counter-culture people at Tompkins Square Park in New York City on Memorial Day, 1967, at the "Yip-in" in Grand Central Station in New York City in April, 1968, and in the "People's Park" riot in Berkeley in May, 1969, which resulted in one person being blinded and another killed. By the end of the decade, the minority group analogy was no longer inappropriate to youth and the counter culture.

REFERENCES

1. Phillipe Aries, *Centuries of Childhood: A Social History of Family Life* (New York: Alfred A. Knopf, 1962), p. 128.

2. Henry Campbell Black, *Black's Law Dictionary* (4th ed., St. Paul, Minn.: West Publishing Co., 1951), p. 71.

3. Gerhard Lenski, *Power and Privilege: A Theory of Stratification* (New York: McGraw-Hill, 1966), p. 407.

4. Garth L. Mangum, ed., *The Manpower Revolution* (Garden City, N.Y.: Doubleday, 1965), p. 249.

5. Alvin Renetzsky and Jon S. Greene, eds., *Standard Educational Almanac: 1971* (Los Angeles: Academic Media, 1971), p. 75.

6. Robert H. Bremner, ed., *Children and Youth in America: A Documentary History* (Cambridge, Mass.: Harvard University Press, 1971), Vol. 2, p. 1383.

7. *Loc. cit.*

8. *Ibid.*, Vol. 1, p. 820.

9. *Ibid.*, Vol. 2, pp. 1523–25.

10. Harold T. Christensen, *Marriage Analysis*, 2nd ed. (New York: Ronald Press), 1958.

11. Aries, *op. cit.*, p. 26.

12. Black, *op. cit.*, p. 1792.

13. Lenski, *op. cit.*, p. 426.

14. Edgar Z. Friedenberg, *Coming of Age in America: Growth and Acquiescence* (New York: Random House, 1965), p. 4.

15. Renetzsky and Greene, *op. cit.*, p. 33.

16. *Ibid.*, p. 34.

17. *Ibid.*, p. 63.

18. Theodore Roszak, *The Making of a Counter Culture* (New York: Doubleday, 1969), p. iii.

19. Steven V. Roberts, "Halfway Between Dropping In and Dropping Out," *New York Times Sunday Magazine* (Sept. 12, 1971), pp. 44–46.

20. Irwin Silver, *The Cultural Revolution: A Marxist Analysis* (Fort Murray, New Jersey: Times-Change Press, 1969).

21. Sara Davidson, "Open Land: Getting Back to the Communal Garden," *Harpers*, 240, No. 1441 (1970), pp. 91–102; and H. Otto, "Communes: the Alternative Life Style," *Saturday Review*, 54 (April 24, 1971), pp. 16–21.

22. Allen Ginsberg, *Howl* (San Francisco: City Lights Books, 1957).

23. Norman Mailer, *The White Negro* (San Francisco: City Lights Poets Series, 1957).

24. Jack Kerouac, *On The Road* (New York: Viking Press, 1951).

25. C. Wright Mills, "Letters to the New Left," *Studies on the Left*, 4, (1961), pp. 63–73.

26. Richard Flacks, "Young Intelligentsia in Revolt," *Transaction*, 7, No. 8 (1970), p. 46.

27. Kenneth Keniston, *Young Radicals* (New York: Harcourt, Brace, 1968), p. 66.

28. See Edward S. Sagarin, *The Other Minorities* (Waltham, Mass.: Ginn and Company, 1971), for an example of this approach to the discussion of minority groups.

29. Flacks, *op. cit.*, p. 48.

30. Renetzsky and Greene, *op. cit.*, p. 33.

31. R. H. Havighurst and B. Neugarten, *Society and Education* (Boston: Allyn & Bacon, 1968), p. 108.

32. Flacks, *op. cit.*, p. 49.

33. Tom Hayden, "Rolling Stone Interview," *Rolling Stone* (October 26, 1972), p. 42.

34. *Ibid.*, pp. 40, 42.

8

THE LIFE AND DEATH OF THE HIPPIE MOVEMENT

In a classic article on alienation, the sociologist Robert Merton differentiated between deviance which entails acceptance of the basic goals of a society, but pursuit of those goals by disapproved means, and deviance which entails rejection of both goals and means.[1]

The hippie movement differed from earlier bohemian movements in the United States in that it was characterized by the latter form of deviance rather than the former. As a result, it made a greater impact on the social system than earlier bohemian movements. It provoked great hostility, but also spurred some important changes.

This chapter will: (1) Briefly compare the hippie movement to earlier bohemian movements in the United States. This discussion will provide a clearer understanding of the relationship between bohemian and mainstream society; (2) Focus on the counter culture itself and on certain commonly found social types in that subculture; and (3) Examine the factors which led to a collapse of the hippie movement.

There have been several periods in American history when a bohemian subculture, always present, has become sufficiently large and vital as to attract public attention. These periods were: 1850 to 1860, the decade prior to the Civil War; the 1890's; 1910 to 1917, the years immediately preceding the United States' entry into World War I; the decade of the 1920's; the latter part of the 1950's with the "beat movement"; and the 1960's, with the "counter culture." The last two movements, a few years apart in time, differ in significant ways from the earlier movements.

Bohemians first surfaced in the United States in New York in the 1850's when a group of young writers, painters, and actors began to congregate in and around Charlie Pfaff's lager beer saloon on lower Broadway.[2] The bohemian as a social type had earlier been popularized in France.[3] He was a romantic figure, a penniless young artist struggling for recognition in a world made callous by the values of the marketplace. Cold soup and drafty garrets were his lot except when the sale of a painting or a story made possible a grand feast at an expensive restaurant. The bohemian saw his natural enemy as the philistine, the citizen of smug, narrow, and conventional views who tended to be indifferent to aesthetic and cultural values. Whereas the bohemian refused to pursue a life of commerce, choosing instead to devote himself to his art, the philistine measured everything by the standards of the marketplace. According to the bohemian, the first question the philistine asked of anything was its monetary worth. The bohemian defined his life as a struggle to maintain the integrity of his art despite poverty and despite the temptation to adopt the philistine's values and "produce" anything which would make money—Christmas card jingles rather than poetry, songs "anyone can whistle" rather than symphonies.

Walt Whitman and a number of lesser-known figures—Ada Clare, Fitz-James O'Brien, Henry Clapp—moved in this first circle of American bohemians. Some wrote or painted or acted. Others were pretenders to artistic talents and interests and haunted Pfaff's for the ambiance. But for all, poverty was viewed as a temporary condition from which artistic success would provide escape.

The bohemian period of the 1890's had many of the characteristics of a fad. Albert Parry wrote:

> In 1894, with almost no warning, like a bolt of lightning out of placid skies, Bohemianism became the sensation and the rage of America. Suddenly, it became respectable and highly desirable for the young and old alike. Everyone talked about it and strove to be considered a Bohemian; one might say that children cried for it.[4]

The inspiration for this wave was the novel *Trilby*, which again offered a highly romanticized version of the life of struggling young artists and models. *Trilby* became a popular play and the name was adopted by businessmen for shoes, ice cream, sausage, a cocktail, a bathing suit, a cigar, a cigarette, shoelaces, socks, garters, and cold cures.

The Trilby craze represented a superficial version of bohemia. More serious was the bohemian colony which flourished in Greenwich Village from 1910 through the period of the United States entry into World War I. John Reed, Eugene O'Neill, Sherwood Anderson, Max Eastman, Louise Bryant, and a host of lesser known persons participated in that subculture, which represented the first significant intermingling of art and radical politics in the United States.

The sociologist Bennett Berger has contended that the bohemians of the 1920's and the activists of the counter culture were similar as regards ideology. Borrowing from Malcolm Cowley's *Exile's Return*, he identified a number of seemingly common elements in the thinking of the two groups and, following Cowley, suggested that bohemians since the mid-19th century have tended to subscribe to the same set of ideas. The ideology of bohemianism includes the idea of salvation by the child, an emphasis on self-expression, the notion that the body is a temple where there is nothing unclean, and a belief in living for the moment, in female equality, in liberty, and in the possibility of perceiving new levels of reality. There is also a love of people and places presumably still unspoiled by the corrupt values of modern society. The noble savages may be blacks or Indians or Mexicans. The exotic places may be Tangier or Tahiti or Big Sur.[5]

But in the view of the present author, the difference between the beat movement and the counter culture, on the one hand, and the earlier American bohemian movements, on the other, is quite profound. Deviant youth of the 1920's simply lived out what many "squares" of the time considered the exciting life—the life of the "swinger." Theirs was the kind of deviance which largely accepted society's definitions of the bad and the beautiful. Lawrence Lipton contrasted values of the lost generation with those of the beatniks, but his remarks are even more appropriate to the differences between the lost generation and the counter culture.

> *Ours was not the dedicated poverty of the present day beat. We coveted expensive illustrated editions and bought them when we had the ready cash, even if it meant going without other things. We wanted to attend operas and symphony concerts, even if it meant a seat up under the roof in the last gallery or ushering the rich to their seats in the "diamond horseshoe" . . . . we had disaffiliated ourselves from the rat race . . . but we had not rejected the rewards of the rat race. We had expensive tastes and we meant to indulge them, even if we had to steal books from the bookstores where we worked, or shoplift or run up bills on charge accounts that we never intended to pay, or borrow money from banks and leave our cosigners to pay it back with interest. We were no sandal and sweatshirt set. We liked to dress well, if unconventionally, and sometimes exotically, especially the girls. We lived perforce on crackers and cheese most of the time but we talked like gourmets, and if we had a windfall we spent the money in the best restaurants in town, treating our friends in a show of princely largess.*[6]

The lost generation wanted the perquisites of the good life, but did not want to do the things necessary to get them. They were a generation which had seen its ranks decimated in World War I and, having a sense of the temporal nature of existence, did not want to wait their turn to live the beautiful life. Their deviance was comprehensible to their elders. They wanted what any "normal" person would want.

Similar to the counter culture and having influence on it was the beat movement. From 1957 through 1960, the beat movement flourished, its major centers being the North Beach section of San Francisco and Greenwich Village in New York. The beat movement and the counter culture are sufficiently close in time for the same individual to have participated in both. Ned Polsky, writing about the Greenwich Village beat scene in 1960, indicated that "the attitudes of beats in their thirties have spread rapidly downward all the way to the very young teenagers (13-15)...."[7] It is not unlikely, then, that some hippies began as beats. There are several reasons for suggesting beat influence on the counter culture. The beat indictment of society is very much like that of the counter culture. Lipton has recounted Kenneth Rexroth's observations on the social system and its values:

> ... as Kenneth Rexroth has put it, you can't fill the heads of young lovers with "buy me the new five-hundred dollar deep-freeze and I'll love you" advertising propaganda without poisoning the very act of love itself; you can't hop up your young people with sadism in the movies and television and train them to commando tactics in the army camps to say nothing of brutalizing them in wars, and then expect to "untense" them with Coca Cola and Y.M.C.A. hymn sings. Because underneath ... the New Capitalism ... and Prosperity Unlimited—lies the ugly fact of an economy geared to war production, a design, not for living, but for death.[8]

In political as well as cultural terms, contemporary youth movements have tended to be dissimilar from earlier movements and to be characterized by lateral rather than vertical deviance.

An analogy was often drawn during the 1960's between the youth movement of the 1960's and that of the 1930's, with both being contrasted to the "silent generation" of youth in the 1950's. In fact, the youth movement of the 1930's and the hippie and post-hippie movement of the contemporary period were vastly dissimilar. The 1930's saw the first mass student movement in the United States but, as Altbach and Peterson have indicated, "the generation gap, so much a part of the political rhetoric of the sixties, was absent during the thirties. Politically active students were generally affiliated with adult political groups and usually took their cues from the adult movement."[9]

The distinction between groups as regards type of deviance is not absolute, of course; it is a matter of emphasis. The student movement of the 1930's may be compared, in some respects, to the student component of the civil rights movement of the early 1960's. The students participating in freedom rides and sit-ins and who went to Mississippi in 1964 as part of "Freedom Summer" were functioning, for the most part, under the auspices of adult civil rights organizations. On the other hand, most of the political and cultural organizations of the young in the hippie and post-hippie periods were not under the direction, or even the influence, of adult organizations.

Bohemianism, then, is an intermittent phenomenon in American history. The beat movement and the hippie movement offered a wholesale rejection of mainstream values, both means and ends. Consequently, the tension between them and mainstream society has been greater than the tension between earlier bohemian movements and straight society. Possibly because their deviance is more wholesale, they have, as is indicated in the next chapter, produced more fundamental changes in mainstream society than have earlier bohemian movements.

THE HIPPIE MOVEMENT

Before the rise of Haight-Ashbury, the aspiring writer or artist from the Midwest fled to Greenwich Village. By the summer of 1967, Haight-Ashbury had replaced the Village as the place to go and, indeed, people were leaving the Village to move to San Francisco. The words of Horace Greeley, "Go West, young man," had rarely been so diligently heeded.

The Haight-Ashbury area was for many years an upper-middle-class neighborhood. Haight Street was named for Henry Haight, a conservative former governor of California, who would have been appalled had he forseen that his name would be associated with the "love generation."

As the city grew and the residents of the area prospered, they moved out and rented their property. Eventually, the expanding black population began to move in and, in the late 1950's and early 1960's, were joined by beatnik refugees from the North Beach area of the city. Eventually, in this relatively tolerant community, a small homosexual colony formed. Even before the hippies appeared, Haight-Ashbury had become a kind of quiet bohemia.

"Hippie" was a generic term. It referred to a general orientation of which there are a number of somewhat different manifestations. There are four social types commonly found on the hippie scene: (1) visionaries; (2) freaks and heads; (3) marginal freaks; and (4) midnight hippies and plastic hippies.

The Visionaries

The visionaries gave birth to the movement. It lived and died with them in Haight-Ashbury. Let us attempt here to understand what happened.

The hippies offered a serious, though not well articulated, alternative to the conventional social system. To the extent that there was a theory of change implicit in their actions, it might be summed up in the phrase "transformation by example."[10] Unlike political revolutionaries, they attempted no seizure of power. Rather, they asked for the freedom to "do their thing," that is, to create their own social system. They assumed, implicitly, that what they created would be so joyous, so dazzling, so "groovy," that the "straight" would abandon his own "uptight" life and come over to their side.[11] A kind of antiintellectualism pervaded hippie thinking; thus, their theory of change was never made explicit.

The essential elements in the hippie ethic were based on some very old notions—the mind-body dichotomy, condemnation of the worship of "things," the estrangement of people from each other, and so on. According to the hippie critique, success in American society is defined largely in terms of having money and a certain standard of living. The work roles which yield the income and the standard of living are, for the most part, either meaningless or intrinsically demeaning. Paul Goodman, a favored writer among the estranged young, caught the essence of this indictment.

> *Consider the men and women in TV advertisements demonstrating the product and singing the jingle. They are clowns and mannequins, in grimace, speech, and action. . . . What I want to call to attention in this advertising is not the economic problem of synthetic demand . . . but the human problem that these are human beings working as clowns; and the writers and designers of it are human beings thinking like idiots. . . .*

> *Juicily, glubbily*
> *Blubber is dubbily*
> *delicious and nutritious*
> *—eat it, kitty, it's good.[12]*

Further, the rewards of the system, the accouterments of the standard of living, are not intrinsically satisfying. Once one has the split-level ranch-type house, the swimming pool, the barbecue, and the color television set—then what? Does one, then, measure his progress in life by moving from a 21-inch set to a 24-inch set? The American tragedy, according to hippies, was that the "normal" American evaluates himself and others in terms of these dehumanizing standards.

These criticisms of the social system have been the standard fare of bohemian movements. The counter culture departed from earlier movements and gained greater significance by virtue of its approach to an alternative. In a sense, hippies inverted traditional values. Rather than making "good" use of their time, they "wasted" it; rather than striving for upward mobility, they lived in voluntary poverty.

The dimensions of the experiment first came to public attention when a number of hippie actions ran directly counter to some of the most cherished values of the society. A group called the Diggers began to feed people free in Golden Gate Park in San Francisco and in Constitution Park in Berkeley. They themselves begged for the food that they prepared. They repudiated the notion that the right of people to satisfy their basic needs must be mediated by money. If they had food, one could share it with them, no questions asked. Unlike the Salvation Army, they did not require prayers as a condition of being fed; unlike the Welfare Department, they did not demand proof of being without means. If a person needed lodgings, they attempted to make space available. They repudiated the cash nexus and sought to relate to people in terms of their needs.

"Free stores" were opened in Berkeley and San Francisco, stores where people could come and take what they needed. Rock groups, such as Country Joe and the Fish, gave free concerts in the park.

On the personal level, a rejection of the conventional social system involved "dropping out." Given the logic of the hippie ethic, dropping out made sense. The school system prepares a person for an occupational role. The occupational role yields money and allows the person to buy things which society says are necessary for the "good life." If one rejects society's definition of the good life, dropping out becomes a sensible action, since he does not want the money to purchase such a life. By dropping out, a person could "do his own thing." And that might entail making beads or sandals, or exploring various levels of consciousness, or working in the soil to raise the food that is eaten.

The hippies had a vision of people "grooving together," and they attempted to remove those things which posed barriers—property, prejudice, and preconceptions about what is moral and immoral.

By the summer of 1968, it was generally felt by those who remained that Haight-Ashbury was no longer a good place. "It's pretty heavy out there on the street," a former methedrine addict remarked as he talked with the author about changes in the community.

In the streets, one sensed despair. Significantly, the agencies and facilities dealing with problems and disasters were still very much in evidence, while those which had expressed the élan and hope of the community either no longer existed or were difficult to find. The free clinic was still there, as was the shelter for runaways and the refuge for persons on bad trips, but free food was no longer served in the parks, and the author looked for several days before finding the Diggers.

Both external pressures (coercion from the police and various agencies of city government) and internal contradictions brought about the disintegration of the experiment, and at the end of this chapter these two factors will be discussed.

The visionaries used drugs, but drug use was not at the core of their behavior. For that reason, a distinction between them and more heavily drug-oriented hippies is legitimate. The public stereotype of the hippie was actually a composite of these two somewhat different types.

Freaks and Heads

Drugs were a common element on the hip scene. At first, the most frequently used were marijuana and hashish, two plant derivatives, and Lysergic acid diethylamine (LSD) and methedrine, two chemical derivatives. Much less commonly used in the beginning were opium and heroin. The plant derivatives are smoked, while the chemicals are taken orally, "mainlined" (shot into a vein), or "skin-popped" (injected under the skin). To account for the use of drugs among hippies, one must understand something of the mythology and ideology surrounding their use.

Marijuana was almost universally used by the hip and by hippies.[18] For some, it was simply a matter of being "in"; others found it a mild euphoriant. A subgroup placed the use of drugs within a religious and ideological context. Both freaks and heads were frequent users of one or more psychedelic agents; the term "freak," however, has negative connotations, suggesting either that the user is compulsive in his drug taking, and therefore in a "bag," or that his behavior has become odd and vaguely objectionable as a result of sustained drug use. The mild nature of marijuana is suggested by the fact that, among drug users, one hears frequent mention of "pot heads" but never of "pot freaks." LSD and methedrine, on the other hand, appear to induce freakiness, the "acid freak" and the "speed freak" being frequently mentioned.

BREAKING OUT   The drug ethic in the counter culture can be partially explained in terms of the middle-class background of most hippies. There is a relationship between social class, drug use, and drug ideology. Drug use and the drug ideology of the counter culture were simply examples of a common middle-class belief in the need to "break out." Encounter groups, sensitivity groups, and various forms of "therapy" are functionally equivalent to drug use in that they serve the same need.

This can be accounted for in the following terms. Many middle-class parents expect from their children high levels of academic performance from the first grade onward. There is also concern with propriety, i.e., with being "nice," with not being vulgar, sweaty, and profane like lower-class children. The parents see themselves as instilling in their children traits necessary to success.

The socialization experience of middle-class children probably gives them the sense of a "divided self," the sense that there is an inner self which is more joyous, more buoyant, freer, and more innocent than the controlled, proper, achieving outer self.

Implicit in the pursuits of these children when they become adults
—encounter groups, being awareness groups, psychosynthesis sessions,
gestalt awareness training—is the belief that there is a psychosocial
interior which is shackled by the "public self." This psychosocial interior
is conceived of as more innocent and guileless than the public self, and it
is thought that somehow life would be better, more honest, if this interior self could be directly expressed rather than being mediated by the
canons of propriety. Different people look for different "keys" to un-
lock the shackles which bind the inner self, and the same person tries a
whole set of different keys—"weekend workshops" in transactional analysis last year, structural integration next year.

The Esalen Institute in Big Sur, California, attended primarily
by middle- and upper-class people, explicitly serves this need. Its cata-
logue lists a number of workshops which will facilitate "breaking out."
According to the description of one of these workshops, "Each of us
carries within him, buried beneath layers of psychic and physical tensions, the fertile seeds of a new self."[14] Participants in the workshop
"will use many of the Esalen body oriented psychological techniques to
allow participants to experience that seed center of self and nourish it."[15]

It is not clear that lower-class people feel this bifurcation, this
schizoid burden. Indeed, middle- and lower-class people appear to have
opposite problems. Whereas middle-class people exert themselves to
facilitate impulse expression, lower-class people strive for impulse control. Whereas the middle class strives to be less "proper," lower-class
people strive for propriety. Encounter groups encouraged people to
touch each other; group members were encouraged to get outside themselves, experience others in sensate ways which violate middle-class conceptions of personal boundaries. It is not clear that lower-class people
feel constrained in the same way.

Middle-class people, then, spend a good deal of time, money, and
energy seeking therapies, experiences, or substances which will enable
them to break out. Lower-class people use drugs but without the elaborate ideology which attends middle-class use. In addition, they use
drugs for a different reason. Whereas middle-class people want to break
out of lives experienced as too confining, lower-class people seek to forget
lives experienced as too harsh and painful.

At first, the drug of choice for those who wanted to go beyond
marijuana was LSD. An elaborate ideology surrounding its use and something of a cult developed around the figure of Dr. Timothy Leary, the
former Harvard professor who advocated LSD as the answer to the
world's problems. The major tenets of the ideology may be summed up
as follows:

(1) LSD introduces the user to levels of reality which are ordinarily

not perceived. The straight might speak of "hallucinations," suggesting that the "acid" user is seeing things which are not real. The user admits that part of his trip consists of images and visions, but argues that part also consists of an appreciation of new and more basic levels of reality. To make the straight understand, some users argue that, if a microscope had been placed under the eyes of a man during the Middle Ages, he would have seen a level of reality for which there was no accounting within the framework of his belief system. He would have spoken of "hallucinations" and demanded that microscopes be banned as dangerous.

(2) LSD develops a certain sense of fusion with all living things. The tripper speaks of the "collapse of ego," by which he means a breakdown of the fears, anxieties, rationalizations, and phobias which have kept him from relating to others in a "human way." He also speaks of sensing the life process in leaves, in flowers, in the earth, in himself. This process links all things, made all things one.

The ideology can be expanded, but these were some of its essential elements.

Three things accounted for the decline of "acid" use in Haight-Ashbury: (1) personal disillusionment on the part of many people with Timothy Leary; (2) rise in the frequency of "acid burns" (the sale of fake LSD); and (3) the rise of methedrine use.

Eventually, methedrine replaced LSD as the major drug in Haight-Ashbury. There is no evidence that marijuana is physically harmful. The evidence on LSD is open to either interpretation. Methedrine, on the other hand, is a dangerous drug. It is a type of amphetamine or "pep" pill and is most commonly referred to as "speed." Taken orally, it has the effect of a very powerful amphetamine. "It uses up body energy as a furnace does wood. . . . When it is shot [taken in the bloodstream], it is said to produce the effect of watching the sun come up from one hundred miles away." In an interview, a former "speed freak" described the effects of the drug to the author:

> You're really going. You know you can do anything when you're high on speed. You seem to be able to think clearer and really understand things. You feel powerful. And the more you drop the stuff, the more you feel like that. It kills the appetite, so over time malnutrition sets in. You're in a weakened state and become susceptible to all kinds of diseases. I caught pneumonia when I was on speed. But I couldn't stop. I was falling apart, but it was like I was running so fast I couldn't hit the ground. It was a kind of dynamic collapse.

Just as beatniks searched for the apocalyptic orgasm, so the head

sought the ultimate high. The search for a better "high" led to a pro-
liferation of the types of drugs available. Thus, eventually, the list was
expanded beyond marijuana, hashish, methedrine, and acid to include
psilocybin, a plant extract, DMT, chemically synthesized, cocaine, a
crystal powder, peyote, a small cactus, and various other old and new
psychogenics. Indeed, the search eventually extended to household items
such as nutmeg, which contains elemicin, an ingredient having hallu-
cinogenic properties.

MARGINAL PARTICIPANTS IN THE SUBCULTURE

Visionaries and freaks were at the core of the movement. The movement, however, became a pop phenomenon, part of pop culture, a successor to the hula hoop and blue suede shoes. Its impact at one level was
as a pop phenomenon. It affected public styles and taste, phenomena
which are highly visible but basically marginal to the important characteristics of the society.

Plastic hippies were the vehicle for the pop impact of the movement. What are here termed "midnight hippies" and "marginal freaks"
account for its more lasting impact.

Plastic Hippies

Everybody is familiar with the story of King Midas who turned
whatever he touched into gold. Ironically, this faculty eventually brings
tragedy to his life and, with it, some insight into the nature of love. In
a strange way, the story of Midas is relevant to the hippie movement.
The hippies repudiated the values of conventional society, particularly
as these related to work and commerce. They decried consumption
mania—the ethic and passion which compels people to buy more and
more. They grieved that so many people are locked into the system,
making or selling things which other people do not need and buying
from them equally useless things. In their view, the system made every
man both victim and victimizer.

Ironically, their repudiation of conventional society brought them
such notoriety that they themselves became a marketable item, another
product to be hawked in the marketplace, and the more they defamed
the commercial process, the more they became a "hot" commercial item.

Those who used the hippie phenomenon to make money appealed
in part to an audience which wanted to be titillated and outraged by
revelations of sex orgies and drug parties, and in part to adolescents and
young people who were not inclined to drop out but who viewed wear-

ing the paraphernalia of the hippie—love beads, headbands, Benjamin Franklin eyeglasses, leather shirts, and the like—as daring and exciting. These were the *plastic hippies*.

Any movement runs the risk of becoming a fad, of being divested of substance and becoming mere style. Symbols which at one time expressed outrage at society's oppression and absurdity become merely fashionable and decadent. Very early, the plastic hippie was common in the land, and leather shirts and trousers sold in Haight-Ashbury shops for more than suits at Brooks Brothers.[16] At the height of media attention to the hippie phenomenon, the author interviewed deans of students at four Bay Area colleges—San Jose State College, Stanford University, Foothill Junior College, and the College of San Mateo. Uniformly, the deans indicated that, despite appearances, there were very few hippies on campus. Despite long hair and beads, most of their students were as career-oriented and grade-conscious as ever. They wore the paraphernalia of the outsider, but were not themselves outsiders.

Plastic hippies had an impact on the hippie movement. In one important respect, their behavior overlapped with the core behavior of the true hippie—many were users of marijuana. Eventually, the demand for "grass" became so great that there was a severe shortage. Beyond the obvious consideration of price, the shortage had two consequences. The number of "burns" increased, a "burn" being the sale of some fraudulent substance—alfalfa, oregano, ordinary tobacco, and the like—as genuine marijuana. And a synthetic marijuana, along with persistent but unsubstantiated rumors that "the mob" (organized crime) had moved in and taken over the lucrative trade, contributed to a deepening sense of demoralization in the hippie community.

The Midnight Hippie

Most hippies were in their teens or early twenties. There were a significant number of people, however, who shared a whole complex of values with hippies, but who were integrated into the straight world to the extent of having families and careers. Most of these people were in their thirties. They were in college during the 1950's and were nonconformists by the standards of the time. Journalists and commentators of the 1950's decried the apathy of youth and spoke of a "silent generation." These people were part of that minority of youth who were not silent. They were involved, even then, in civil rights and peace and the other issues which were to engage the passions of youth in later years.

There was no hippie scene into which these people could move. They could have dropped out of school, but there was no Haight-Ashbury for them to drop into. Consequently, they finished school and moved into the job world. Significantly, many were in professions which accommodated a certain amount of bohemianism. They taught in colleges and universities and thus avoided working the conventional nine-to-five day, or worked as book salesmen on the college and university circuit. Relatively few were in occupations such as engineering or insurance or banking; rather, they were in jobs amenable to new ideas and to experimentation with new life-styles.

The *midnight hippie* provided an important link between straight society and the hippie world. The straight found hippies strange, weird, or disgusting. Therefore, he viewed any action taken against them as justified. The midnight hippie, on the other hand, looked straight. He had a straight job, and did not evoke the same immediate hostility from the straight. The midnight hippie's relative social acceptance allowed him to articulate and justify the hippie point of view with at least some possibility of being listened to and believed.

Marginal Freaks

The identification of visionaries and freaks with the hippie phenomenon was complete and their involvement in the life of the community, complete. On the other hand, as awareness of the existence of the new subculture spread, it began to attract large numbers of young people only vaguely aware of its content and only tentatively committed to its values. These people may be called *marginal freaks*. Their level of awareness and commitment was greater than that of plastic hippies, but they were either unable or unwilling to commit their whole lives to the experiment. Among the marginal freaks were teen-age runaways and high school dropouts, as well as older persons spending a semester or more out of college trying on the new life-style, to decide whether it felt comfortable.

While symbols of the new left and political activism were ever-present among marginal freaks ("Che" posters, antiwar posters, and the like), few of those encountered in a summer of research in Haight-Ashbury had any active involvement in the civil rights movement or the peace movement or the then developing "Peace and Freedom" Party. Although they seemed to have left college for the purpose of participating more fully in the counter culture, most marginal freaks expressed the intention of returning to school. Interviews indicated, however, that they had little use for school, which they regarded as irrelevant to their education but necessary to their credentials.

Their remarks reflected disillusionment and resignation. Myron J., formerly a doctoral candidate in philosophy at a Bay Area university, asked,

> *How long can you go on being concerned with the esoterica of philosophy while Oakland is burning? I got into the antipoverty program—poor people felt they were being screwed by the poverty program, and by liberals. There's a lot happening at Berkeley but it's not happening in the classroom except with a few guys. You got to make a choice though. Either you drop out and become a professional revolutionary—screw school and screw the system—or you go back and get a degree so that you're less vulnerable. You have a job, you make a few bucks, and you still fight the system.*

This orientation will be discussed in the next chapter where attention is turned to "vocations for social change."

The marginal freaks had an instrumental view of higher education. It was not worth anything in itself, but it helped you get where you wanted to go. Although the visionaries and freaks had probably not had worse experience with higher education than the marginal freaks, they were less willing, apparently, to accommodate what was viewed by both groups as irrelevant classroom instruction, senseless course requirements, and constraining social regulations. Younger marginal freaks were more critical of high school than older ones were of college, and some of the younger group entertained hopes that college would not have the shortcomings of high school.

THE DEATH OF HAIGHT-ASHBURY

Both internal contradictions and external pressures brought about the death of Haight-Ashbury.

The internal contradictions related principally to the failure of voluntarism as a mechanism for allowing the community to meet its needs and to the failure of the community to develop mechanisms for protecting itself against predators.

The hippies assumed that voluntarism (every man doing his thing) was compatible with satisfying essential group needs and with the maintenance of a social system in which there was an absence of power differentials and invidious distinctions based on wealth, sex, or race. The assumption is open to question. Voluntarism can work where the participants in a social system have enough of a shared understanding of the needs of the system to be willing to do things which they do not want to do in order for the system to persist. Put somewhat differently, every system has its own needs, and where voluntarism prevails, the participants must both understand what needs to be done and be willing to do it.

An illustration may help to clarify this point. The author asked one of the Diggers why they were no longer distributing food in the park:

Well, man, it took a lot of organization to get that done. We had to scuffle to get the food. Then the chicks or somebody had to prepare it. Then we got to serve it. A lot of people got to do a lot of things at the right time or it doesn't come off. Well, it got so that people weren't doing it. I mean a cat wouldn't let us have his truck when we needed it or some chick is grooving somewhere else and can't help out. Now you hate to get into a power bag and start telling people what to do but without that, man, well . . . .

By refusing to introduce explicit rules designed to prevent invidious power distinctions from arising, such distinctions inevitably began to appear. Don S., a former student of the author's who had moved to Haight-Ashbury, commented on the decline of the communal house in which he had lived:

We had all kinds of people there at first and anybody could stay if there was room. Anybody could crash out there. Some of the motorcycle types began to congregate in the kitchen. That became their room, and if you wanted to get something to eat or a beer you had to step over them. Pretty soon, in a way, people were cut off from the food. I don't mean that they wouldn't give it to you, but you had to go on their "turf" to get it. It was like they had begun, in some very quiet and subtle way, to run things.

This episode also relates to the second problem, one which was also inherent in the experiment itself. The system had no way of protecting its own integrity. As each day brought a new wave to Haight-Ashbury, the coherence of the community began to break down. A sense of common purpose and vision began to erode. Newcomers came for a variety of reasons not related to the core values of the community's earlier inhabitants.

The language of the counter culture lost meaning, becoming a vehicle for selfish and antisocial ends. Young men attracted to the area in hopes of finding free and easy sex castigated women who would not provide immediate gratification as "hung up," "uptight," and "bourgeois." The counter culture's vocabulary of spontaneity and openness became a weapon used by men seeking to exploit women sexually. Small-time street hustlers pushing fraudulent or dangerous drugs tried to allay the buyer's suspicions with vivid descriptions of the apocalyptic high to be obtained, interlaced with hints that the buyer was really square and unhip if he did not at once consummate the deal. Both the vocabulary and the social structure of the counter culture served the ends of the hustler, the con man, and the rip-off artist. Life on the streets in Haight-Ashbury became nasty, brutish, and dangerous, crowded with speed freaks, motorcycle toughs, hustlers, runaways, and 15-year-olds strung out on bad dope and talking about "communing with the billion-year-old wisdom in their cells."

Even in the absence of external pressures, the internal contradictions of the hippie ethic would have led to a collapse of the experiment. There were also external pressures, however, and they hastened the decline.

Obviously the counter culture was an affront to straights. For straights to have reacted with anything other than severe condemnation would have been to grant legitimacy to values and behavior which mocked and devalued their own. The "niggerization of youth" has been discussed in the previous chapter.

Summary

The Haight-Ashbury experiment collapsed because of external pressures and internal contradictions. The external pressures took the form of police coercion and of cooptation by the larger society of some of the symbols of the movement. The internal contradictions were probably more important as they suggest that the movement would have collapsed even in the absence of external factors.

The failure of Haight-Ashbury did not extinguish the impulse which had given rise to the effort in the first place. The next chapter focuses on alternative and, in a certain sense, more viable expressions of the same impulses.

REFERENCES

1. Robert Merton, "Social Structure and Anomie," in *Social Theory and Social Structure* (Glencoe, Illinois: The Free Press, 1957), pp. 131–161.

2. Albert Parry, *Garrets and Pretenders: A History of Bohemianism in America* (New York: Dover Publications, 1960), pp. 14–61.

3. For a brief discussion of the emergence of the bohemian as a type, see: Malcolm Cowley, *Exile's Return: A Literary Odyssey of the 1920's* (New York: Viking Press, 1960), pp. 56–57.

4. Parry, *op. cit.*, p. 162.

5. Bennett Berger, "Hippie Morality—More Old Than New," *Transaction*, 5, No. 2 (December, 1967), pp. 19–20.

6. Lawrence Lipton, *The Holy Barbarians* (New York: Grove Press, 1959), p. 284.

7. Ned Polsky, "The Village Beat Scene: Summer 1960," *Dissent*, 3, No. 3 (Summer, 1960), p. 341.

8. Lipton, *op. cit.*, p. 150.

9. Philip G. Altbach and Patti Peterson, "Before Berkeley: Historical Perspectives on American Student Activism," in *The New Pilgrims: Youth Protest in Transition* (New York: David McKay, 1972), p. 19.

10. Interestingly, Martin Buber, in *Paths In Utopia* (Boston: Beacon Press by arrangement with the Macmillan Co., 1968), suggested that the example of the kibbutz might transform the rest of society. The values of the kibbutzim and those of the hippie movement are not dissimilar.

11. We shall have occasion to speak frequently of "straights." The derivation of the word is even more obscure than that of "hippie." At one time, it had positive connotations, meaning a person who was honest or forthright. "He's straight, man," meant that the referent was a person to be trusted. As used in the hippie world, "straight" has a variety of mildly to strongly negative connotations. In its mildest form, it simply means an individual who does not partake of the behavior of a given subculture (such as that of homosexuals or marijuana users). In its strongest form, it refers to the individual who does not participate and who is also very hostile to the subculture.

12. Paul Goodman, *Growing Up Absurd* (New York: Vintage Books, 1960), pp. 25–26.

13. Marijuana, also known as "weed," "pot," "grass," "maryjane," and "reefers," has not been proven to be physically addictive. It is one of a number of "natural" hallucinogens, some of which are found growing around any home: Jimson weed, Hawaiian wood rose, common sage and nutmeg, and morning-glory seeds. There were claims in Haight-Ashbury that the dried seeds of the bluebonnet, the state flower of Texas, have the same property. In California, the bluebonnet is called "lupin" and grows wild along the highways, as does the Scotch broom, another highly praised drug source.

14. *The Esalen Catalog*, 11, No. 2 (1973), p. 7.

15. *Ibid.*, p. 8.

16. Malcolm Cowley suggested a similar cooptation by straight society of some of the values of the bohemian subculture of the 1920's. These values were redefined in such a way as to become instruments in the hands of business. He writes that *"self-expression and paganism* encouraged a demand for all sorts of products—modern furniture, beach pajamas, cosmetics, colored bathrooms with toilet paper to match. *Living for the moment* meant buying an automobile, radio, or house, using it now and paying for it tomorrow. *Female equality* was capable of doubling the consumption of products—cigarettes, for example—that had formerly been for men only." *Exile's Return* (New York: Viking Press, 1960), p. 62.

AFTER THE FALL:
Communes, New Religions, Vocations for Social Change

The collapse of Haight-Ashbury did not bring a collapse of the youth movement. Coexistent with Haight-Ashbury and surviving it were three developments, each representing a different kind of adaptation of youth to the pressures and contradictions within the counter culture.

Some youth went into rural communes. This represented a continued effort to realize the values of the counter culture, but in a less threatening environment.

Others adopted new religions, either of a Christian fundamentalist variety or derived from Eastern, principally Indian, thought. This phenomenon is more complicated than the commune movement. The interpretation taken here of the move toward new religions is that the adoption of Eastern religions is another way of expressing the same degree of alienation from mainstream values that was found in the counter culture. It is a mode which excites less public hostility and retaliation. The public signs of Eastern religiosity—in the case of Krishna Consciousness, flowing robes and shaved heads—are regarded by the public as "weird," "strange," or "exotic" rather than dangerous. Young people in Krishna Consciousness are permitted to be "mad" because their madness is not seen as a threat to old values and established society. On the other hand, the Jesus phenomenon is a way in which youth can reestablish identification with traditional values.[1] It does not reflect the kind of psychic estrangement that Krishna Consciousness does; rather, it marks "the way home."

It may be, however, that neither communes nor new religions are the most important product of the counter culture. Both are peripheral to the major institutions of the society. Both are a retreat from the attempt to effect major institutional change. The most important survival of the youth movement may be "vocations for social change."

COMMUNES

With the death of Haight-Ashbury, the commune movement became a more important and self-conscious phenomenon. An underground literature on communes rapidly developed. Circulation of the *Whole Earth Catalog*, first published in the fall of 1968, leaped from

1,000 copies to 160,000 by the fall of 1969. The *Catalog* provided information for those trying to make their way without the assistance of commercial and industrial culture. It informed the reader how to build dwellings, fix cars, grow food, and the like. *Alternative Society*, published out of Canada, listed plots of rural land for sale. In a perceptive piece, Sara Davidson wrote about communes:

> *The impulse to return to the land and to form "intentional communities," or communes, is being felt in the sudden demand for publications like* The Green Revolution, *founded in the 1940's to promote rural revival, and* The Modern Utopian, *produced by "Alternative Foundation" in Sebastopol, California, which also runs a commune matching service.*[2]

It would not be correct to say that youth revived the communal movement in the United States. The utopian experiments of the early 19th century never entirely died out. There are still 25,000 Hutterites scattered about the country in over 150 communal settlements. Groups like the Reba Fellowship (a Christian community founded in 1957) predate the youth movement, and the pacifist Catholic worker movement has had communes since 1936.

Personal disillusionment motivated an exodus from Haight-Ashbury, but many of those who moved on sought to realize essentially the same values and ideals in a new setting. Rural communes, however, faced some of the same problems that had ripped apart Haight-Ashbury. For example, hostile relations with the outside world were inevitable. The counter culture persona is an affront to the straight world. Pressures on communes from the outside world took the form of charges that included harboring runaways and draft deserters and violating health and safety codes. Most of the time, these charges were accurate, for the life-style of the communes disavowed the values which the draft laws and the various health and safety codes happened to reflect.

Sanctions from the outside world were less crucial to the survival of rural communes, however, than solving problems of internal organization. There are no data available, but it can be plausibly argued that for every commune hounded out of existence by the authorities there must be three or four which collapsed from problems with internal organization.

The major problems confronting communes included at least the following: (1) Who can become a member? Is membership open to anyone or is it limited to people who either display a certain ideological commitment or appear to be "compatible"? (2) To what extent should there be explicit rules about the division of labor? (3) To what extent are elements of a private, noncommunal identity permitted? In other words, can people retain personal and private possessions? Is monogamy permitted? (4) How are decisions made? Are they made communally, or by a select few, or by one person? (5) How does the commune support itself economically? (6) How does it maintain nonhostile relations with the outside world?

To some extent these are issues any group faces, but they become more difficult for communes to solve in that they repudiate the answers society offers for most of these questions. They try to formulate their own answers and inevitably face problems in doing so.

There seem to be better and worse answers, however. Below, two models or types of organization seen among the new communes will be described.

Many adherents of the new commune movement subscribed to a kind of Rousseauian notion that man is born good and then corrupted by society. The concept of society is generalized to mean any social setting with rules, including the home, the classroom, and the business office. From this perspective came the attempt to establish communes free of structure. Morning Star Ranch was an early effort of this sort. Founded by Lou Gottlieb, a singer with a kind of homogenized folk group known as the Limelighters, Morning Star had one governing precept: Access to the land would be denied to no one. With no rules and no organization, members felt that hostilities would not arise and that people could be reborn by living in harmony with the earth. Morning Star operated on the premise that

> *God is the sole owner of the land and we, as his children, are not meant to fight, quarrel and kill over the land, but rather to share this natural resource—to each according to his needs. . . . The land itself selects the people. Those who do not work hard to build shelter and provide for their basic needs do not survive on the land.*[3]

Some communes of this sort were based on the anarchist principle of voluntary cooperation. There were "no rules or structure; people helped each other because they saw a need and wanted to be of service. The community was open to anyone and no one could be asked to leave."[4]

An alternative concept posits the necessity of structure but one without invidious status distinctions. People are assigned specific tasks and responsibilities, generally on a rotating basis, but neither the distribution of rewards nor participation in decision-making is influenced by notions that some people are more capable or more important than others. The decision-making structure is formalized, and individuals who fail to meet their responsibilities may be sanctioned. In addition, candidates for admission are screened to determine whether they genuinely subscribe to the values of the commune.

Typical of this approach was a commune visited in central Oregon, which will be discussed later. It and Morning Star worked out their problems very differently.

Morning Star very quickly began to experience the consequence of granting access to all: "As the word got out that Morning Star was an 'open commune,' more and more people split from the city, especially the Haight-Ashbury. These transient hippie types would visit for a weekend or sometimes for a week or two and then leave."[5]

The facilities at Morning Star, never good to begin with, began to collapse. The toilets were constantly broken. The capability of feeding people fell off. And as Morning Star was "open," there was little commitment on the part of its many transients to doing the work necessary to preserve it.

> Due to the lack of toilet facilities, most people used the woods. Many were careless and did not bury their feces and paper adequately. Thus, this lack of sanitation constituted a serious health hazard. Buildings on the property, including barns and sheds, provided only fourteen small but habitable rooms. Some of these rooms were claimed by permanent residents as "private space" and this space was seldom disturbed. The newest transients crammed into the two small houses. As a result both houses deteriorated rapidly and bathrooms, kitchens and floor surfaces required major repairs. Such crowding increased the danger of disease as well as social stress.[6]

It did not appear that the land was selecting the people but that the people were destroying the land. The escalating crisis forced permanent residents at Morning Star to institute regular meetings for the purpose of deciding what had to be done and soliciting volunteers to do it.

Morning Star also excited the hostility of its neighbors, but its major problems were internal. It simply recreated in a rural setting a social system which had proven not to be viable in an urban setting, with the consequence that its physical facilities were overwhelmed and its natural resources destroyed.

Fairfield and Sardoval, after a national survey of communes, formulated a set of principles with regard to structure and survival:

> People who are new to each other and refuse to develop any sort of structure, group consensus or methods of dealing with problems, inevitably become enemies rather than friends. The larger the size of the group, the worse the problem, i.e. the more need for structure. Two people may be able to live together, if they are reasonably

compatible, without structure but five or ten people will need some
sort of framework for dealing with the inevitable variety of problems
which will arise. A basic rule of thumb for new communes organizing
is: The more people, the more structure; the less thoroughly mem-
bers know and understand each other, the more structure. And
finally, the less time members spend together, the more structure.[7]

The Oregon commune was more viable. Its population consisted of
six adults and five children. The adults formed monogamous pairs, although there had been some talk of sex sharing. There was an attempt
to establish affective parent-child ties among all the adults in the house
and all the children. The adults participated in regular sessions on
management of the house, and the children were often brought into
these discussions. In the past, anyone had been admitted who wanted
to stay, but this policy had proven unwise because some people either
clashed in personality with residents in the house or threatened to become permanent free-loaders. Consequently, new members were screened
for compatibility and seriousness of intent. Most of the adults in the house
held outside jobs, but the communal arrangement did not make it man-
datory that everybody work all the time.

There were certain practical problems. The house was a large, old
structure sitting on about an acre of land. Although there were hopes
of buying it, the landlord had not yet agreed to sell. In order to move
in in the first place, it had been necessary for one of the members of the
group to approach the landlord pretending to be straight. The landlord
was not really aware of what was going on in his dwelling, and the man
who had initially dealt with him had to continue playing the role of
responsible citizen in their subsequent encounters. In addition, some of
the children were of elementary school age and had, in their innocence,
made comments about their home life which had aroused the curiosity,
if not the suspicion, of their teachers.

For all of its difficulties, this approach is probably more viable than
the "open land" ideal.

The Twin Oaks commune in Virginia is even more elaborately
structured. Founded in 1967 by a number of people interested in ideas
which the behavioral psychologist B. F. Skinner had propounded in
Walden Two, it underwent many changes of membership and suffered
an onslaught of would-be members in the late 1960's when interest in
communal living was on the upsurge.

A limit was eventually set on the number of members that would
be admitted and a waiting list was established. People were admitted
from the waiting list according to whether their skills were needed by

the commune at a given time. Thus, number three on the list might get in ahead of number two if he had needed skills in major and minor appliance repair and number two did not.

A membership manager recommended admission to a board of planners who could submit it to a vote of members if the applicants from among whom a choice was to be made were known to the members.

A "labor credit system" was used for getting work done. Each member had to earn the same number of labor credits per week. The labor credit manager posted the necessary jobs each week, and members selected the jobs they preferred; the amount of credit depended on the desirability of the job selected. The more people who selected a job, the less credit it carried. People who selected the less desirable jobs or who were assigned to jobs no one selected (and which, therefore, were totally undesirable) worked fewer hours per week because that job carried more credit.

There have been modifications in this system at Twin Oaks, but the basic principle of labor credit has remained.[8]

An explicit decision-making structure allowed Twin Oaks to censure persons whose behavior undermined the survival of the enterprise and to expel those who were incorrigible. It also allowed them to "manage" their relations with the outside world in such a way as to minimize the hostility that the square world is prone to feel toward communes.

These successful communes shared some of the characteristics of successful 19th-century communes described by Kanter in *Commitment and Community*, but they departed dramatically in other respects. Kanter indicated that "almost all of the successful nineteenth-century communities did not permit nonresident members, whereas more than half of the unsuccessful groups had nonresident members."[9] As indicated here, this seems to be true in the contemporary situation. It relates to the degree of "investment" participants have in a commune. Members have to invest time, energy, and emotion in the enterprise and therefore are more committed to making it work. In both eras, communes with selective membership were more successful than those without such a policy.

Successful communes also had certain rituals, such as regularized group contact, which reinforced the values that held the group together; "the meetings held by the successful Utopias tended to be more frequent than those held by the unsuccessful."[10] In the contemporary situation, participation in decision-making sessions and regular meetings to discuss matters of mutual concern differentiated successful and unsuccessful communes.

On the other hand, many successful 19th-century communal groups —Harmonists, Shakers, Oneidans—isolated their members from the outside world much more totally than contemporary groups. They tended to be much more regimented and to leave much less latitude for individuality than successful contemporary communes.

Those residents of successful communes who remain committed appear to be people who reject some of the major values of the society. They do not strive for "success" or material wealth or status.

The residents of stable communes appear to be heterosexual pairs who share dissent from mainstream values and who find their social life in a communal setting. Their communes, however, do not move toward the style of many 19th-century totalistic communes, where most facets of life were closely regimented and isolation from the outside society was virtually complete.

Successful contemporary communes vary in the degree to which they reject mainstream values and life-styles. The living room of the commune in Oregon was dominated by a large color television set which everyone enjoyed watching. On the other hand, Tolstoy Farm, which managed to stabilize itself after a disastrous open-land experience on the order of Morning Star, has no modern conveniences—no electricity, flush toilets, or clocks.

As was indicated earlier, there has always been a core of people interested in communal living. The peak of youth interest in communes has passed and, of the new communes formed as a consequence of that interest, only a few will survive.

THE NEW RELIGIONS

The new religions found among youth are a more complicated phenomenon, both socially and psychologically, than the communes. They derive principally from Eastern thought and from fundamentalist Christianity. There are certain similarities between Krishna Consciousness and the Jesus movement: both remove youth from drugs, politics, protest, and casual sex, and both foster surrender to a "higher power." They differ principally in that Krishna Consciousness integrates youth into a sect that is alien to conventional society. The Jesus movement, on the other hand, provides a more direct mechanism for reintegration with straight society.

Krishna Consciousness

Like the commune movement, some of the "new religions" of youth predate the youth movement. The Krishna Consciousness movement was started in New York in 1961 by the followers of A. C. Bhartivedanta, an Indian expatriate. The Swami was believed to be a direct link to the deity Krishna, and his name was invoked as the "spiritual master" in each holy ceremony. In a decade, membership in Krishna Consciousness grew from a handful in Greenwich Village to several thousand. The movement came to public attention in the late 1960's as the hippie movement began to disintegrate. Initiates of Krishna Consciousness appeared on the streets, wearing long diaphanous robes, the males having shaved their heads.

Many members of Krishna Consciousness hold jobs, but life centers around the temple. Tithing supports the upkeep of temples. Initiates, some of whom live in the temples, cook and clean sacred objects. Daily meals in the temple provide an occasion for reinforcing group identity and solidarity through chanting, the discussion of sacred writings, and the sharing of food.

Krishna Consciousness offers for its membership the possibility of safe deviance. It imposes a rather rigid code of behavior. The consumption of meat, fish, and eggs is prohibited. Intoxicants, as well as coffee and tea, are forbidden. Sexual congress is prohibited except between married couples once a month after several hours of chanting to cleanse the mind. Ideological deviance is not tolerated. The internal organization of the group is hierarchical and authoritarian. Members accept the four divisions of the Hindu caste system as divinely ordained. There is an acceptance of their own "place" within a system in which others are seen as possessing legitimate authority over them.

For the initiate, the ideology of the organization provides a rationale for the hierarchal organization and extreme asceticism. The individual's present life is seen as only a transitional state to higher spirituality and eventual reunion with Krishna, or toward spiritual descent and reincarnation in a baser state. To achieve higher spirituality requires unquestioning acceptance of the teachings of Krishna and the eschewing of material encumbrances and sensate distractions.

By mainstream or straight standards, the principles of Krishna Consciousness are bizarre but harmless. The very persona of its members, chanting on street corners and playing finger cymbals and drums, dissuades the passerby from viewing it as an organization which must, in a political sense, be taken seriously. Indeed, it becomes a form of diversion, sidewalk frolics for weary urban travelers, something interesting to talk about back home for the tourist. Certain forms of deviance are publicly perceived as harmless, eccentric, or mildly amusing, and are therefore tolerated. Other forms of deviance are seen as dangerous and calling for public action. Krishna Consciousness clearly falls into the former category.

For the convert, Krishna Consciousness offers a relatively safe vehicle for the expression of deep estrangement from mainstream culture.

It also provides a way for youth, facing a personal crisis concerning the values and life-style of the counter culture, to back off without dropping back into mainstream society. For the person having a problem coping with extensive drug use or the idea of extensive drug use, it places a prohibition on all drugs. For the youth disoriented by the casual, open, and, indeed, implicitly compulsory, sex of the counter culture, it provides very explicit rules for sexual behavior. For the young person unable to arrive at a personal system of belief within the intellectual anarchy of the counter culture, it offers an encompassing and explicit belief system.

Krishna Consciousness offers strong organizational support, for its refugees from the hippie collapse, in the form of a fictive family. Further, it offers external symbols of deviance that mainstream culture does not view as dangerous. It provides a mechanism for alienated youth to express their alienation without the harassment attending a more conventional counter-culture persona, and it also provides a mechanism for coping with some of the pressures in the counter culture. It is not clear how stable the membership of Krishna Consciousness is. It itself may be only a mode of transition for youth disenchanted with the counter culture. In any event, it is exotic and attention-getting, but ultimately peripheral to an understanding of youth in the post-hip era.

Jesus Revisited

The Jesus movement provides a way for dissident youth to be reintegrated into society. Its ethic calls upon youth to eschew all that was dangerous and problematic in the counter culture—drugs, promiscuity, and radical politics. The values emphasized are those of the clean-cut, wholesome, 100-percent American youngster circa 1950—faith in God, love of country, and obedience to those in authority. The major difference is that Jesus people in their external style reflect the hippie movement. They have longish hair and the mode of dress introduced by the counter culture in the mid-1960's, but, as was indicated in the previous chapter, this style has been adopted by youth in general—young Republicans as well as hard-core dopers.

The Jesus movement is not a unitary phenomenon. There are a variety of fundamentalist groups claiming the allegiance of formerly dissident youth.

The Jesus movement and Krishna Consciousness differ in that affiliation with Krishna Consciousness ultimately alienates the individual from American society. The initiate in Krishna Consciousness assumes, from the mainstream perspective, the role of crank or fool. He is seen as strange but harmless, weird but vaguely amusing. The Jesus movement is more directly connected to Americana. It represents one version of a fundamentalist Christianity whose roots go back in American history to the late 18th century and, before that back to Europe and the highly emotional millennialist movements which flourished in the late 17th century.

Adams and Fox in their study of the phenomenon have indicated that members of the Jesus movement have a high incidence of past drug use, 62 percent of those over 18 having used dope. Only a few individuals were extremely light users, usually of marijuana.[11] They suggest that the emotional ecstasy of fundamentalist Christianity—speaking in tongues, coming forward to be "saved"—may be the functional equivalent of a drug experience. "Both are subjective and experientally oriented. . . . A common description of the conversion experience is: 'It's a rush like speed.' "[12] The form and the implications of the form are significant. Getting high on Jesus is not publicly seen as having the same threatening implications as getting high on "grass."[13]

Most of the Jesus people reported a shift in political values coincident with their religious conversion. In practice, this seems to have meant a withdrawal from political activism, repudiation of the liberal dictum that man makes himself, and the adoption of a kind of political fatalism. The general stance was one of political apathy. On specific issues, the positions articulated were conservative and included hostility to the peace movement and to new left and liberal politics. The allocation of sex roles tends to be traditional—women do the cooking and other housework, men work outside the home. Sex relations outside of marriage are frowned upon.

The Jesus movement provides a break from the kind of estrangement from traditional behavior reflected in the counter culture. It provides a mechanism for reintegration and a relatively safe outlet for certain kinds of tensions. Thus, teen-age females—Jesus boppers—attending concerts at which "Jesus Rock" groups appear, sometimes display the same ecstasy that was formerly shown at concerts given by big name rock groups. Conventional rock musicians, however, often indulged this ecstasy by having intercourse with the girls. The sexual prohibitions of the Jesus movement make such an event unlikely. Put somewhat differently, the teen-age girl at a rock concert, indulging her developing sexuality and exploring its limits, might, if she approaches a rock musician, have to face the possibility of being pressured into intercourse. The limits at Jesus rock concerts do not extend to this kind of emotionally and socially threatening situation.

The Jesus movement offers less threatening norms than the counter culture. The counter culture offered the norm of "doing your own thing." This freedom placed on individuals either the awful burden of individual decision-making or the uneasy acquiescence in those norms of the counter culture which defined what each person's own thing should be—drugs, sex, dropping out. The norms of the Jesus movement are more consonant with American verities—sex outside of marriage is bad; drugs, except for cigarettes and sometimes alcohol, are bad; and everyone should work hard and be well groomed. Acquiescence in these norms causes fewer problems for many of the young than does acquiescence in the norms of the counter culture.

Many middle-class youth who participated seriously in the counter culture were downwardly mobile. They lived in shabby apartments in low-rent districts and wore secondhand clothing. They were short on money and sometimes went hungry. Reintegration involves an attempt to regain social status. Those that dropped out of school must return. Those who have not held a steady job must develop reliable work habits. The fundamentalist religions not only provide supports for avoiding the sinful pleasures of the counter culture, but they also reinforce the kind of behavior necessary to regain class position. It is not enough to move back into the parents' suburban home; to retain the parents' class position entails finishing college, obtaining a certain type of job, and displaying the proper behavior. Affiliation with the fundamentalist groups of the Jesus movement may help refugees from the counter culture to regain middle-class status.

Jews for Jesus

Brief mention may be made of a small group called Jews for Jesus. Moishe Rosen, an ordained Baptist minister, founded the group and served for a time as a member of the American Board of Missions to Jews in the United States. Rosen founded Jews for Jesus in San Francisco, calling it the "radical wing" of the Hebrew Christian movement. He describes himself as a "Jew who believes that Jesus Christ is the 'true messiah.'" Most members of the Jews for Jesus, according to Rosen, observe the High Holy Days and attend synagogue. They are, he indicates, both Jews and followers of Christ.

The reception of the movement in the Jewish community has not been entirely gracious. Rosen has observed, "Our statements about the satisfaction we have found in Christ have been answered with either ridicule or silent contempt. We find ourselves shunned by the Jewish community and we have been accused of spiritual treason, idolatry, and of deserting our people and our heritage."[14]

Jews for Jesus is a minuscule phenomenon. Its social and psychological roots remain obscure. In the spectrum of the youth movement, it is unusual but not influential.

VOCATIONS FOR SOCIAL CHANGE:
THE NEW POLITICS OF YOUTH

Under the turbulent surface of American society lies more turbulence. Radical activism has traditionally focused on politics, in the narrow sense of the word. It has entailed running candidates for office, demonstrating, picketing, and sitting-in for a wide variety of causes.

For many youth, the massive protest movements of the 1960's culminated in the attempt to create a viable set of alternative institutions. This attempt sprang from two aspirations. First, there was the desire for a more meaningful work life, work that would meet the criterion of being useful rather than personally and socially degrading or destructive. Second, there was the desire to facilitate progressive social change.

Paul Goodman and other social critics have argued that there is little useful work in which the young can engage. The teacher fresh out of college finds herself locked into an educational system which systematically discriminates against blacks and other minority groups; the social worker finds that the job entails being an overseer of the poor; the architect discovers that the builders for whom he works are implicated in perpetuating racial and ethnic residential segregation; the young intern finds that the right to life is mediated by the ability to pay, with the poor being relegated to overcrowded and understaffed city hospitals while the well-to-do enjoy the best that American medicine can offer. The poet discovers that he can make a good living writing jingles for underarm deodorants, but nothing writing poetry.

In response to the moral ambiguity inherent in many occupations in mainstream institutions, a movement toward vocations for social change has come into being. In the broadest sense, reference is being made to the orientation of many youth to occupational settings where training as a professional in law, medicine, teaching or other such areas can be employed explicitly and directly in the public interest.

The rise of such areas as "advocacy" planning and "advocacy" social work reflect the desire of many young professionals to use skills and training on behalf of have-not populations and directly in support of progressive social change.

The term is used here to refer to a broad orientation, but it was borrowed from an organization which reflects that orientation in crystalized form. As an organization, Vocations for Social Change is a collective in Canyon, California, which acts as a clearing house for "people working, or wishing to work, towards building an alternative society." In their newsletter, the collective discusses Vocations for Social Change as a concept:

To explain what we mean by "Vocations for Social Change" we will break it down into "vocation" and "social change." In the current jargon of guidance counseling, "vocation" has become synonymous with "career." The original definition of "vocation" as being a person's calling is closer to our definition. When we say or write "vocation" we mean the life's work of a person—the cause or search to which a person's life forces are dedicated. "Social change" is the process of making fundamental changes in our basic institutions so they meet our collective needs and of working out our interpersonal relationships so they no longer manipulate or limit our growth. . . . A "Vocation for Social Change" . . . is a way people can work for social change on a protracted basis by becoming part of the social change process itself."[15]

In education, there are a remarkable number of efforts at creating new schools. Typical of the effort is the notice placed in the newsletter *Vocations for Social Change:*

We would like to get it together with people interested in opening a new type of school in Los Angeles around February or September 1972. Basically, the school (ages 4-17) would be a free school. This school, however, would attempt to avoid the racism, elitism, and sexism perpetuated by most free schools. Also, contact would be established with teachers and students in an attempt to begin work against the oppression in public schools. Lastly, tuition would be necessary, but based on ability to pay. The school would be structured to enable children to experience: Knowledge derived from practice, reality and personal and collective needs—themselves and others as important just for being and not for doing or competing —learning in a supportive and loving environment—human relationships and behavior free from conventional sex roles—human culture in its entirety, including the cultures of African, Latin American, Asian, and Native peoples.

The school also would offer older members an opportunity to research and organize around community institutions. Staff people are needed with a radical/revolutionary analysis of society and social change, people who also recognize that the creation of new values and relationships is an integral part of the struggle to create a new society. The school would operate as a collective.[16]

The *New Schools Exchange Newsletter* is the major vehicle for transmission of information about alternative education. The following is a typical notice:

> *A group of us in the area of Southern New England are trying to establish a small alternative education community near Voluntown, Conn. called Ahimsa (a Sanscrit word meaning "reverence for life"). We have a small, very lovely acreage with several cabins and a lodge with cooking and bathroom facilities. We are looking for two or three people who would be interested in helping us set up this community, take a lot of initial responsibility in formulating the program and clarifying the philosophy, help with recruiting of other residents, etc. Should be people who have had some experience in the area of alternative education and who have an easy rapport with children. All of us, unfortunately, have commitments on our time which make it impossible for us to involve ourselves fully, but we are all willing to help in every way we can. Our need is for someone to spearhead the formation of this experiment in ed. Anyone coming should be prepared to work for the first few years for subsistence.[17]*

It is also a medium for persons seeking to affiliate with new schools, as the following indicates:

> *BA-Studio Art, 2 years keeping open classroom in "closed" school, ages 11-18; dev. methods of using discards as art materials. Also strong background in poetry/theatre and music, incl. 9 years singing, playing bass and harp, and writing for rock bands. Love animals, growing and eating pure foods, hiking, reading. Subsistence pay. Will consider any area. Thanks . . . .[18]*

> *25, interested in working with children in a nonrestrictive school setting. Especially interested in art, math, crafts, and poetry. 3 years teaching experience. K-9 credential. MA in Learning Disabilities. Salary open. Location—anywhere (especially in the mountains) . . . .[19]*
> *Free school trouble-shooter on the road, had 5 years experience in administration and problem solving with staff, parents and kids. Will exchange skills for room, board plus some travel expenses . . . .[20]*

There are also efforts being made to establish alternative institutions in the health area.

> *We're starting construction for a small, private, nonprofit health clinic in this low-income neighborhood in the San Joaquin Valley. This will be the fourth Salud clinic, although like the others it will*

be completely autonomous. We have no outside funding, only debts.

The staff will function in many ways like a collective, with no hierarchy of authority or income. Services will be flexible, bilingual, and as widely comprehensive as possible, on a pay-as-you-can basis, accessible to as many people as we can handle. (We're not here to work out our guilt feelings; we'll work at a reasonable pace, suitable for a permanent institution. We will try to build a better lifestyle as we work, individually and together.)

Right now we'd like to find a compatible person as business *manager and administrator; someone who has some idea how to carry on business matters in general, be responsible for keeping the books, etc. Also we could use another R.N. or P.H.N., man or woman, preferably bilingual, or an excorpsman from the war who'd like to develop a physician-assistant role, with or without formal credentials. In the long run we'd like to hear from anyone who feels she/he has something to contribute to this project, whether or not it's closely related to "health" care. We can offer long hours, low (but steady) pay, frustration, and some excitement. Whatever else you may get out of it is pretty much up to you, but the potential is here. Visitors welcome . . . .[21]*

And in economics:

The Food Conspiracy is an effort to provide an alternative food source for the community of Berkeley and surrounding areas. Simply, it avoids the impersonality made necessary by corporation-type food distributors. Overhead and profit motives are not involved, allowing us to move to a cheaper and more reliable food system.

The Conspiracy is presently in need of individuals willing to work on gardening vacant lots, picking orchards, researching agri-business and food marketing, communicating with rural communes and other small farmers, making contacts beyond the current young white conspiracy community, printing, and silkscreening, and more.[22]

There are even alternative research outfits.

Aquarian Research Foundation is a research project designed to find ways of breaking down resistance to social change so that a new age can come quickly and peacefully, avoiding unnecessary suffering. They are involved in psychic research, development of natural methods of healing and birth control, encouraging people to set up block radio stations, scientific study of psychic and spirit world phenomena, and anything else that might reduce society's resistance to change.[23]

The most distinctive form of social organization found among the politically oriented is the "collective." The collective generally brings people together for clearly defined tasks; thus, there are law collectives, medical collectives, and teaching collectives.

The collective has brought changes in both style and substance to staid professions such as law. Stylistically, the law collective is likely to project the image associated with new life-styles: longer hair, casual dress, beads, and peace symbols. Substantively, it is likely to have a heavy load of cases relating to political dissent and the new culture: black panthers, dopesters, and political dissenters. In addition, status differences are repudiated so that "staff" and lawyers share in decision-making on matters of general concern. Some law collectives even take the radical step of paying everyone—partners and clerks, lawyers and secretaries—the same amount, with allowances for dependents.

It is not clear whether the movement toward alternative institutions is viable. In some sense, the "underground press" has been an alternative institution, providing a definition of "news" and a perspective not found in the mainstream press. Some underground papers such as the *Village Voice* have survived more than a decade to become "established"; others, seemingly viable, have been rocked by factionalism, the *Berkeley Barb* and the *Los Angeles Free Press* being the major examples.

It may be that persons involved in vocations for social change are drawn disproportionately from the category defined in the previous chapter as "marginal freaks"—persons attracted to the hippie manifestation of the counter culture but who still maintain commitments and aspirations in the straight world.

Youth active in the new left, a category not given much attention in this book, has probably also contributed members to this movement.

THE FUTURE OF THE YOUTH MOVEMENT

The question of the future of the counter culture breaks down into a number of separate questions. What will become of the commune movement? What will become of vocations for social change? Will some of the attitudes and values associated with the counter culture be absorbed into mainstream culture and survive the disappearance of the counter culture as such?

Fred Davis, a sociologist, has argued that "we may all be hippies some day." Davis has stated that hippies engaged in a form of "anticipatory socialization." We are, he has contended, moving toward a society in which cybernation and other forms of technological change will make work less and less necessary while goods become more and more plentiful. Therefore, the relationship between work, the distribution of goods, and self-identity must be reexamined. Currently, access to goods and services is mediated by salary earned from work. In addition, self-image and the sense of self-worth are, for many people, related to the type of work they do. If work ceases to be necessary, ego-strength and the sense of worth will have to be based on other attributes and qualities. By repudiating work and the cash nexus, hippies are providing society with alternative models for determining personal worth and a sense of selfhood. Therefore, Davis has concluded, we will all be hippies some day.[24]

In the long run Davis may be correct, but in the short run the hippie phenomenon itself seems to have lost its social base. It was the author's contention at the beginning of this section that the counter culture is the product of an alienated, young intelligentsia, oriented to social change and not plagued by fears about "making a living."

It is likely that the counter culture message will have an impact, although the messenger will be repudiated. In other words, social conditions in the United States are such as to allow for implementation of some of the changes demanded by radicals and the counter culture. Changes in economic conditions, however, have reduced the likelihood, in the short run, that many youth will be drawn to the more extreme forms of counter cultural life.

Clearly, the economic slowdown which began in 1969 has had an impact on the motivation and values of the stratum from which adherents of the counter culture came. Suddenly, after a prolonged period of prosperity, a significant number of people are again worried about "making a living." College seniors who had their pick of jobs in the 1960's find themselves working in post offices or driving cabs. Fellowships for graduate students have dried up, and students finishing graduate work at the master's or doctoral level find the academic marketplace glutted.

Within youth subculture, considerations of "making a living" are no longer scorned.

In short, the economic conditions necessary to produce a population attracted to the counter culture no longer exist as of the early 1970's. Even the hippies have had to resort to short-term odd jobs. They worked in the post office or waited tables and some managed to get on welfare. "Gigs" were tougher to obtain after 1969, and it was harder to get on welfare. The hippie phenomenon flourished in an atmosphere in which people were not worried about getting by economically and in which it was possible to exist on the fringes of a prosperous economy. By the early 1970's neither condition obtained. It appears unlikely that the kind of total "cutting loose" necessary to move into the commune scene will be very common, at least in the first part of the decade.

In addition, many facets of the social system offered by the counter culture were simply not viable. Speed (methedrine) did kill. The rock music scene did come to be characterized by the "hype," with untalented musical groups being foisted upon the public for a quick financial killing from an album and a few tours. Voluntarism did not work. Significantly, some of the saints of the movement and some of its hallowed events are becoming objects of ridicule among youth. For several months in 1973, four years after Woodstock, a group of satirists, performing at the Village Gate cabaret in Greenwich Village before nightly packed audiences of persons of undergraduate age, did devastating parodies of Bob Dylan, Joan Baez, and other heroes and heroines of the movement. The effect was to delegitimize certain values connected with the movement, to make the vocabulary seem mindless and muddled, and to portray former counter-culture gods and goddesses as self-serving, avaricious, hypocritical, or simply foolish.

On the other hand, it is not at all clear that the reformist impulse of significant numbers of youth has declined. Vocations for social change afford an opportunity to make a living while at the same time being faithful to certain humanistic values. This trend suggests the channel through which the counter culture may continue to have an impact on the society. Those involved in vocations for social change seek both to bring about reform and to establish the validity of alternative institutions. They are pursuing certain counter-culture ends by means of political activity and community organizations. Such activity is found in a wide range of areas, including ecology, alternative education, gay liberation, health collectives, alternative media, and women's liberation.

An attempt has been made in this section to provide a historical overview of the counter culture and an analysis of its predominant trends in the 1970's. Certain superficial aspects of the phenomenon have had a broad impact on the society: men wear their hair longer and dress in a more flamboyant manner, and even the most encrusted traditionalists use phrases like "where it's at." The widespread use of marijuana, particularly among the young, represents a more important impact of the phenomenon on the society. Pot is no longer confined to hip and marginal people. Fraternity boys and associate professors are as likely to light up a joint at a party as the hairiest freak. But the greatest impact of the counter culture has been through the commune movement and the movement to create alternative institutions, and the point of view taken here is that the latter of these two movements will have the most lasting impact on the direction of change in our society.

It might be appropriate to close this section with some observations on the positive societal functions of personal and social deviance. Popular thinking and some of the literature of the social sciences tend to view deviance as "bad," "sick," "pathological," or "undesirable." From a certain perspective, the psychological state of counter-culture people is irrelevant. They could be mad as hatters, yet their critique of society could still be correct.

On the other hand, a number of social scientists have commented on the social role of the "the outsider," "the stranger." The outsider can comment on a society in new and fresh ways and can suggest alternatives not perceived by insiders. The outsider does not accept the myths of the tribe. He is not a part of the picture and therefore can stand apart from it and see it as a whole.

Counter-culture people are outsiders. They are not members of the tribe. By virtue of being outsiders, they have a view of the society that is unique. They are also able to try out new life-styles and, in doing so, provide models which more conventional citizens may find meaningful enough to integrate into their own lives.

We cannot say whether Roszak is correct in suggesting that the counter culture poses the most meaningful alternative to an Orwellian future. We do believe, however, that his comment underscores the importance to society of having people who consciously strive for styles of life and forms of meaning that go beyond the ordinary.

Return to the "Silent Generation"

While important currents of dissent still flow through youth culture, the raging tide of the late 1960's is no longer present. If "vocations for social change" does become a coherent, defined alternative, it might be for only a small percentage of youth. It is necessary to contemplate a more pessimistic judgment of the youth movement. The general change in economic circumstances may be one factor in the demise of youth militance, but there are other possible explanations, explanations which raise questions about the nature of the youth movement overall.

The movement was always characterized by both broad idealistic goals (end racism; end poverty) and certain more immediate objectives (abolish dorm closing hours; change the grading system to pass/no-credit; do away with required courses; end the draft). While the broader, macroscopic goals have obviously not been achieved, to a remarkable extent the proximate goals bearing on conditions of life on campus have. Colleges are now freer and more open places than they were when the youth movement began. The concept and practice of *in loco parentis* has been abandoned. Colleges no longer regard it as their obligation to protect the virginity of their coeds. Many colleges have gone to new grading systems, experimentation in higher education is the norm, and students participate in decision-making in ways that would have been considered unthinkable in the mid-1960's.

In short, the steam may have gone out of the college-based phase of the youth movement because the proximate goals of that movement have been largely realized.

If the privatism of American students during the 1950's is returning, the late night movie is not the only place where reruns occur.

REFERENCES

1. Robert Lynn Adams and Robert John Fox, "Maintaining Jesus: The New Trip," *Transaction*, 9, No. 4 (February, 1972), pp. 50–56.

2. Sara Davidson, "Open Land: Getting Back to the Communal Garden," *Harper's*, 240, No. 1441 (1970), p. 96.

3. Dick Fairfield, "Communes, USA," *The Modern Utopian*, 5, Nos. 1, 2, 3 (1972), p. 110.

4. *Ibid.*, p. 130.

5. *Ibid.*, p. 110.

6. *Ibid.*, p. 111.

7. *Ibid.*, p. 130.

8. *Ibid.*, pp. 48–74.

9. Rosabeth Moss Kanter, *Commitment and Community: Communes and Utopias in Sociological Perspective* (Cambridge, Mass.: Harvard University Press, 1972), p. 81.

10. *Ibid.*, p. 91.

11. Adam and Fox, *op. cit.*, p. 53.

12. *Loc. cit.*

13. *Loc. cit.*

14. *New York Times*, September 5, 1972, p. 32.

15. *Vocations for Social Change Newsletter* (November-December, 1971), p. 4.

16. *Vocations for Social Change Newsletter* (September-October, 1971), p. 10.

17. *New Schools Exchange Newsletter* (October 31, 1971), p. 7.

18. *Ibid.*, p. 6.

19. *Loc. cit.*

20. *Loc. cit.*

21. *Vocations for Social Change Newsletter* (September-October, 1971), p. 13.

22. *Loc. cit.*

23. *Op. cit.*, p. 12.

24. Fred Davis, "Why All of Us May Be Hippies Someday," *Transaction*, 5, No. 2 (1967), pp. 10–18.

THE
REVOLT
OF THE MASSES

10

PUBLIC POLICY

and the White Working Class

The relationship of this chapter to the rest of the book may at first appear tenuous, but it, too, focuses on social movements and social change.

This chapter deals with the causes and consequences of the absence of a strong, progressively-oriented movement among the white working class in the United States. The American left seems to have its base in a segment of the middle-class intelligentsia and among have-nots such as blacks. This fact has certain consequences for the way public policy is formulated and for the content of such policy.

This chapter focuses, then, on three issues. First, how has public policy in the United States been affected by the absence of a left-oriented movement among the white working class? Second, what is the situation of the white working class? Are white workers well-off? And third, what accounts for the orientation of the white working class with regard to public policy?

The United States lacks many types of social welfare programs taken for granted in other industrial democracies,[1] and the consequences of this lack are borne by broad sections of the population. Much attention in this regard has been focused on the poor, but a far larger segment of the population, including most of the white working class, also feels the consequences of this lack. Both the poor and the economically marginal would benefit enormously from social welfare programs. Paradoxically, however, the white working class, unlike nonwhites and some segments of the white intelligentsia, scarcely conceives of the need for new and more adequate social welfare programs. Consequently, as such programs come into existence, they are popularly viewed as being for blacks or other minorities. This interpretation reinforces white working class resistance to them.

In simple Marxist terms, the white working class manifests "false consciousness." The political scientist Robert Lane has indicated that the members of this class moralize downward rather than upward,[2] becoming indignant about the welfare mother who receives a few dollars a year over her allotted stipend but shrugging off the price-rigging businessman who might have bilked the public of millions. This chapter discusses the foundations of this perspective and its consequences for social welfare policy in the United States.

Social scientists, like other Americans, have traditionally been concerned with the powerful and with social outcasts. Consequently, as Peter Schrag observed of the white worker, "there is hardly a language to describe him, or even social statistics." Poverty and affluence are the subject of endless studies and books; yet white workers are neither poor nor affluent. Their life-style can be conveyed in literature, but social scientists have no adequate conceptual category to define their existence. Schrag attempted a summation: "between slums and suburbs, between Scarsdale and Harlem, between Shaker Heights and Hough, there are some eighty million people (depending on how you count them)." It is the world of American Legion posts, neighborhood bars, the Ukrainian club, and the Holy Name Society. Its inhabitants live in tract homes in Daly City, south San Francisco, Bay Ridge, and Canarsie, "bunting on the porch rail with the inscription 'Welcome Home Pete.' The gold star in the window."[3] This population is culturally square and traditionalist. Rock music and movies as an art form are not within their cultural purview; that which the hip regard as "camp" they take seriously; that which the hip take seriously they regard as boring, annoying, or disgusting. It is a measure of the partial validity of the term "forgotten American" that they cannot be as precisely defined as those at the bottom or those at the top.[4]

This chapter is divided into three parts, the first two of which take up the question of whether the white working class has a set of interests which might reasonably be served by changes in social welfare policy. In the first section, "comparative social welfare policy," the United States and other industrial democracies are compared. This comparison demonstrates that the United States lacks a number of social welfare programs commonly found in other industrial countries. In the second, economic characteristics of the white working class are discussed, and it is indicated that its members are far from being affluent. These two sections lay the foundation for the third, which identifies and analyzes those factors which generate and sustain white working-class perspectives on social welfare policy and their seeming hostility to more generous welfare policies, even when these would benefit them.

This chapter rests on the assumption that public policy is formed partly in response to the pressures to which office-holders are subjected. Here, the pressures to be focused on are those of the white working class as an interest group. Their attitudes and behavior cannot be accounted for in terms of any simple Marxist model. The issue is one that has agitated American radicals for decades; it is also an important question for political sociology. And, of course, it is important in grasping the tone and direction of American society.

COMPARATIVE SOCIAL WELFARE POLICY

The United States is thought of as the most advanced nation in the world. It can be plausibly argued, however, that in many ways the country is backward, for it lacks a number of social welfare programs taken for granted in Western democracies. This circumstance has important consequences for the quality of life in our society, and it can be explained partly by the absence of any strong sense of class interest or political consciousness among white workers, those who are here termed economically marginal.

The dearth of social welfare programs in this, the most advanced nation in the world, has been noted by several commentators. For example, Alvin Schorr has observed with regard to family allowances that "a majority of the countries of the world and all of the industrial West, except the United States, now have such programs."[5] James Vadikan points out that family allowances "constitute a means of redistributing income in such a way as to benefit the child-rearing portion of the population."[6] In most countries, it is a fairly modest sum. Under the Canadian system, for example, the amount per child ranges from $6 a month to $10 a month, depending on the child's age. By contrast, the French system is quite generous.[7] "The payment there varies according to region, the number of children in the family, and their ages. In Paris in 1964, for example, a family with four children received between 380 and 450 francs ($77 to $111) a month, exceeding the legal minimum wage at the time. In addition, various special payments may be made during pregnancy, at birth, [and] for improved housing."[8]

Edgar Z. Friedenberg has remarked that the United States "still provides less in the way of social services, especially to the ill and aged, than an Englishman or Scandinavian would expect as a matter of right." National health insurance plans are found in one form or another in all of the industrial democracies, although the extent of benefits varies from place to place. In Great Britain, complete medical, surgical, pharmaceutical, and dental services are offered. In Australia, one finds restricted pharmaceutical benefits, hospital benefits, and various other kinds of services. But there are basically three types of national health programs: the government may own facilities and hire the professionals; patients may pay fees and be reimbursed; or professionals may render services under contract to the government. Most West European countries have the third type of program. There is a good deal of nonsense talked in the United States about the British system. No doctor is forced to join the national health service, but 95 percent have chosen to do so. Their income is lower than that of doctors in the United States but higher than they were before Health Service came in and higher than that of other professionals in Great Britain.

Social welfare policy extends beyond the provision of certain kinds of services and income redistribution to include the creation of opportunities. All developed nations have specified policies with respect to manpower and employment. These policies vary in the extent to which they sustain the worker during periods of unemployment and facilitate his reemployment. Sweden has a number of sophisticated manpower programs, leading Carl Uhr to observe that "we in the United States have not yet developed as comprehensive and coordinated a set of labor policies and institutions as have evolved in Sweden." In addition to a variety of training programs for older workers whose skills have become obsolete and younger people without marketable skills, there are mechanisms for matching up workers with jobs. "Workers living in labor-surplus areas," says Uhr, "are induced by a system of allowances to move to available jobs, known to the employment service, in labor shortage areas. Unemployed persons who need and want to move great distances to job opportunities in other locations may apply for and receive travel expenses to seek new work in these areas. If they locate jobs, they may immediately receive a 'starting allowance.' This is in substance a grant which becomes repayable in part only if they do not hold the new job for at least 90 days." Other problems associated with worker mobility are anticipated: "If housing for their families is not available in their new work location, they may receive 'family allowances' for the separate maintenance of wife and children for up to 9 months in their former location. These allowances pay the rent for the family up to a maximum figure, plus a cash allowance for the maintenance of wife and children."[9]

Few critics argue that the United States should simply mirror other industrial democracies with regard to social welfare policy and programs. These approaches are not ends in themselves but are designed to alleviate kinds of mass deprivation, deprivation that is visible and persistent in this country. Some scholars have pointed to what they believe to be the tangible consequences of the paucity of comprehensive social welfare measures in the United States. Daniel Patrick Moynihan has stated,

> *The teeming disorganized life of impoverished slums has all but disappeared among North American democracies—save only the United States. It requires some intrepidness to declare this to be a fact, as no systematic inquiry has been made which would provide*

*completely dependable comparisons, but it can be said with fair
assurance that mass poverty and squalor, of the kind that may be
encountered in almost any American city, simply cannot be found
in comparable cities in Europe or Canada or Japan.*

Robert Heilbroner echoes this: "I maintain that to match the
squalor of the worst of the American habitat one must descend to the
middle range of the underdeveloped lands."[10]

Infant mortality rates in the United States are considerably higher
than those in other industrial democracies. In 1968, with a rate of 22.1
infant deaths per 1,000 live births, the country ranked above most other
Western industrial democracies. It is estimated that the nation ranks
eighteenth in the world, just above Hong Kong. Some might argue that
this is a consequence of the extraordinarily high rate among nonwhites,
but even if we consider the rate among whites only (in Mississippi, for
example, 23.1 among whites; in Pennsylvania, 20.3; Maine, 22.8; New
Hampshire, 20.1; Illinois, 20.3; West Virginia, 24.8), the national performance is inferior to that of other Western countries.[11]

Vadikan has observed, "Almost 40,000 babies die in America each
year who would be saved if our infant mortality rate was as low as that
in Sweden. In 1967, one million babies, one in four, [were] born to
mothers receiving little or no obstetric care."[12]

To reiterate, whether the United States is the most developed or
underdeveloped nation in the world depends upon the dimension one
examines. If one looks at the number of automobiles per 1,000 population, the United States leads the field. If one looks at infant mortality
rates, or number of hospital beds per 1,000, or number of doctors per
1,000, or average rates of unemployment over time, the country lags and,
along some dimensions, lags badly.

Some might counter that the United States has programs that other
democracies lack (New Careers, Head Start, Upward Bound, and so
forth). However, these programs have been directed at the poor and
have not been intended to meet the needs and problems of those who
are marginal. Indeed, the Nixon Administration has been able to threat-
en the existence of many "Great Society" programs precisely because
they were seen as benefiting only the "unworthy" poor. Secondly, although international comparisons are difficult to make, it does appear
to be true that all things taken together (save education), the United
States spends less on social welfare than many other countries. Bert Seidman has observed,

*It generally surprises most Americans to find out that their country,
the wealthiest in the world, uses less of its natural wealth for the*

> social welfare of its citizens than other advanced industrial nations
> and frequently less than many poor and developing nations which
> make considerable sacrifices to do so. For example, an International
> Labor Organization Report published in 1964 shows that West
> Germany, Luxemburg, Austria, and Italy used 17 percent, 16.8 per-
> cent, 14.8 percent, and 14.7 percent, respectively, of their gross na-
> tional product for social welfare measures. None of the 15 nations
> in Western Europe, except Spain and Portugal, spent less than 8.9
> percent. This contrasts with 7 percent of the gross national product
> spent by the United States for such programs.[13]

The United States spends more on education and has a much
higher proportion of its college-age population in college than West
European countries. This is partially a consequence of having different
channels of access to employment. The lower proportion of the European college-age population in college does not mean that there is mass
unemployment or that jobs go begging; rather, the system of matching
up man and job is different. There is a school of thought, however,
which contends that European technological development and entrepreneurial efficiency may be hurt in the long run by not having a work
force with as much formal education as that in the United States. If
that occurs and European countries move to spend more on education,
the relative position of the United States in terms of social welfare
spending would remain unchanged.

Mike Harrington has indicated that "the American percentage of
the gross national product devoted to direct social benefits has yet to
achieve even half the typical European contribution."

Let us now look more closely at the economic status of white workers.

THE POOR AND THE MARGINAL

It is assumed by many observers that the white working class has
become conservative because it has become affluent and therefore does
not need amplified social welfare legislation. Actually, about 12 percent
of the white population is poor, while another 55 to 60 percent is economically marginal.

Like poor nonwhites, poor whites have been clearly identified by
demographers, economists, and sociologists. In 1967, of the 26,146,000
people in the country defined as poor, 17,764,000 were white.[14] Among
the 619,000 young men in 1972 who were 20 to 24 years of age and unemployed, 501,000 were white and 118,000 were nonwhite; 562,000 of
707,000 unemployed young men aged 16 to 19 in 1972 were white.[15] In

December, 1972, 2,160,000 white males 16 years of age and over were un-employed, and 475,000 nonwhites. The nonwhite rate was higher, of course, but the figures and the rates belied the notion that unemployment was solely or primarily a black problem.

The economically marginal white is much harder to identify. His existence proves the inadequacy of the simple dichotomy between the poor and the affluent. Below, five quantitative measures are employed to define this class: income distribution, standard of living, real income, credit status, and liquid assets. These measures cover a number of years in order to establish that marginality is a stable condition of the white working class rather than a transient condition.

As regards income distribution, in 1966 31 percent of white families made less than $5,000, and 39 percent made $5,000 to $9,999, while another 30 percent made more than $10,000 a year.[16] Seven families of ten, then, were poor or marginal. But income figures per se mean little unless they are related to purchasing power and standard of living. An inference with regard to the meaning of the income of white workers can be made by an analysis of reports published by the Bureau of Labor Statistics, U. S. Department of Labor. The bureau regularly devises a "standard family budget" for a four-person family consisting of a working husband, a nonworking wife, a son, age 13, and a daughter, age 8. This pattern closely approximates actual family structure. The budget is derived from "scientific and technical judgment regarding health and social well-being" and is designed to indicate the cost of a "modest but adequate" standard of living in urban areas. In 1967, the required sum ranged down from $10,092 in Honolulu to $9,744 in the San Francisco–Oakland area, $9,079 in Philadelphia, and $8,641 in Durham, with a low of $7,952 in Austin, Texas. The average for 39 cities and metropolitan areas was $9,243.[17]

In the same year, production and nonsupervisory workers on non-agricultural payrolls averaged just over $5,000 a year, ranging from a high of $8,060 for construction workers to a low of $4,264 for those in wholesale and retail trade. All fell well below the government's own figure of the amount needed to enjoy a moderate standard of living in urban areas.[18] The mean income of craftsmen and foremen was $9,310, otherwise, no workers year-to-year even approach the average of the Standard Family Budget.

Further, the effects of inflation erode the money gains made by the blue-collar class. Between 1965 and 1969, the average wage of 47 million production and nonsupervisory workers in private industry went up $14.74 from $96.21 to $110.95 per week; at the same time, the worker with three dependents saw his tax rise by $4.80 a week. The four-year increase in prices from a base of 100 in 1965 was $11.18. Adding the price rise to the tax increase and subtracting from the 1969 wage, the worker had $1.24 per week less to spend in 1969 than in 1965.[19]

The pace of inflation in the 1970's has not improved the situation of the working class with regard to purchasing power but, rather, has made it worse.

Obviously, the American blue-collar and working class does not live in misery and desperation. Nonetheless, it is undeniable that the members of this class are far from affluent, that life is probably a worrisome thing for them, and that their opportunity to get very far ahead seems more and more distant.

Apart from the bureau's "modest but adequate" standard, we also have to look into consumer finance to find the meaning of dollar income. The Economic Behavior Program of the Survey Research Center of the University of Michigan yearly collects detailed information on "family income, financial assets and debt, automobiles, other durable goods, and housing." Multi-stage area probability sampling is used to select a sample that is representative of the nation.

The debt status of economically marginal whites can be summed up as follows. About 55 percent of the families in the income category $5,000 to $7,449 had installment debt, and 61 percent in the income category $7,500 to $9,999. Being unmarried and having no children reduced the probability of being in debt. About 65 to 70 percent of households with children were in debt. In 1967, the mean amount of debt for all families was $1,260. Payments for automobiles were most common but were closely followed by payments on other durables and on personal loans.[20]

The meaning of debt is amplified if viewed in terms of financial assets at the command of workers. About 80 percent of wage earners making $5,000 to $10,000 a year in 1967 either had no checking account or had less than $500 in an account. Sixty-three percent of families making $7,500 to $9,999 had no account or had less than $500 in an account. The amount of liquid assets then, is meager, and most families are a paycheck or two away from public assistance.[21]

The life-style of the marginal class is suggested by other data. Less than half take vacations, and those who do rarely spend much money on them. It is not the case, then, that there is an affluent blue-collar or working class. Most white families are either poor or economically marginal. If they are marginal, they had only a slight rise in real income from 1965 on despite a rise in paper income. Federal data suggest that they may barely make enough for an adequate standard of living. They have acquired certain household goods and durables by going into debt and have the slenderest resources to sustain themselves in a crisis.

The American worker has to purchase out of his pocket services that are publicly provided in many other industrial democracies. He is taxed, but there is no commensurate return in public services. For example, the American worker, except under highly restricted circumstances, bears out of his own pocket the cost of moving to a locale where he may find work, the cost of supporting his family while looking for work, and the cost of moving them. A whole complex of expenditures which, as we saw, is a matter of public responsibility in Sweden, is paid for privately by the American worker.

Social scientists have devised a number of classificatory systems to describe the American population. To delineate further the position of economic marginals within the society, a rather gross system will be formulated here which nevertheless makes certain important distinctions.

For purposes of this discussion, the American population can be divided into four categories.

At the bottom, there are the poor (a disproportionate percentage of the black population and of Indians, Mexicans, and Puerto Ricans; a disproportionate percentage of the elderly and of families headed by a female). The poor subsist on public monies, inadequate incomes, or both. They are unable to make ends meet and thus may suffer from malnutrition or a wide variety of debilitating, untreated medical conditions. A segment of the black population and, increasingly, parts of the Indian, Mexican, and Puerto Rican populations show some degree of political consciousness and some conception of the need to develop national policy approaches to the problems of the deprived.

Then there are the marginals. Most of the white working-class population falls into this category and, indeed, most of the population. Their characteristics have already been described.[22]

Above them is a class that has substantial money income but does not own or control wealth. (The distinction between income and wealth is important.) They sell brain power and relatively uncommon skills and are handsomely rewarded. In this category are such persons as the upper-echelon professors at the more prestigious universities, the new experts at information control, systems analysts, middle- and upper-echelon advertising and media men, most business management people, and the like. These people are affluent, and some of them have influence with the powerful (Henry Kissinger, for example). Basically, however, they are well-paid laborers. The politics of this group spans the spectrum, and it is difficult to tell what the factors are that account for value differences.

Last, there are the true magnates, the corporate elites, the people who own or control the wealth of the country. The upper 5 percent of consumers in the country control 53 percent of the wealth. There is much greater inequality in the distribution of wealth than there is in the distribution of income, accounting for the class of income-affluent persons.

The marginals appear, for reasons we shall explore, to consider themselves closer to the top than to the bottom when, in fact, they are much closer to the bottom than to the top.

POLITICAL VALUES OF THE WHITE WORKING CLASS

It should be clear by now that the white working class is not afflu- ent. Neither, of course, are white workers poor. They make enough to meet daily living costs and are able to acquire appliances, durables, and some other kinds of goods through installment buying. They have little in the way of liquid assets and are highly vulnerable in the event of loss of job, illness, or any of a number of other kinds of misfortunes. They would benefit enormously from a wide variety of social welfare measures that are quite conventional in other industrial democracies. But they are not politically active in the pursuit of these or other social welfare measures and have left lobbying and agitation for more effective and broadly based programs up to blacks and to white liberals and radicals.

They are the people whose sons were drafted and sent to Vietnam and whose children are less likely to get into college even when they are extremely capable. Inadequate opportunity for higher education is generally seen as a problem of nonwhites. The existence of inadequate educational opportunities is widespread, however. With regard to higher education, Project Talent, a survey funded by the United States Office of Education, revealed a "marked relationship between reported family income and college entry." Data were gathered on 60,000 students. Basically, the findings were that males in the 98th to 100th percentile were likely to go to college irrespective of family income. Below that social class became very important, with the mediocre male at the 50th percentile whose family made $12,000 a year or more being more likely to have entered college than the talented boy at the 89th percentile whose family made $3,000 a year or less. The reality behind these data are neither perceived nor translated into political reality by poor and marginal whites.

Why are economically marginal whites not further to the left politically? Why are they not active in promoting the kinds of policy approaches and programs that would appear to serve their own interests?

To be a supporter of movements for the kinds of social welfare policies discussed earlier in this chapter implies that one (a) recognizes the existence of certain kinds of problems, (b) accounts for these prob- lems in system terms and, therefore, (c) calls for given policy approaches to cope with them. Obviously, if an individual either does not recognize the existence of particular problems or accounts for them in personalistic terms, then he does not seek system changes or new policy approaches.

Evidence on how the white worker defines his own situation is vague and inconclusive. The data provide no basis for anything other than hypothesis and speculation. Therefore, let us hypothesize and speculate.[23]

The results of public opinion polls suggest that white workers have a sense of the inadequacy of their position but are at a loss to explain it. Something is wrong but they are not clear about what. Lloyd A. Tree and Hadley Cantril, reporting on a representative national sample, indicate that personal economic conditions and employment status were cited by three out of four persons as their most pressing concerns.[24] This finding seems to have surprised the researchers. "Even in affluent America, the leading item mentioned under personal wishes and hopes was an 'improved or decent standard of living.' As one Arizona housewife pointed out, 'They say it's prosperous now, but I sure as heck don't notice it.'"[25] This chapter suggests that the Arizona housewife was more nearly correct than Tree and Cantril.

Alongside an appreciation of their precarious material situation was complete confusion with regard to policy and meliorative approaches. The overwhelming majority of respondents making $10,000 a year or less favored government programs to accomplish social ends, but only one third believed that the government should use its power more readily. Less than one third believed that corporate powers should be curbed, while almost half favored greater government control over labor unions.

The task, then, is to make sense of this contradiction, to understand it, to grasp the underlying logic and rationale. If there is an underlying logic and rationale, it is probably something on this order: "Yes," the worker says, "I would benefit from various kinds of government programs; they would help me meet real and pressing material problems. Those problems, however, are caused by other segments of the population. Therefore, alternatively, the government might force these people to stop doing the kinds of things which cause problems for me."

Contemporary workers who recall the desperate and hungry souls populating "Hoovervilles" during the depression are likely to feel comparatively well off. Those too young to have experienced the depression undoubtedly have it recalled for them by parents. Their dollar income is substantially greater, the number of household possessions is greater, and they have greater job security. This relative satisfaction with having enjoyed a certain amount of mobility probably decreases the workers' proclivity to critize the politico-economic system or view it as inequitable and unjust. It decreases any sense of a need to agitate for new policy. It is also the case, however, that the worker still has trouble making ends meet.

These difficulties, implicitly, pose a question for him. "If I'm so much better off and make so much more money than guys made before, how come I'm still having a rough time?" His belief that the system has afforded him the opportunity for a better life decreases the likelihood that he will account for his difficulties in terms of system defects. If the system were not benign, he would not now be in a position where he should be enjoying a better life. In absolving the system he also absolves those who, in some sense, run it.

There are a number of ready-made scapegoats the worker can focus on in attempting to account for his difficulties (blacks, communists, hippies, liberals, "peace creeps"); of these, blacks are the most plausible and the most accessible. As blacks demand programs to deal with poverty, as they demand a guaranteed annual income or an improved system for distributing food to the needy and the hungry, as they demand a whole complex of social welfare legislation, they must seem to the white worker to be unwilling to take advantage of the opportunities he believes exist for any person willing to work. They seem to be making vigorous raids on his pocketbook. They appear to be cheaters, people unwilling to play by the rules, people who "want something for nothing." And he believes the something comes out of his pocket.

This kind of explanation posits genuine misperception on his part. An alternative (psychologically "deeper") approach might posit displacement of frustration and hostility onto scapegoats. According to this approach, the worker has some glimpse of the precariousness of his position and some sense of the reasons for it. However, to entertain conscious notions of system defects would be to harbor ideas that are "un-American" or "communist-inspired." And for the man who pastes his American flag decal on the car windshield and puts an "Honor America" sticker on his bumper, this might be no small matter. It might be the political equivalent of a hard-hat admitting that he has sexual thoughts about other men. Rather than countenance thoughts that he has come to view as subversive and immoral, he displaces his hostility onto out-groups—blacks, hippies, "bleeding hearts," "limousine liberals," and other freaks of nature.

In addition, there are important differences within the white working class which militate against the expression of common sentiments about problems and their solutions. The 80 million or so people who comprise the marginal class are differentiated by geography, ethnicity, and occupation. A number of students have discussed the persistence of ethnic identity in American communities. Michael Parenti has observed that "in a single weekend in New York separate dances for persons of Hungarian, Irish, Italian, German, and Polish extractions are advertised in the neighborhood newspapers and the foreign language press."[26] Herbert Gans[27] and Gerald Suttles[28] have discussed the persistence of a close network of relationships among Italians living in Boston and in Chicago. Occupationally, the $5,000 to $10,000 category includes secretaries and assembly-line workers, senior clerks and cab drivers. Geographically, workers spread out over the South, with its racially dominated politics, the Midwest, where fear of communism is a serious sentiment, and the Northeast, where problems of traffic congestion and state financial support for parochial schools excite political passions.

In other words, there are a number of cross-cutting loyalties and interests that reduce any sense of common identity.

The trade unions encompass a larger portion of the American working class than any other organized body. The union movement itself, however, is internally fragmented. In addition, (not counting about two million blacks who are trade union members) only about 14 million whites in a work force of over 70 million are union members. The American union movement very early fell into the trap of racism: excluding blacks and thereby creating a pool of strikebreakers for employers, and depressing the wage level of whites by insuring low wage levels for blacks. The unions neither ideologically nor organizationally are prepared to define radically progressive policy alternatives.

The muted role of the trade unions has been crucial. The political interests of most citizens are mediated through organizations. This is particularly important for populations (white workers, for example) less likely to participate electorally in the political process. Thus, for example, the underrepresentation of blacks at the ballot box is counterbalanced somewhat by the existence of a variety of politically vigorous organizations (the N.A.A.C.P. and the Urban League are the oldest and most resilient). Traditionally, these organizations have been the vehicles of the black bourgeoisie. Recently, however, a number of groups drawing their membership from street and ghetto blacks have become prominent; the Black Panthers, the Black Muslims, and DRUM, an organization of black workers in automobile plants, are the most vigorous.

Many of those who have written on the white lower class suggest that they have "a deficient sociocultural milieu"; that they possess undifferentiated and unsophisticated notions with regard to the nature of the socio-politico-economic system, and that they are bigoted and suspicious.[29] The lower middle class is seen as rigidly moralistic and concerned with propriety. The self-defeating definitions of the situation entertained by these two groups go unchallenged by major alternative formulations put forth by the trade unions. They have not played the educational role vis-à-vis white workers that civil rights groups have played vis-à-vis blacks. In regard to social welfare legislation, the orientation of the unions has been to conserve and preserve rather than significantly expand or explore.

The white worker is not wholly unmindful of his economic interests,[30] but he does not translate this knowledge into any consistent conception of major programmatic and policy change. This process is left to a segment of the black movement, thereby decreasing further the likelihood that white workers will subscribe to such views.

We have already seen one consequence of this political orientation of the white working class in the relatively poor showing of the United States with regard to social welfare programs. Another important consequence is that the pursuit of more adequate social welfare legislation becomes equated with the pursuit of racial justice.

The black movement has focused attention on the deprived status of blacks. There has been no equivalent movement among whites to sensitize policy-makers to the marginal status of most whites. While there are a variety of ethnically-based organizations—Hibernian clubs, Sons of Italy, Polish-American clubs, Greek-American clubs—none has a clearly formulated program with regard to the class problems of its members.[31] Many nonwhite groups, however, are so oriented. The black movement is too well known to need discussion. Among Mexicans, La Huelga has mobilized many Mexican-American agricultural workers in California and the Southwest, while Rijes Tijerina and "Corky" Gonzales have rallied Mexicans in New Mexico and Colorado. Recently, Indians have demanded that attention be paid to their economic and social problems.[32]

Consequently, meliorative policy is formulated implicitly (and sometimes explicitly) in racial terms. Seligman has observed that everyone connected with the formulation of the poverty program "accepted the political view that the War on Poverty was mainly for Negroes." In fact, blacks and other nonwhites do participate more extensively than poor whites in federal programs; consider, for example, the percentages of blacks and other nonwhites in the following programs: New Careers, 67 percent; Concentrated Employment Program, 72 percent; Neighborhood Youth Corps, Summer, 56 percent; in school, 76 percent; out of school, 52 percent.[33] Many colleges and universities have begun to deal with the problem of educational opportunity by recruiting more heavily from among blacks and other nonwhites, ignoring the lack of opportunity among poor and marginal whites precisely because poor and marginal whites have not articulated a position reflecting any grasp of their own position in the society.

Social welfare policy in the United States is discussed with the vocabulary of race rather than that of class. In addition to posing analytic problems, the excited hostilities and passions of poor and marginal whites make it difficult for even meagerly financed and minimally intrusive programs to survive or to function successfully. In the meantime, they themselves do without.

REFERENCES

1. It is a measure of American thinking that the very term "welfare" is equated with husbandless mothers receiving public assistance. In the broader sense of the term, it refers to policies intended to redistribute national wealth in terms of need. Pekka Kuusi, the Finnish social scientist, Gunnar Myrdal, and other European scholars have written extensively on social welfare. See, for example, Richard Titmuss, *Commitment to Welfare* (Pantheon Books, New York, 1968).

2. Robert Lane, *Political Ideology: Why the American Common Man Believes What He Does* (Glencoe, Illinois: Free Press of Glencoe, 1962), pp. 330–331.

3. Peter Schrag, "The Forgotten American," *Harper's*, 239, No. 1431 (August, 1969), p. 27.

4. Christopher Jencks and David Riesman, "On Class in America," *The Public Interest*, No. 10 (Winter 1968), p. 6.

5. Alvin Schorr, *Poor Children: A Report on Children in Poverty* (New York and London: Basic Books, 1966), p. 148.

6. James Vadikan, *Children, Poverty, and Family Allowances* (New York and London: Basic Books, Inc., 1968), p. 6.

7. Some people might object to the introduction of a program of this sort into the United States on the grounds that it would have the effect of raising the birth rate. Vadikan concludes, however, that "Based on worldwide experience over a considerable period of time, it would appear safe to conclude that a program of family allowances of modest size such as exists in Canada or such as might be considered in the United States could have no significant effects in increasing the birth rate." (*Op. cit.*, p. 101). Not even in France where family allowance benefits average one-fifth of family budget of low-income people has it accelerated the birth rate.

8. Schorr, *op. cit.*, p. 148.

9. Carl Uhr, "Recent Swedish Labor Market Policies," *The Man-Power Revolution*, (Garth Mangum, ed., Garden City, New York: Anchor Books, 1966), p. 376.

10. Robert L. Heilbroner, "Benign Neglect in the United States," *Transaction*, 7, No. 12 (October, 1970), p. 16.

11. Seymour Kurtz, ed., *The New York Times: Encyclopedic Almanac 1970* (New York: The New York Times, Books and Educational Division, 1969), pp. 245–299; and U. S. Bureau of the Census, *Statistical Abstracts of the United States*, (1955 edition; Washington, D. C., 1970), p. 5.

12. Vadikan, *op. cit.*, p. 24.

13. Bert Seidman, "The Case for Higher Social Security Benefits," *The American Federationist*, 74, No. 1 (January, 1967), p. 5.

14. Kurtz, *op. cit.*, p. 301.

15. Department of Labor, Bureau of Labor Statistics, *Employment and Earnings*, 19, No. 7 (January, 1973), p. 122.

16. George Katona, James N. Morgan, Joy Schmiedeskamp, and John A. Sundquist, *1967 Survey of Consumer Finances* (Ann Arbor, Michigan: University of Michigan, 1967), p. 11.

17. Department of Labor, Bureau of Labor Statistics, *Monthly Labor Review*, 92, No. 4 (April, 1969), p. 8.

18. Department of Labor, Bureau of Labor Statistics, *Employment and Earnings*, 16, No. 7 (January, 1970), p. 67.

19. Nathan Spero, "Notes on the Current Inflation," *Monthly Review*, 21, No. 2 (June, 1969), p. 30.

20. Department of Labor, Bureau of Labor Statistics, *Monthly Labor Review* (1973) 96, No. 2, p. 111.

21. Katona et al., *op. cit.*, pp. 15–43.

22. For an excellent discussion of this population, one roughly parallel to the discussion undertaken here, see "Middle Class Workers and the New Politics" by Brendan Sexton in *Beyond the New Left* (Irving Howe, ed., New York: McCall, 1970), pp. 192–204.

23. Among the useful works on poor and marginal whites are: *Uptown: Poor Whites in Chicago* by Todd Gitlin and Nanci Hollander, (New York: Harper and Row, 1970); Eli Chinoy, *Automobile Workers and the American Dream* (Garden City, New York: Doubleday, 1955); Lee Rainwater, Richard Coleman, and Gerald Handel, *Workingman's Wife* (New York: Oceana Publications, 1956); Lee Rainwater, *And the Poor Get Children* (New York: Quadrangle Books, 1960); and William F. Whyte, *Street Corner Society* (Chicago, Illinois: University of Chicago Press, 1943).

24. Lloyd A. Tree and Hadley Cantril, *The Political Beliefs of Americans* (New York: Simon and Schuster, 1968), pp. 9–10, 96, 99, 190, 195–196, 218.

25. Tree and Cantril, *ibid.*, p. 96.

26. Michael Parenti, "Ethnic Politics and the Persistence of Ethnic Identification," *American Political Science Review*, LXI (September, 1967), p. 719.

27. Herbert Gans, *The Urban Villagers* (New York: Free Press of Glencoe, 1962).

28. Gerald Suttles, *The Social Order of the Slums* (Chicago: University of Chicago Press, 1968).

29. See, for example, Albert R. Cohen and Harold Hodges, "Lower Blue Class Characteristics," *Social Problems*, 10, No. 4 (Spring, 1963), pp. 303–334. Jack L. Roach, "A Theory of Lower-Class Behavior," in *Sociological Theory: Inquiries and Paradigms* (Llewellyn Gross, ed., New York, Evanston and London: Harper and Row, 1967), pp. 294–315.

30. See S. M. Lipset, *Political Man* (Garden City, New York: Doubleday, 1960), pp. 97–130; and S. M. Lipset and Earl Raab, "The Wallace Whitelash," *Transaction*, 7, No. 2 (December, 1969), pp. 23–36.

31. This is no longer wholly true. In both Cleveland and New York, ethnically based groups have begun to stir. The major impetus has probably been the surge of the black population, but these groups may turn out to have objectives which are not simply anti-black.

32. For a discussion of protest movements by these other minorities, see John R. Howard, *The Awakening Minorities: American Indians, Mexican Americans, and Puerto Ricans* (Chicago: Aldine, 1970).

33. U. S. Department of Labor, *Handbook of Labor Statistics, 1970* (Washington, D.C.: Bureau of Labor Statistics, 1970), p. 123.

11

THE RADICAL RIGHT AS A MINORITY GROUP

There is a growing body of literature in which the concept of minority group is employed to understand the problems and status of women, youth, the aged, the physically handicapped, and various other categories of persons. This literature suggests that concepts and models originally developed in the study of racial and ethnic categories may have analytic utility when applied to populations not ordinarily thought of as minority groups. This chapter is addressed to the question of whether the radical right can be usefully conceptualized as a minority group. Its conclusions can be summed up as follows:

1. In a structural sense, the radical right is not a minority group as that concept is conventionally understood.

2. The perspective of many persons on the far right is similar, however, to that of members of a minority group. In terms of political values and attitudes, many manifest what the historian Richard Hofstadter has referred to as "the paranoid style."[1]

3. The perspective of the right derives from certain persistent strains and tensions in the American social system and is important because occasionally it breaks through to affect broadly the course of political events.

4. The persistence of these strains and tensions can be better understood if we employ a conceptualization of the minority group that departs from that ordinarily found in the literature.

THE RADICAL RIGHT

The right can be identified in terms of certain organizations and/or in terms of a constellation of attitudes held by certain segments of the population. Both are important. Rightist organizations speak for broad masses of people; if they reflect widely shared beliefs and attitudes, then obviously they become something more than sectarian curiosities, the object of contempt and amusement.

The Organized Right

A substantial number of the organizations on the right are sweaty, transient affairs consisting of hardly more than one zealot and a packet of letterhead stationery. Among the more tenacious right-wing organizations are the Christian Crusade, the John Birch Society, and the Ku Klux Klan. Borrowing from the terminology of the right, one can refer to the members of these organizations as hard core. They differ from each other in orientation, but the spectrum they represent comes close to embracing the range of thought on the far right. Their constituencies overlap, but there are differences in the profile of the typical member. In discussing these organizations, one can both survey the range of radical right thinking and describe the characteristics of members and supporters.

The three broad orientations found among these organizations are Christian fundamentalism (the Christian Crusade), anticommunism (the John Birch Society), and racism (the Ku Klux Klan). They overlap in doctrine but differ in emphasis.

The Christian Crusade was founded by the Reverend Billy James Hargis, a graduate of Ozark Bible College. The Crusade is centered in Tulsa, Oklahoma, and sponsors speaking tours, radio programs, and special schools.

Hargis articulates a straightforward kind of fundamentalism:

> *Never did the founding fathers of America intend that our government become one which denies God. Never did they intend for our government to "shield" our children from the saving knowledge of God's truth by banning the Bible and prayer from the public schools. The first great American president, George Washington, made it clear that it is impossible to govern the world without the Bible.*[2]

The Christianity of Hargis rests on the belief that the mission of the church is to save souls, not correct social ills. He identifies as communist in inspiration those actions of clerics which are ecumenical in intent or which spring from the social gospel.

Hargis' strength seems to be in the Southwest and the South. His radio program is carried more frequently by stations in those areas than by stations in the East. His appeal seems to be to the small-town and rural white Anglo-Saxon Protestant.

The John Birch Society deals primarily in fear of communism. It intensifies that fear and then presents its own program for combatting the communist beast. Its anticommunism is expressed mainly through militant nationalism in foreign affairs and opposition domestically to policies intended to improve the lot of have-not groups, such as blacks and the poor.[3]

The supporters of the Society tend to be more affluent than those of the Christian Crusade and they are less likely to live in rural areas. A California poll of attitudes toward the Birch Society suggested that the profile of the average person with a positive attitude was as follows: male, traditionally Republican, Protestant, either some college or a college graduate, medium to high economic level, a businessman, professional, or retired.[4] "Its sociological profile," observed Hofstadter, "is that of a group enjoying a strong social position, mainly well-to-do and educated beyond the average, but manifesting a degree of prejudice and social tension not customarily found among the affluent and the educated."[5]

The Ku Klux Klan must by now be regarded as an old American institution, part of our national heritage. It has experienced several reincarnations but in each of its lives has traded principally in racism. On the whole, its members and vocal supporters seem to be inferior in socio-economic status to those of the Birch Society and less staid and respectable than the Christian Crusade followers. It is not easy to get reliable data on the Klan, but Vander Zanden managed to obtain information on 153 Klansmen. They held such jobs as gas station attendant, grocery store clerk, truck driver, garage mechanic, machinist, and carpenter.[6] David Chalmers indicated that, whereas in parts of the South the White Citizens' Councils drew businessmen, bankers, and lawyers, the more openly and violently racist Klan recruited "mechanics, farmers, and storekeepers."[7]

There are hundreds of right-wing organizations. These three represent three major orientations: religious fundamentalism, anticommunism expressed as strong nationalism and opposition to domestic social welfare programs, and racism.

Among right-wing groups that have paraded across the national stage are the Action Patriots, the Alerted Americans, the Minutemen, the American Patriots Defense Committee, the Conservative Society of America, the Vigilantes of America, Americans Awake, Operation Survival, and the Alert Americans Association. Most of these groups have played bit roles in the American political drama. The three groups focused on have drawn more attention and shown more durability. Most right-wing groups have represented *ad hoc* responses to events which are perceived as threatening, such as court-ordered school integration. Relatively few survive for very long, although the sentiments which give birth to them are persistent.

No one knows how many members these organizations have had, but that is not wholly to the point. The number of supporters is much greater than the number of members.

The interests of their constituencies are not always wholly consistent; Birchers, for example, are probably more conservative on economic questions than are the less affluent members and supporters of the Klan. Consequently, there is often bitter strife between organizations on the right despite the core beliefs they share.

THE MINORITY GROUP CONCEPT AND THE RIGHT

To ask whether the radical right is a minority group is to ask any or all of three questions:

1. Can the theoretical models commonly employed to account for negative attitudes toward racial and ethnic groups be used to explain popular views toward the right?

2. Have members of the right collectively and historically been victimized because of their political beliefs?

3. Does the radical right show a collective perspective similar to that of ethnic or racial minorities?

Below, each of these questions is explored.

There are at least three theoretical approaches widely employed to account for negative attitudes toward minority groups: the frustration-aggression displacement theory, the repression projection theory, and what for want of a better term can be called "interest" theories. None of these accounts for popular views toward the radical right. Briefly, the frustration-aggression-displacement approach suggests that racial and ethnic hostility is a consequence of displacing upon these groups the anger arising from sources of which one is unaware or over which one has no control. The right is not an object of popular contumely, largely because many people are unaware of its existence. Most people are unaware of the existence of right-wing organizations. The John Birch Society is one of the best-known conservative organizations; yet a Gallup poll taken in February, 1962, on a national sample indicated that seven persons out of ten had either never heard of the Society or had no opinion about it.[8]

The repression-projection process has been used analytically to explain such matters as the sexual overtones in the anti-Negro stereotype. The sexually repressed individual is presumably able to have his psychological cake and eat it, too, by indulging in all sorts of fantasies about Negro sexuality while feeling indignant at the reality he supposes his fantasies represent. Clearly, there is no analog in the image of the right.

The interest group approach suggests that racism is a device which allows certain groups to secure and rationalize unfair privileges. Thus, allegedly, management uses it to drive a wedge between white and black workers, and white workers use it to keep blacks in the lowest-paying and dirtiest jobs or out of work altogether. Again, this model is clearly inapplicable to the right.

As regards the second question, there is no evidence that rightists collectively experience discrimination. Unlike Jews and blacks, they do not have a historically formed collective identity based, in large part, on having been the victims of severe and pervasive discrimination. The sociologists Shibutani and Kwan suggest that "a minority group consists of people of low standing—people who receive unequal treatment and who therefore come to regard themselves as objects of discrimination."[9] In this sense, the right is not a minority group.

In regard to the third question, the right does in many striking ways reveal a perspective similar to that of minority groups. Minority groups commonly develop a certain view of the world. There is a tendency toward obsessive concern with the characteristics which define one's status, to see it as mediating every interaction. There is a tendency to view all of those who are not a member of one's group as hostile, and to feel that one's compatriots are peculiarly prone to "selling out." There is what might be termed a "collective ego." That is, any triumph or failure of a member of the group is felt to have meaning for the status and future of the entire group.

The perspective of racial, ethnic, and religious minorities is grounded in reality. Historically, they really have been the victims of discrimination and prejudice. The collective ego develops as a response to the tendency of nonmembers to assign collective blame or virtue.

The persecutions visited upon the right are less visible to the dispassionate observer. It is not so much that the right is persecuted as that it believes it is. There are certain key elements in the world view of the minority group member: a sense of being blameless and possibly even praiseworthy, and a belief that others not only do not recognize one's virtue but are actively engaged in malicious actions. There is a sense, then, that the members of the group must band together, that they must "all hang together or hang separately." These elements are prominently displayed in the thinking of the radical right. The extreme conservative radio commentator, Paul Harvey, communicated the sense of being innocent yet put upon:

> *Youngster, let me tell you what it was like in the Old Country. We had fun in the Old Country . . . . we didn't concentrate on learnin' tricks of the trade; we learned the trade . . . . religion and education were all so mixed up together when I was a boy you couldn't tell where one left off and the other began. Patriotism was*

taught in every school class every day. Our national heroes were honored, almost revered, in the Old Country.

. . . Folks who worked harder were rewarded for it, so everybody worked harder.

We had no card-carrying Communists; we had no cross-carrying Christians . . . in the Old Country. We told dialect jokes and everybody laughed because all of us were "mostly something else," in the Old Country. It isn't there anymore.[10]

The sense of moral virtue of most rightists comes from perceiving themselves as the guardians of an older and finer ethic. Ezra Taft Benson, Secretary of Agriculture during both Eisenhower administrations and later a vocal spokesman for various right-wing organizations, expressed this point of view when he said:

I wonder what our founding fathers would do and say about America today if they were here . . . . They would be concerned with the alarming growth of a something-for-nothing philosophy, a failure of people to stand on their own feet. They would find some bad examples by unscrupulous politicians and by delinquent parents, and possibly a weakening of religious training, and the substitution therefore of a faith-destroying materialism.[11]

There is an obsessive quality to the minority group world view. Many blacks see all their dealings with people as mediated by color. They are sensitive to the smallest nuances from others. If the media do not portray blacks, they are angry; if the media do, they question the sincerity of media executives and the honesty of the portrayal. There is literally no phase of existence which cannot be filtered through colored lenses. Likewise, the hard-core rightist tends to be obsessive in his thinking. Issues which are ordinarily not deemed political are interpreted by him in terms of the need to maintain vigilance against communists, liberals, and other enemies. Thus, there is a rich literature on the dangers of mental health programs—for example, Kenneth Goff's *Facts On Mental Health,* Tom Sullivan's *Mental Health,* Martin Gross's *The Brain Watchers,* and Lewis Alesen's *Mental Robots.* Virtually every political or economic issue is interpreted in terms of the evil manipulations of communists. Thus, the gold crisis was "explained" in Major George Racey Jordan's *The Gold Swindle,* the income tax in Frank Chodorov's *Income Tax: Root of All Evil,* student discontent in E. Merrill Root's *Brainwashing in the High Schools.* Rightists see themselves as living in a world in which evil people have power, a world in which the things they believe in are under attack and the goods they possess are not securely theirs.

Enemies are seen as so powerful that efforts to expose them are often futile; thus, Robert Welch, founder of the John Birch Society, anguished over the commercial failure of Medford Evans' *The Secret War for the A-Bomb:*

> *It should have rocked the nation from one end to the other. Instead it sold twenty-six hundred copies. There is no clearer proof of the effectiveness of the blanket of obfuscation, with which communist influences have been able to keep the truth about their activities from being known.[12]*

The Birch Society has spoken out on many issues including the following:

Medicare:
> *. . . the principal object of "medicare" is to destroy the independence and integrity of American physicians. . . .*

The economic situation:
> *The conspiracy can produce a total economic collapse any time that it decides to pull the chain.*

The federal government:
> *Communist domination of many of the departments of the Federal Government is too obvious to require much comment.[13]*

The world view of the rightist is not unlike that of the member of a minority group. There is the same obsessive quality, but political values take the place of race or ethnicity in pervading every situation, in ordering reality, and in ranking people. There is the same sense that one's vital interests are threatened, that one's enemies are in control of the situation. There is something of the same sense of being outnumbered and beleaguered. The radio commentator Paul Harvey expressed an attitude found among many persons on the right: "I am a displaced person though I never left my homeland. I am a native-born American. I never left my country. It left me."[14] There is the sense in that statement of viewing oneself as a member of a minority group, a stranger in the land.

Is it correct to call the radical right "sick"? Would it be correct to refer to them as paranoid in a clinical sense? The answer is probably no. Just as the world view of the black or Jew or Puerto Rican or woman has some basis in reality, in a subtle way that of the radical right does also.

The radical right cannot be explained solely in psychological terms. They are, paradoxically, an inevitable product of those facets of the American value system which emphasize egalitarianism and openness, the need to give every man a chance. Their fury is fueled by public politics which seek to close the gap between American rhetoric and American reality. They are not hypocritical but rather stand to pay a price for a more open society.

This view is enlarged upon below.

AMERICAN SOCIAL STRUCTURE
AND THE RADICAL RIGHT

A value system such as that in the United States, which assumes that every man has a chance to be upwardly mobile and that talent and ambition are required for such mobility, also assumes that those who are not mobile may be lacking in talent and ambition. Robert Lane's discussion of the attitudes of a selected group of adults in an Atlantic seaboard community which he called "Eastport" dealt, in part, with this assumption. There was in the community "a tendency to believe that men in high places deserve the power and honor and responsibility; otherwise they wouldn't be there. . . . Those who are unsuccessful are . . . thought to have failed, in considerable part, because of 'playing the ponies,' drink, laziness, or shiftlessness."[15]

The Meaning of Status in American Society

If an individual has internalized this value system, then there is a linking of class position and the conception of self. This link exists not only subjectively for the individual but also for others in the society as they view him. There is a tacitly assumed link between the slot an individual occupies in the stratification system and the kind of person he must be. Hence, the first question one asks in this society if one wants to learn about another is, "What does he do for a living?" The answer is assumed to give a rough indication of status and, from this, inferences are made about the other characteristics an individual must have.[16] As Edgar Z. Friedenberg indicated with regard to a Department of Health, Education, and Welfare study, *Work in America*, "the major findings of the report are probably familiar to many readers; its more publicized conclusions are that work is absolutely central to identity in

America; who you are, in other words, depends on how you earn your living."[17]

For those with high status, there are certain psychological gratifications in possessing culturally approved characteristics. The potential for a positive self-conception is greater when the possession of a high status position is assumed tacitly or explicitly to be the consequence of possessing certain approved personality characteristics. For those with low status within the society, there are certain psychological pressures; a tacit or explicit assumption of their position is that they are personally inadequate. The literature on mobility suggests that downwardly mobile persons resist identifying with the class into which they have fallen, while the upwardly mobile become, in some respects, overidentifiers with the class into which they have moved. It can be reasonably inferred that the need for a sense of personal adequacy helps to account for both tendencies. Within the society, it becomes psychologically important for those with position to attempt to conserve it and equally important for those without position to seek to achieve it.

The ethic of openness implies to the individual that he has no immutable claim to comfort for himself or his progeny. It has built into it, therefore, an element of insecurity. Unless one assumes that room at the top is unlimited, an ethic which emphasizes merit as the criterion of status has a built-in insecurity factor; if they are honest, people must recognize that there will inevitably be someone who is more intelligent, more hard-working, more dedicated than they (or, if not them, their children). Insofar as an ethic of openness posits that no one has an immutable claim to high status but must presumably yield in the face of superior claims, it has tension and insecurity built into it. The only way to allay this insecurity is to attempt, consciously or unconsciously, to "fix" the system—thus, we come to the radical right.

A society can distribute rewards to its members because of their position along either achieved or ascribed dimensions. American society, of course, explicitly emphasizes the former, while reward distribution in closed societies is based on the latter. Both play a role in every society and it is a matter of the relative weighting attached to each. This means that some people in the United States may, because of their ranking along both dimensions, be able to invoke claims to status (rich and WASP), while others, because of their ranking along both dimensions, may be unable to invoke any claims (poor and black). Yet others may be able to invoke claims because of their ranking on one dimension or the other. It is possible, then, to classify people in terms of the following four categories: (1) high ascription, high achievement; (2) high ascription, low achievement; (3) low ascription, high achievement; and (4) low ascription, low achievement.

Those in different categories have different constellations of experience and are exposed to different kinds of pressures. The status-linked pressures of each category create a perspective for those in that category which makes the ideology of particular kinds of deviant political organizations meaningful. Categories (1) and (2) seem to yield a perspective supportive of rightist organizations because these organizations ultimately invoke ascription to justify status claims.[18]

High Ascription, High Achievement

Those high on both of these dimensions in the United States have traditionally been the middle, upper-middle, and upper class, white, Anglo-Saxon Protestants. Hofstadter has commented on this group:

> *These people, whose stocks were once far more unequivocally dominant in America than they are today, feel that their ancestors made and settled and fought for this country. They have a certain sense of proprietorship in it. . . . These people have a considerable claim to status which they celebrate by membership in such organizations as the D.A.R. and the S.A.R. . . . although very often quite well-to-do, they feel that they have been pushed out of their rightful place in American life, even out of their neighborhoods. Most of them have been traditionally Republican by family inheritance and they have felt themselves edged aside by the immigrants, the trade unions, and the urban machines in the last thirty years.[19]*

This group subdivides into an Eastern urban and urbane wing and a Midwestern, Southern, and Western small-town provincial wing. These two groups differ in several ways. The Eastern segment tends toward the more intellectualized Protestant denominations such as Congregationalism, the Midwestern element toward denominations with a more literal interpretation of scripture and a less ecumenical outlook.[20] The Midwestern group tends toward a greater puritanism, that is, prohibition of the use of alcohol, concern with "smut," rejection of "foreign" ideas.

Threats, insofar as this group is concerned, relate both to pressures within the society to widen the channels for upward mobility, thus facing the group with a whole host of new competitors for the rewards of the society, and to measures which, in promoting universalistic principles, undermine their ascriptive-based claims to status. For a period during the 1960's, this group was in precipitate cultural decline.[21] Their style, values, and privileges were eroding. They saw an Irish Catholic assume the presidency, a black senator, black city councilmen in many municipalities, and Jews in a variety of higher-level government posts. They saw the civil rights movement undercut their claims along the ascribed dimension.

Franz Neuman has suggested the effects which such changes can produce: "In every society that is composed of antagonistic groups there is an ascent and a decent of groups. It is my contention that persecutory anxiety—but one which has a real basis—is produced when a group is threatened in its prestige, income, or its existence."[22]

In order to conserve their status, one would then expect those in this category to react to moves toward further openness in the society by accentuating the importance of the ascribed dimension, and by attacking those measures which broaden the channels for mobility from below. The kinds of deviant political organizations which draw their membership largely from persons in this category do show these two characteristics in their goals and their ideology.

The John Birch Society probably draws the bulk of its support from persons in this category, as does the Christian Crusade and many of the other older, more stable right-wing organizations. The Birch program, involving as it does attacks upon trade unions, the civil rights movement, welfare measures, civil liberties organizations, etc., can be seen as advocating measures which would have the effect of introducing greater closure into the society, thus conserving the status of this group. The Birch conception of Americanism seems to be synonymous with a set of attitudes and policy positions which would have the consequence of making the status and cultural style of the fundamentalist, small-town oriented "old Americans" unassailable.[23]

While threats related to policy proposals that broaden the opportunities for have-nots are important in generating a right-wing perspective, the decline of their cultural style also plays a role. Style and taste reflect values and, to the extent that one's values are regarded as primitive and faintly amusing, one's style is regarded as vaguely absurd.

The conservative writer Kevin Phillips has listed some of the differences between conservative Americans and those of an "elite liberal" persuasion. Among other things, it was a matter of preferring Lawrence Welk, John Wayne, and Billy Graham to Leonard Bernstein, Marlon Brando, and Father Groppi, and charcoal steak and Pepsi-Cola to Quiche Lorraine and Beaujolais Fraise. While Phillips is referring to a broader category than the radical right, he does suggest some of the stylistic differences between those who are considered "square," "old fashioned," and traditional, and those who view themselves as "hip" and "with it."[24]

Persons on the right not only see their position threatened in a concrete way, but sense or believe that their style is increasingly viewed as vaguely ridiculous by trend-setters and opinion-makers.

High Ascription, Low Achievement

Those in this category have traditionally been working-class or poor whites in the South and Southwest who have enjoyed higher status by ascription than blacks, Mexicans, or other racial minorities. There is a tendency toward greater conservatism in this group than one would expect, given their class position. To the extent that public policies intended to open channels for upward mobility also involve supporting the principle of universalism (judge all people by the same standard), persons in this category will be opposed to them. Widening channels for mobility might or might not benefit them, while undermining the ascribed basis for their status definitely would not. Thus, status is best conserved by opposing any measure which introduces universalism, even if that measure also promises to widen the channels for upward mobility.

As was indicated, Klansmen tend to be persons whose only un-equivocal claim to status is along the ascribed dimension. Thus, in the face of moves to open the society further, they gravitated to political organizations accentuating the importance of the one dimension along which they have high status.

James Boggs, autoworker and author, writing from a left perspective, has observed, "Fascism in the United States is unique because it is developing from the grass roots rather than from the top down. Today such organizations as the Minutemen, the White Citizens' Councils, the America Firsters and scores of others . . . are made up of workers, skilled and unskilled."[25] While the use of the term "fascism" may be questioned, radical right organizations do find greater support from among workers than might be expected.

In summary, the radical right is not a minority group in the conventional sense, although its members manifest the perspective of a minority group which feels itself persecuted. Their fears about the erosion of caste and status privilege have some foundation in reality. The black movement, the women's movement, the Chicano movement, etc., have made certain gains. Greater equity in the society means that members of these traditional privileged groups will have to compete for status rather than having it conferred on them as a birthright.

Although the style may be paranoid, the people are not paranoid in a clinical sense.

The conventional idea of a minority group only partially encompasses the radical right. An alternative conceptualization of the minority group phenomenon, which would embrace the right as well as youth, women, racial and ethnic minorities, and other persons to whom the category is conventionally related, is needed.

Toward a New Conception of the Minority Group

"When they speak of stratification, sociologists are referring to the ranking of categories of people, not the ranking of individuals. Some persons live in comfort while others endure deprivation, not because of their . . . personalities, but because of their social status."[26]

Minority groups, as conventionally conceived of, are found in certain kinds of stratified societies. The minority group is disadvantaged as regards the opportunity to acquire wealth and power. The disadvantaged position of the minority group is rationalized and justified by privileged persons on the basis of the alleged negative aspects of certain ascribed characteristics of the minority group—for example, "women are too emotional to make good executives," "students are too young and immature to be able to set their own social codes," "blacks are too dumb to be promoted to skilled jobs."

Let us take a member of the working class, a 28-year-old semiskilled white worker with a wife and two children, making $9,000 a year. Let us say that, when the wife works parttime, the family income goes up to $12,000 a year. Let us say that this worker is antiblack and that he opposes the black movement, feeling the blacks are demanding unfair advantages, that they do not want to work for what they get.

This worker is better off than many blacks, but relative to the top executives of the plant for which he works he is more disadvantaged than blacks are disadvantaged relative to him. A large body of research has indicated that the distribution of wealth is greatly skewed in the United States.[27] A small number of people are very wealthy, but the great majority of wage earners are only a paycheck or two away from disaster. Most do not realize this fact, but it is as true of the college professor as it is of the factory hand.

The white worker, with his constant worry over time payments and his chronic shortage of funds, is far from affluent. He is better off than the black, but he is not particularly well off. This is equally true of the small entrepreneur, the salesman, the small farmer, the elderly retired, and others who help to make up the legions of the right.

As regards per capita share of the wealth, the white worker and minor entrepreneur are much closer to blacks than they are to the top executives in the 100 largest firms in the country.

The persistence of tax loopholes and various kinds of subsidies and allowances for the rich indicates that they have enough power to make laws beneficial only to themselves and to deflect efforts to alter these laws.

The mythology subscribed to by much of the public, the ideology of the common man ("you can make it if you only try"), has the consequence of rationalizing and justifying the interests of economic and political elites while not really serving the interests of nonelites. In other words, in moralizing downward to "welfare chiselers" but not upward to corporate thieves, the worker serves corporate elite interests rather than his own. Much of the public mythology about success being a result of "working hard" and "getting ahead on your own" has the consequence of undermining social welfare policies which might, in fact, provide sounder structural supports for mobility and a decent standard of living. Popularly, members of minority groups are deemed to suffer a low estate because of certain innate failings. In a similar fashion, the worker or small businessman falling on hard times through circumstances largely beyond personal control is likely to be deemed to have "lacked the stuff" to make a go of it.

In short, the position taken here is that vis-à-vis elites, everyone is a member of a minority group. Some know it and some do not. The typical Bircher thinks he is in a privileged position. But in focusing on the threat from below of the nonwhite rather than on the political and financial advantages of those above him, he saves himself a fraction in terms of status advantage but at the cost of seeking changes which might genuinely improve his situation.

If credence is given to the notion of a power elite, then everyone is a member of a minority group vis-à-vis that elite. Some are privileged members of the minority group (as the black bourgeoisie is among blacks) but in a larger sense all are disadvantaged.

In terms of the conventional conception of the minority group, supporters of the radical right fit only marginally into that group; in terms of the conception suggested here, of course, they are a minority group.

In the approach taken here both you and I are minority group members. We may differ only in perception of what we are.

REFERENCES

1. See Richard Hofstadter, *The Paranoid Style in American Politics and Other Essays* (New York: Knopf, 1964).

2. Billy James Hargis, *Communist America: Must It Be?* (Tulsa, Okla.: Christian Crusade, 1960), pp. 32–33.

3. For an articulation of the views of the Society's founder, see Robert Welch, *The Blue Book of the John Birch Society* (Published by the Society, Belmont, Mass.: 1961).

4. Seymour Martin Lipset, "Three Decades of the Radical Right," in *The Radical Right* (Daniel Bell, ed., New York: Doubleday, 1964), pp. 422–25.

5. Hofstadter, *op. cit.*, p. 71.

6. James W. Vander Zanden, *Race Relations in Transition* (New York: Random House, 1965), pp. 41–43.

7. David Chalmers, *Hooded Americanism: The First Century of the Ku Klux Klan, 1865–1965* (Garden City, N.Y.: Doubleday, 1965), p. 345.

8. Lipset, *op. cit.*, p. 422.

9. Tamotsu Shibutani and Kian M. Kwan, *Ethnic Stratification* (New York: Macmillan, 1965), p. 35.

10. Paul Harvey, "Why Not Return to the Old Country," *Human Events* (September, 1963), p. 4.

11. Ezra Taft Benson, *The Red Carpet* (Salt Lake City: Bookcraft, 1962), pp. 239–40.

12. Welch, *op. cit.*, p. 23.

13. William F. Buckley, Jr., "The Birch Society, August 1965," *National Review* (October 19, 1965), pp. 916–18.

14. Harvey, *op. cit.*, p. 4.

15. Robert Lane, "The Lower Classes Deserve No Better Than They Get," in *Poverty in Affluence* (Robert E. Will and Harold O. Vatter, eds., New York: Harcourt, Brace and World, 1965), pp 66–68.

16. In a closed society, one might ask, "What family?" "What lineage?" "What clan?" What the individual is assumed to be is a consequence of the category into which he was born.

17. Edgar Z. Friedenberg, "Public Documents: The Hostile Delusions of the Working Class," *Harpers*, 246, No. 1477 (June, 1973), p. 12.

18. The other two categories tend to yield a left of center perspective. For a discussion of these categories, see John R. Howard, "The Social Basis of Political Extremism: A Comparison of the Black Muslims, the John Birch Society and the American Communist Party," presented at the meetings of the Pacific Sociological Association, April, 1970.

19. Hofstadter, *op. cit.*, pp. 54–55.

20. For a discussion of variations in degree of intellectualization in Protestant denominations, see H. Richard Niebuhr's *The Social Sources of Denominationalism* (New York: Meridian Books, 1960). For a discussion of the religious styles of particular regions, see John Dollard's *Caste and Class in a Southern Town* (New York: Doubleday, 1957), August Hollingshead, *Elmtown's Youth* (New York: Science Editions, 1961), and W. Lloyd Warner, *Yankee City* (New Haven: Yale University Press, 1963).

21. One interesting indicant of the decline of this group is the change in practice with regard to finding names for movie stars. Prior to the 1950's, most movie stars had Anglo-Saxon names, the principal exceptions being those who were obviously foreigners. Presumably, changing names which had an ethnic identity resulted from the fact that white Anglo-Saxon Protestant identity was the cultural ideal. Thus, Julius Garfinkle became John Garfield, Bernard Schwartz became Tony Curtis, David Kaminsky became Danny Kaye, and Jerome Levitch became Jerry Lewis. In the last decade, however, Marilyn Novak was changed only to Kim Novak, the ethnic last name being retained, while neither Annette Funicello nor Anthony Franciosa changed their names.

22. Franz L. Neuman, "Anxiety in Politics," *Dissent* (Spring, 1955), p. 135.

23. An implication of the position being taken here is that anticommunism, as such, is not an explanation for Birchism. Rather, the Birchers identify the things they do not happen to like with a currently very unpopular movement, as a result of a not uncommon human tendency to identify whatever happens to be inimical to personal interests with something widely regarded as evil.

24. Kevin Phillips, "Conservative Chic," *Harpers*, 246, No. 1477 (June, 1973), p. 70.

25. James Boggs, "A Black View of the White Worker," in *The White Majority: Between Poverty and Affluence* (Louise Kapp Howe, ed., New York: Vintage Books, 1970), p. 106.

26. Shibutani and Kwan, *op. cit.*, p. 28.

27. See for example, Clair Wilcox, *Toward Social Welfare* (Homewood, Illinois: Richard D. Irwin, Inc., 1969), or Ferdinand Lundberg, *The Rich and the Super Rich* (New York: Lyle Stuart, Inc., 1968).

CONCLUSIONS

12

GETTING IT ALL TOGETHER AGAIN

In the late 1950's, an air of self-satisfaction prevailed in the United States. Active political dissent from the left was practically unknown, thanks in part to the right-wing vigilantism inspired by Senator Joseph McCarthy earlier in the decade.

Intellectuals, traditionally critics of the social system, were among its most enthusiastic celebrants. Birnbaum and Sagarin indicate that there were intellectuals who contended that the United States "had solved, or was on the way to solving most . . . social problems without violence by institutionalizing an equitable way of settling class grievances through the two-party system."[1] They observed that "many of those who hailed these successes were once social critics of the left who, reacting to their acceptance by establishment elites and to Stalinism ended by renouncing their former critique of capitalism."[2]

Celebration of the "American Way of Life" was made plausible by the absence of vigorous social protest movements. Beatniks, fore-runners of the hippies, were limited largely to Greenwich Village and the North Beach section of San Francisco. The black movement was largely confined to the South and had receded from public view following the boycott against segregated seating on buses in Montgomery, Alabama, and the Little Rock school integration effort.

The national ego was shaken a bit when the Soviet Union took the first step into space by launching Sputnik in 1957, but in the waning days of the second Eisenhower administration the prevailing sentiment was that the United States had "made it."

The "American celebration" persisted through the end of the Eisenhower period and into the Kennedy years. The reporter David Halberstam commented on the perspective of that era.

> When we went into Vietnam, we thought the world was ours, that we were supermen in a supercentury, that America could do no evil, that American soldiers always gave away chewing gum. And that the rest of the world—even Vietnamese peasants—wanted our values, wanted our protection.[3]

The war, the assassinations, and massive protest by a variety of have-not groups shattered this illusion. The celebration had masked reprehensible conditions—sexism, racism, poverty—but eventually rain did begin to fall on the American parade.

A host of problems, domestic and international, economic and political, suggest that the nation's resources are finite and its powers limited. There are intimations of national mortality.

Unique to the time is the fact that a number of groups have revolted simultaneously, including women, racial and ethnic minorities, homosexuals, and youth. Collectively, they reflect the widespread nature of status disadvantage, and they all call for a massive redistribution of opportunities and privileges as well as major ideological and cultural changes. It is unlikely that any society could make shifts in status and power for so many groups simultaneously without severe conflict.

In some spheres, the conflict assumes the character of a zero sum game. Gains by the minority groups may in some instances decrease the opportunities of the majority by removing unfair advantages they have enjoyed. An end to discrimination against women in employment, an end to male "penis privilege," forces men to compete and faces some with the prospect of losing out in that competition.

In other spheres, conflict revolves around ideas and life-styles. Many middle-class intellectuals view Archie Bunker with contempt, while gas station attendants in working-class neighborhoods wear Archie Bunker T-shirts. Feminists write letters to *The New York Times* referring to Bunker's wife, "Dingbat," as an insult to women, but working-class women, the putative objects of this insult, are not heard in any forum.

The status of every group in the society is in flux, as is the distribution of power. There is a lower degree of normative consensus than in the period of the American celebration and a wider range of life-styles. It is not yet clear when or how a new consensus will be established. It is not clear whether that consensus will involve the legitimation of the values of blacks, women, gays, and youth and a substantial redistribution of power in their favor or will involve their repudiation in favor of groups which feel threatened by them.

The conflict is waged in the political arena, each group attempting to develop enough political power to see its goals become public policy.

The goals of the minority groups taken together pose a radically different future for the United States from that envisaged by defenders of the *status quo ante*.

Alan Wolfe, a political scientist, has discussed revolution and counter-revolution in the American context:

Counter-revolutions, by definition, require revolutions to counter, and the ferment of the 1960's hardly qualifies with the French,

Russian, and Cuban examples. True there was a great deal of activity. There were even significant changes—not so much in concrete institutions as in people's attitudes toward education and American society. But that was all prelude, first steps in a long process. The visibility, however, had the effect of convincing people that it was the real thing.[4]

There is sufficient substance to minority protest to pose genuine threats to major segments of the society. In this struggle, the role of a national administration becomes critical. Does it dispatch federal marshals to Mississippi to protect black voting rights or take a hands-off policy? Does it talk about fighting poverty or about "the specter of busing"?

The administration of President Nixon clearly opted for less change and against a redistribution of power. It spoke on behalf of those who had a real or imagined stake in inequality, and the basis of its appeal was summed up in its phrase "the New Majority."

Since at least 1932 every presidential administration except that of Dwight Eisenhower has tried to convey its sense of purpose by means of a slogan; thus the Roosevelt administration spoke of a "New Deal," the Truman administration of a "Square Deal," John Kennedy of the "New Frontier," and Lyndon Johnson of a "Great Society."

The slogan of the Nixon administration, the "New Majority," differs significantly. The earlier phrases suggest a vision of a good society. They convey idealism and a sense of purpose, a fair deal for all, a square deal for all. They suggested that there were ills in the existing system but that there was a better system toward which all could strive. The call for a "New Majority" is fundamentally different from these earlier phrases. It does not speak to a vision of a unified society. If there is a new majority, then there is also, by implication, a new minority, top dogs cast down into the dust. It does not suggest any effort to meliorate social ills. It speaks more to power than to ideals. It implies a divided society rather than one which is integrated, but reflects its times more accurately than the visionary phrases employed by previous administrations.

·The new majority embraces a variety of groups which feel threatened by minority protest. Kevin Phillips, the conservative analyst of the social system and an advocate of administration strategies to solidify a new majority, has indicated that "the bonds that unite the New Majority are largely negative. There are a lot of things that people just don't want done any longer."[5]

He identified the composition of the New Majority, indicating that it "really has two vital components. The first is most of traditional

Republican America . . . suburbia, business, big and small; the more prosperous agricultural areas of the nation. The second . . . is the increment of conservative Democrats from the South, the Rocky Mountains, and the Catholic ethnic areas of the North."[6]

Some groups are not part of the New Majority; others are welcomed:

> Black may not be too beautiful in the Administration's eyes . . . but "ethnic" certainly is. These days, Presidential receptions for leaders of the New Majority invariably include Chicago Poles, Cleveland Hungarians . . . and Italo-American War Veterans commanders. In state after state, GOP ethnic clubs and associations are being formed.[7]

Nor does the New Majority include the liberal intellegentsia, academics, and intellectuals of the sort associated with the Kennedy administration. *The New York Times* and the *Washington Post* are in disfavor, as is the *New York Review of Books* and the left intellectuals who form its readership. Phillips comments, "Quite a few Nixon people carry an anti-Ivy League chip on their shoulders. Two former Presidential advisors, John Mitchell and Chuck Colson, turned down admission to Harvard for reasons of inverted snobbery. Colson insults Harvard and the Ivy League any chance he gets."[8]

The fears of the ethnic and blue-collar segments of the New Majority are compounded by the kinds of economic problems discussed in Chapter 10. They are not affluent, nor are they poor; they are marginal and what the social analyst S. M. Miller has referred to as "subaffluent."[9] As indicated in Chapter 10, the position of this group has been eroding. The political scientist Kim Moody has observed that, "taxes and inflation, endemic to the crisis, affect all sections of the working class."[10]

The architects of a New Majority have based their appeal not only on resistance to the claims of have-nots but also on the promise of relieving the economic problems of the marginal by freezing or eliminating programs for the poor. Basically, they promise a programmatic income transfer from the poor to the marginal. Moreover, in an economy in which the problem of unemployment exists, New Majority architects are attacking "affirmative action" efforts with regard to minority employment, thereby supporting traditional, often discriminatory, hiring practices.

Minority protest has generated a counter ideology. Those opposed to change have begun to support ideas and belief systems which rationalize and justify their privileged position. One of the major tenets of this ideology is that problems of inequality can be explained by inadequacies among the have-nots rather than by imperfections in the social system.

Thus, racism is enjoying a revival with the writings of the psychologist Arthur Jensen.

Richard Herrnstein and Edward Banfield have also advanced positions which rationalize the status quo and suggest the inevitable failure of efforts at social reform. Banfield in *The Unheavenly City* argues that certain cultural traits of the poor prevent them from utilizing opportunities to move out of poverty. They are, he suggests, oriented mainly toward gratification in the present. They lack the discipline to make the sacrifices necessary to accumulate the capital or acquire the skills that would move them out of poverty.[11] Herrnstein contends that inherited intellectual ability determines success and status and that, as discriminatory barriers fall, stratification will be based on innate differences among people. Implicit in the argument is the idea that a major portion of contemporary stratification in the United States already reflects such differences.[12]

In different ways, Jensen, Herrnstein, and Banfield are each responding to the efforts at social reform in the 1960's, particularly as this reform was directed at meliorating the situation of blacks and the poor. An extensive set of programs and policies was developed, including Job Corp, Head Start, open admissions, and Upward Bound. All were intended to broaden opportunities for blacks and the poor to become upwardly mobile. The adherents of the "new inequality" argue, basically, that these programs were doomed to failure because of the intractable inadequacies of the poor. The poor are poor, not because the system has denied them an even break, but because they lack the intelligence and character to rise out of poverty.

In the history of racism as an idea, its popularity and acceptance have never rested on scientific grounds. Indeed, some anthropologists question whether there is, in a genetic sense, any such thing as race. As an idea, racism has always served to rationalize and justify extreme degrees of inequality. The scientific foundation of Jensen's theory has been cast in doubt by many critics. That his ideas are discussed as if they might have some validity is a reflection of the tensions arising from black protest.

Literature which supports racist beliefs is frequently published; whether that literature receives wide dissemination depends on whether large segments of the white population feel the need for fresh ideological justification for racial privilege. Thus, Aubrey Shuey's *The Testing of Negro Intelligence* was published in 1959 without great fanfare. A decade later, with the demands of the black movement ringing in the air, Jensen's writings struck a more responsive chord; many whites preferring to ask questions about black intelligence rather than about the social system in which blacks and whites live.

Conclusions

As was indicated in the first chapter, if black gains come to threaten whites, if they fear for their own jobs or security, if they fear that black advances will limit their opportunities or those of their children, then a revival of racism may occur. Counter ideologies have a political function. They provide a rationalization for forestalling further advances and possibly even for returning to the *status quo ante*.

A direct inference from these ideas is that the resources and influence of government should not be used on behalf of these groups.

The rapidity with which ideas contributing to a counter ideology are adopted and the number of people who adopt them reflect the extent to which a movement evokes fears. The black movement has provoked an extensive counterattack, as reflected in the works discussed above. The women's movement has not stimulated as substantial a trend towards a counter ideology. Sexism was never as discredited as racism, and thus there was less need for a massive attempt to reestablish its legitimacy. Lionel Tiger in *Men In Groups* has suggested the inevitability of male domination, and there are other works of this genre. Not even among women is sexism wholly discredited. In this respect, the two movements differ. While there are disagreements among blacks on strategy there is no dissent from the idea that blacks do not have a satisfactory position in the society. It is not clear that the premises of the women's movement are universally shared by women. If they were, a much more vigorous antifeminist counter ideology would develop.

The student movement has receded from public view. Those few phenomena which do receive attention, including Krishna Consciousness and Jesus Freaks, are regarded as strange, or exotic, or vaguely "interesting," rather than dangerous.

Vocations for social change, possibly the impetus for renewed vigor in the youth movement, is thus far rather obscure. Literature articulating a counter ideology with regard to the youth movement has ceased to appear because the youth movement has eroded.[18]

The gay movement is a phenomenon largely of the big cities and has not had the national impact of the black movement or the women's movement. It is not perceived by most people as having as much relevance to their own fortunes as the black and women's movements. Thus, although there has been some counter literature, it is not nearly as voluminous as that on blacks or women.

Essentially, the counter ideology revives ideas of a social Darwinist character. Some of the formulations in this ideology posit inherent or genetic factors to account for the position of the disadvantaged, principally blacks; other formulations focus on cultural factors. These cultural factors are assumed, however, to be resistant to change. In many respects, the concept of a "subculture of poverty," in vogue among liberal reformers during the 1960's, has been picked up by those resistant to reform. But whereas liberal reformers assumed that the poor could be weaned from their bad habits, proponents of the New Inequality argue that these habits strongly resist alteration.

The outcome of this conflict is in doubt. The move to form a "New Majority" represents an effort to achieve a coalition composed of those threatened by change, and it is not at all clear that the fate of this effort hinges on the personal fate of Richard Nixon. The shape of the new equilibrium will depend on the relative strength of those seeking a redistribution of rewards and those resisting it.

In essence, the question is whether the movements of disprivileged groups have enough power to forestall or prevent a successful counter movement.

Below, this question is discussed, first in terms of the possibility of a coalition between the protesting minorities and the white working class, and then in terms of a coalition of the minorities.

WAITING FOR LEFTY

Analysts of the American social system who employ a critical or Neo-Marxist framework often argue the necessity of nonelite protest groups forming an alliance with the white working class. These analysts view the working class as the key to progressive change. It is argued that they benefit less from the system than they should and that, as a result of being shut out of decision-making both by union bosses and by management, they are alienated from the system and are therefore subject to mobilization for progressive change.

Many of these critics see the first task of dissident protest groups as that of forming an alliance with the working class. Otherwise, it is argued, protest is bound to fail. The working class is seen as providing the social base necessary for revolution.

Although their analysis of the condition of the working class is accurate, there is little to justify the assumption that the working class is therefore predisposed to form a coalition with other nonelite groups. As Chapter 10 demonstrates, American workers are much less affluent than many assume them to be. They manifest a high degree of alienation. They work at hard and monotonous jobs and have little control over their immediate work environment, much less any voice in how the plant or factory itself is run.[14] As indicated, however, their grievances do not result in identification with other nonelites.

It is not that workers are more bigoted than other groups in the population. They appear to be no more racist than anyone else. When queried, many express a verbal belief in equal opportunity.[15] The leadership and some of the members of certain unions—the United Auto Workers, for example—have consistently supported civil rights and other progressive causes. And there have been instances of worker association with progressive elements. Thus, in 1969, Local 1-561 of the Oil, Chemical, and Atomic Workers in California "voted to accept student help and even to endorse the demands of the Third World Students at San Francisco State."[16]

Most trade unionists, however, have shown no such enthusiasm. The working class has not in recent times been the base of any left-of-center movement. The peace movement was largely the vehicle of middle-class intellectuals and students. As indicated in Chapter 7, those whites who became involved in the civil rights movement were from affluent, liberal, and left-oriented homes. Many of the whites involved in the farm workers strike also came from this class (see Chapter 4).

Many left theorists, wedded to the notion of the working class as the vanguard of progressive change, have labeled students and intellectuals active in left protest a "new working class." The presumed factory-like conditions of colleges and universities were seen as analogous to the assembly line and the plant floor and therefore allegedly created discontent and a spirit of revolt. This argument would have been more persuasive had the old working class shown any signs of movement into left-oriented politics.

The most spontaneous and therefore probably most meaningful instances of working-class activity (whatever their sentiments as revealed in public opinion polling) have for years consistently reflected hostility to groups espousing liberal or radical causes. Thus, peace demonstrators were beaten up in several big cities, and rank-and-file hostility to the peace movement lasted long into the Nixon administration.

In regard to the relationship between the dissident minorities and the working class, reference may be made to a depression-era play by Clifford Odets called *Waiting for Lefty*. The plot involves a group of workers who are poor, hungry, frightened, and brutalized by the bosses, coming to a meeting to talk about striking. Each man bears his own fears, terrified of losing the little he has, but yearning for a better life. The workers wait for Lefty to come. Lefty will pull things together, Lefty will help them strike, Lefty will lead them in confronting and overcoming the bosses. Then the word is received that Lefty is not coming because the bosses have had him killed, and they realize that if they are to strike they must do it on their own.

For dissident minorities, the evidence suggests that the white working class is not coming, at least not very soon. And if they are to seek progressive change, they must, at least initially, embark on that task by themselves.

Moody has observed, "In the context of class struggle, groups within the class do not 'wait' for other groups to move."[17] There are vastly different degrees of consciousness among nonelite groups, just as there are within a group. Among women, for example, some are fully attuned to the women's movement, while others are opposed to it. To be "conscious" means to have an understanding of the position of one's group in the stratification system. From this understanding comes a conception of the systemic changes required to eradicate the exploitation and degradation of the group.

As indicated in Chapter 10, the white working class manifests "false consciousness." Moody suggests that the example of other, more militant groups may raise the consciousness of workers and cites historical examples. "Remember that the fights waged by CIO workers brought forth an enormous upsurge among AFL workers, even though the AFL bureaucracy went to great lengths to convince their members that CIO efforts were a threat to them."[18] The reaction to the movements discussed here has been negative, however. Apparently, AFL craftsmen can identify with CIO industrial workers and perceive common interests more easily than they can associate themselves with the protest of women and racial and ethnic minorities at the present time.

There is the question, of course, of why the working class should come along. If there is a zero sum element in the game, if they are fighting to hold on to scarce resources, then is their resistance not rational?

Ultimately, their resistance would be wholly rational only if one assumed that the size of the pie could not be made larger. As has been indicated at several places in this book, elites benefit from a populace more inclined to excoriate welfare "chiselers" than to question the overall distribution of wealth and income. In an area such as taxation, for example, it is unnecessary for any but the most unsophisticated elites to break the law, given that existing laws already provide ample "legal" advantages in the form of tax-exempt income from bonds, accelerated depreciation on property which is then sold at higher than original prices, depreciation allowances, and the like.

It is the basic assumption of this book that the size of the total pie could be made larger were there a common political front of non-elites against elites. A variety of policies bearing on improvement in the quality of distribution of resources might be forthcoming.

The game retains a zero sum quality as long as the total resources available for the public good do not increase, and it is unlikely that these will increase except by an alignment of the white working class with the dissident minorities in this book.

Ironically, even where the actions of dissident minorities have managed to broaden opportunities not only for themselves, but also for the white working class, the white working class has still tended to repudiate the mechanisms which accomplished this. Thus, the colleges within the New York City system adopted "open enrollment" after sustained protest in 1969 by blacks and Puerto Ricans. Open enrollment is a kind of open door policy similar to that which California has had for years except that the support services for students are greater.

Despite the fact that a majority of the students admitted to the city system are white, the white working class is much more critical of the practice and is much more likely to view it as having "lowered standards" than are blacks or Puerto Ricans.

Thus, the pie is bigger now and many members of the white working class who previously could not get a taste can now do so, yet because the pie was baked by blacks and Puerto Ricans they say it does not taste good.

It is a very complex matter. It is obvious that the participation of the white working class in the struggles of other non-elite groups might increase the proportion of the nation's resources available to all, thereby reducing the zero sum character presently found in certain areas of conflict among non-elites. It is equally obvious that the processes whereby this participation might materialize are still very obscure.

POSSIBLE AREAS OF CONFLICT AND CONSENSUS WITHIN THE MOVEMENT

Turning to the question of coalitions of protesting minorities, there are a number of factors which inhibit such a coalition but a few important factors which make it conceivable on a limited basis.

Given the position advanced at various places in this book, that conflict between minorities and entrenched groups is, in part, a consequence of competition for scarce resources and rewards, it follows that some of these minorities might come into conflict with each other over access to highly desired but limited goods. This conflict is most likely to occur in the occupational sphere between blacks and women. A number of employers, ranging from institutions of higher education to symphony orchestras, have felt pressure to change their hiring policies and increase the number of minority group persons on the payroll. In reality, the number of jobs available is limited and commitment to hire blacks may limit the opportunities for women (except, of course, black women).

The potential conflict between the black movement and the women's movement over access to limited opportunities has a forerunner in the conflict between blacks and Mexican Americans in California over antipoverty funds and jobs. The Mexican Americans felt that blacks dominated the program and denied them their fair share. Affinity between the two groups had never been great, and conflict over influence in the poverty program exacerbated the tension between them.

Black women, potentially a bridge between the two movements, tend to identify with the black movement. Thus, on campuses where there is a black student organization and a women's organization, most black women with any organizational affiliation belong to the black students' group, but relatively few also belong to the women's group.

As was indicated in Chapter 6, most activists in the women's movement are middle-class and white. The black woman is likely to have grown up in a largely black environment and her cultural style and references derive from that environment. Since the rise of the second feminist movement has been a relatively recent occurrence, the black woman has internalized an identity as black and has only lately been asked to think of herself as a woman first and a black second.

Ironically, the campus is a setting in which one perceives conflict over scarce resources. Much of white support for the civil rights movement was drawn from the campus. Thousands of white college students in 1964 went to Mississippi for "freedom summer." A decade later there are traditional student government groups on campus, often mostly or entirely white, and there are black student organizations. They compete, sometimes bitterly, for the limited funds available for student activities. Black students view the purposes for which white students would spend limited funds (festivals of old movies, rock concerts, lectures on transcendental meditation) as frivolous, and define their own intentions (visits by black poets or black writers) as serious and political and essential to helping black students gain a better understanding of their own culture and heritage.

A second factor militating against coalition is protest-group nationalism. This was most in evidence in the cultural nationalism of the black movement, but has analogs in the women's movement, the gay movement, and the youth movement. Nationalism is an orientation which turns the perspective of members of a movement inward. It generally reflects the sectarian fragmentation of a minority movement. Nationalists use ascriptive characteristics in evaluating persons politically. Thus, for cultural nationalists, all whites were rejected, thereby, of course, making coalitions impossible. Indeed, those blacks who did not accept nationalist dicta were themselves attacked as not being part of the black movement. The women's movement has also seen what might be referred to as sexual nationalism. This tendency was touched on in the chapter on women and is exemplified in the point of view of those women who claim that only a lesbian orientation shows integrity within the movement. The youth movement, in its disavowal of the possibility of trusting anyone over 30, revealed age chauvinism. This orientation tends to isolate a group politically, not only from other movements, but also from other segments of the same movement.

A third factor undermining coalition is selective cooptation by elites of the leadership of a protest movement. Insofar as elites are elite because they possess control over resources, they can channel those resources selectively to dissidents in the effort to blunt protest. Where there is competing leadership, they can, in effect, tip the balance one way or the other. Thus, the influence and power of the accommodationist black leader Booker T. Washington among blacks at the turn of the century was based, in large part, on his access to white philanthropists and the white political elite. He was able to dispense favors to blacks in a period when the black condition in the United States had reached its nadir. By contrast, the more militant W. E. B. DuBois was never lionized by political and corporate elites.

The risk for the leader of a protest group is that he will inevitably be accused of "selling out." But if his patrons allow him to channel at least some gratuities to his needy followers, he may secure their compliance over more militant spokesmen who cannot provide any kind of tangible assistance.

The impediments to coalition are formidable, but there are areas of common interest which provide grounds for shared activity.

Many of the objectives of one group speak to the needs and problems of another. Thus, efforts of the women's movement to have day-care centers for working mothers benefit black women as well as white. Black households show a higher percentage of working wives than do white households. Therefore, the availability of day-care centers is as important to black women as to white.

The right of abortion also crosscuts the two movements. Abortions have always been available to women who had the financial means to travel to Tiajuana, Mexico, or similar places. Laws against abortion have fallen most heavily on women who were too poor to have abortions done out of the country or who lacked the influence to secure them legally in this country through loopholes in the law. Abortion reform, then, has served the interests of black women as well as white.

The National Association for the Advancement of Colored People and other civil rights organizations have always lobbied vigorously for a higher minimum wage. Insofar as a disproportionate number of women, as well as blacks, concentrate in low-income occupations, the interests of both groups are served by such legislation.

While there have been conflicts between black and white students on campus, the protest of each has been beneficial to the other. White college youth have sought successfully to expand student influence in college government and in the determination of curricula. They have made vigorous assaults on the departmental organization of knowledge and have questioned the assumption, common before the contemporary student movement, that 40 courses at three hours each, taken over four years for 120 "credits," bear any relationship to whether one has acquired enough education to be considered a civilized person, or even enough training to perform adequately on the job.

The expansion of student power as a result of the protest of white students has meant greater opportunity for black students to voice their needs in regard to curricula and support services, and the protest of black students has increased faculty and administration willingness to consider the counsel of both. This protest has set in motion a process of self-examination in higher education and a willingness on the part of many schools to experiment with new curricula and new programs.

In addition, the vocations for social change pursued by some youth entail work in support of the poor, of blacks, of women, of homosexuals, and of other disadvantaged groups. In some respects, vocations for social change create opportunities for the middle class, principally in the establishment of alternative schools. In other respects, they provide advocacy for have-nots and help to devise alternatives to the generally indifferent or abusive public bureaucracies which serve the needy.

In many tangible and programmatic ways, then, the interests of protesting minorities coincide. The points of conflict are many, but there are common interests which create a basis for cooperative action.

Moreover, some of these goals are consonant with the interests of the white working class. Under the impact of inflation, an increasing number of women in that class will seek employment outside the home, thereby needing day-care centers.

It has been suggested at several points in this analysis that there is a zero sum quality to some of the conflicts between the working class and protest groups. There is also a potential for such conflict between women and blacks. Strategically, however, all of these groups benefit more by cooperative action to increase the total resources from which each draws than by protecting their respective interests in a static or even receding level of resources. Programmatically, this cooperation would translate into a broad-based left movement. But, again for reasons already discussed, a working-class component of this movement is not yet in evidence.

The kinds of objectives which might integrate the various movements of protesting minorities fall short of the French Revolution or the Russian Revolution or the Cuban Revolution, but they do speak to the needs of a significant segment of the population.

These movements have set in motion a period of intense change in the society, and it is not yet clear what the substance of a new equilibrium will be. Even if their goals are realized, the degree of social transformation would fall far short of some of history's more dramatic examples of massive institutional change.

They do not offer the French Revolution, but for those oriented to progressive change, they are, at the present time, the only revolution the United States has.

REFERENCES

1. Arnold Birenbaum and Edward S. Sagarin, *Social Problems: Private Trouble and Social Issues* (New York: Charles Scribner's Sons, 1972), p. 3.

2. *Loc. cit.*

3. David Halberstam, "Playboy Interview," *Playboy* (August, 1973), p. 58.

4. Alan Wolfe, "The Ideology of Counter Revolution," *Nation* (July 2, 1973), p. 14.

5. Kevin Phillips, "Conservative Chic," *Harpers* (June, 1973), p. 70.

6. *Ibid.*, p. 66.

7. *Ibid.*, p. 68.

8. *Loc. cit.*

9. S. M. Miller, "Sharing the Burden of Change," *The White Majority* (Louise Kapp Howe, ed., New York: Random House, 1970), pp. 279–295.

10. Kim Moody, "Can The American Worker Be Radicalized," in Howe, *ibid.*, p. 250.

11. Edward Banfield, in *The Unheavenly City* (Boston: Little, Brown, 1970), offers this argument.

12. Richard Herrnstein, "I.Q.," *Atlantic*, 228 (September, 1971), pp. 43–58.

13. Lewis Feuer's *The Conflict of Generations* (New York: Basic Books, 1969), falls into this category.

14. James O. Toole, *et al*, in *Work in America* (Cambridge, Mass.: M.I.T. Press, 1972), discuss worker satisfaction and alienation.

15. Richard F. Hamilton, "Black Demands, White Reactions, and Liberal Alarms," in *Blue Collar World* (Sar A. Levitan, ed., New York: McGraw Hill, 1971), pp. 129–153.

16. Moody, *op. cit.*, p. 251.

17. *Ibid.*, p. 251.

18. *Loc. cit.*

A

Aberle, Sophie, 114
abortion reform, 266
achievement, and status, 245–48
Acker, Joan, 147, 149, 154
Adams, R. L., 94, 208
"advocacy" movement, 210
AFL-CIO, 96, 263
Ali, Muhammed, 78
Alianza Federal de Mercedes,
    100–101
Alinsky, Saul, 96
Altbach, Philip G., 184
alternative institutions, 212–14
Alternative Society, 200
American Indians:
    in the American psyche, 108–9
    living conditions of, 109–10
    mobility of, 90
    power movement, 115–17
    U.S. policy toward, 110–17
American Way of Life, 255
Aquarian Research Foundation,
    213–14
Aries, Philippe, 163, 165
ascription of status, 245–48
Atlanta pogrom, 21

B

"bad motherfucker," 44
Badillo, Herman, 103, 107–8
Bachelors-for-Wallace, 125
Baker, Ray Stannard, 21
Baker, Ross, 47, 53
Banfield, Edward, 259
Barbaro, Fred, 74
Baron, Harold, 15, 69
beat movement, 183–85
Beauvoir, Simone de, 149
Benson, Ezra Taft, 242
Berger, Bennett, 182

Bhartivedanta, A. C., 205
Bieber, Irving, 131
Bienstock, Herbert, 103
Birch Society, *see* John Birch Society
Birnbaum, Arnold, 255
Black Liberation Army, 53
Black Muslims:
    ideology of, 61–64
    recruits to, 54–61
Black Panthers, 36–37, 41–53
    ideology of, 49–51
    persecution of, 49–53
    reorientation of, 52–53
    "style" of, 48
black power, 13, 15, 41, 70–86
blacks:
    civil rights movement, 12–13,
      14–15, 23–28, 30
    community welfare movement,
      28–32
    history of, 11–38
    organizations of, 12
    and other minorities, 223,
      264–65, 267
    in politics, 13, 15, 36–38, 41,
      46–48, 67–86
    power movement, 13, 15, 41,
      70–86
    prejudice against, 12, 16–22, 29,
      34, 42–43, 79–80, 90–91, 233,
      259–60, 262
    protest movements, 36–37, 41–64
    segregation of, 14–15, 17, 19,
      24–25, 30, 92
    separatist movements, 33–35
    street, 42–46
    urbanization of, 22, 70–71
    violence against, 18–22
    white support for, 46–48, 78
Blatchford, Herbert, 116
Boggs, James, 248

bohemians, 133–35, 181–85
Bond, Julian, 44, 78
Boy Scouts, 164
Bradley, Thomas, 85–86
"breaking out," 188–89
Bremner, Robert, 164
Brophy, William, 114
Brown, Antoinette, 142
Brown, Warren, 104
brown power movement, 100–101
Browne, Robert S., 34, 35

C

Cantril, Hadley, 231
Carmichael, Stokely, 41, 45, 145
caste, 12, 16–22, 90
    color and, 16–17
    rituals of, 19–20
Catholic worker movement, 200
Causa, La, 95–97
Chalmers, David, 239
change, see social change
Chavez, Cesar, 96, 97–98, 100
Cherokees, 111–12
Chicago race riot, 21–22
Chisholm, Shirley, 78
Christian Crusade, 238
city government, blacks in, 70–86
Civil Rights Act of 1964, 25–26
civil rights movement, 12–13 ,14–15,
    23–28, 30
Clark, Del, 132
Clark, Kenneth, 32
Clark, Mark, 51
class, see social structure
Cleaver, Eldridge, 44, 46, 50, 51, 52
coalitions of minorities, 261–68
collective perspective, 241–44
college students, 217–18, 267
color:
    and caste, 16–17
    and prejudice, 105
"coming out of the closet," 129–30
communes:
    forerunners of, 199–200, 204–5
    organizational problems of, 200–5

Community Alert Patrol, 42
community control of schools, 30
Community Service Organization, 96
community welfare, black, 28–32
conflict, minority:
    intergroup, 3
    intragroup, 264–68
    with the majority, 3–4, 256–57
Congress of Racial Equality, 25–26
Connor, Evord, 45
consciousness, false, 221–22, 263
consciousness raising, 154–55
contagious stigma, 124
Convention of Free Colored People,
    33
cooptation, 266
counter culture, 171–78
counter ideology, 20, 49–51, 61–64,
    123, 125–26, 131–32, 258–61
Cowley, Malcolm, 182
"crazy nigger," 44
cultural conflict, 4
Curvin, Robert, 76, 82

D

Daughters of Bilitis, 132–33
Davidson, Sara, 200
Davis, Fred, 214
Davis, Ossie, 78
Dawes Act, 113
day-care centers, 266
Delaney, Martin Robinson, 33–34
Delano grape strike, 97–100
delinquency, juvenile, 169–70
Deloria, Vine, 109, 110, 113, 116
desegregation, 14–15, 30
deviance:
    social function of, 217
    subcultures of, 133–35
    vertical and lateral, 167–68
Diggers, 187
discrimination, see prejudice
"dropping out," 187
drug subculture, 188–91
Dubois, W. E. B., 37, 266
Dunne, John Gregory, 99

E

education:
  of blacks, 29–31
  of white working class, 230
  of women, 139–40, 141–42
  of youth, 163–65
Elijah Muhammad, 54, 61
elite class, 229–30, 249–50
employment programs, national, 224
Equal Rights Amendment, 153
Esalen Institute, 189
ethnic minorities, 11–117
ethnic stratification, 89–91
Evans, Medford, 243
expressive-affective orientation, 172
expressive groups, 154

F

Fairfield, Dick, 202
false consciousness, 221–22, 263
family allowances, 223
Farb, Peter, 110, 111
Farmer, James, 25
Feminists, The, 149, 150
Flacks, Richard, 173, 175
Flexner, Eleanor, 141, 144
Foner, Philip, 42, 45
Food Conspiracy, 213
Fox, Robert John, 208
Franklin, Raymond S., 81
freaks, drug, 188–91
freaks, marginal, 193–94
free schools, 211
Free Speech Movement, 165
free stores, 187
Friedan, Betty, 149, 153, 154
Friedenberg, Edgar Z., 166, 223, 244
frustration-aggression-displacement
    theory of prejudice, 240

G

Galarza, Ernesto, 96
game theory, 12
Gamio, Manual, 92
Gans, Herbert, 232
Garvey, Marcus, 34
Gary, Indiana, 71–85

gay movement (*see also*
    homosexuals)
  early movements, 122–26
  gay liberation, 126–35
  ideology of, 123, 125–26, 131–32
  media involvement in, 121–22
  public perception of, 260
  radical perspective of, 133–35
  "straights" and, 124–26
  tactics of, 130–31
Gibson, Kenneth, 73, 76
Gittings, Barbara, 131
Glazer, Nathan, 105
Goffman, Erving, 127
Gonzalez, "Corky," 100
Goodman, Paul, 186, 210
Gottlieb, Lou, 201
Greenwich Village, 134, 183
Greer, Edward, 72
Greer, Germaine, 154
Gregory, Dick, 78
groups, expressive and instrumental,
    154

H

Haight-Ashbury, 185–96
Halberstam, David, 255
Hampton, Fred, 51
Hargis, Billy James, 238
Harrington, Michael, 226
Harrison, Linda, 50
Harvey, Paul, 241, 243
Hatcher, Richard, 73
Havighurst, R. H., 175
Hayden, Tom, 177
"heads" (drug users), 188–91
health insurance, 223–24
Heilbroner, Robert, 225
Henry, George W., Foundation, 122
Henry, Milton, 35
Henry, Richard, 34
Herrnstein, Richard, 259
Himes, Joseph, 90
hippie movement:
  forerunners of, 181–85
  sex roles in, 145–46
  social types in, 185–96

Hofstadter, Richard, 237, 239, 246
homosexuals (*see also* gay
    movement)
  prejudice against, 121, 123–26,
    128
  and psychologists, 131–32
  sanctions against, 135
  self-identity of, 128–30
  social life of, 127–28
  stereotypes about, 122–23
Homosexuals Intransigent, 126–27
Horton, John, 43
Howard, Mary D., 147, 149, 154
Huelga, La, 97–100
Hutterites, 200

I
ideological conflict, 4
ideology, minority, 20, 49–51,
    61–64, 123, 125–26, 131–32,
    258–61
Indian power movement, 115–17
Indian Reorganization Act, 113–15
Indians, *see* American Indians
infant mortality, 225
inflation, 227–28
instrumental group, 154
integration, 14–15, 30
intellectual class, 174–78, 258
interest-group theory of prejudice,
    240

J
Jackson, Andrew, 111–12
Jefferson, Thomas, 33
Jensen, Arthur, 259
Jesus movement, 207–9
Jews for Jesus, 209
Jiminez, Cha Cha, 106
John Birch Society, 238–39, 243, 247
Jones, Le Roi, 76
Jordan, Winthrop, 108

K
Kanter, Rosabeth Moss, 204
Kelley, Florence, 139

Keniston, Kenneth, 173
Kerr, Edward, 85
Kinsey report, 124–25
Kochman, Thomas, 43
Kopkind, Andrew, 27, 85
Krishna Consciousness, 205–7
Ku Klux Klan, 239
Kwan, Kian M., 90, 241

L
Labor Statistics, Bureau of, 227
Lane, Robert, 221, 244
Latin America, racism in, 89–90
law collectives, 214
Leary, Timothy, 189
left, *see* radical left
Lenski, Gerhard, 163, 165
lesbian movement, 132–33
Liberia, 33
Lincoln, Abraham, 33
Lipton, Lawrence, 183, 184
Los Angeles, 85–86
LSD, 189–90
lynching, 18–19
Lyon, Phylis, 132

M
majority, conflict with, 3–4, 256–57
Malcolm X, 46
Mangum, Garth, 163
manpower programs, 224
marginal class, 226–30
marijuana, 188
marriage, 148–51
Marxist social analysis, 221–22,
    261–64
Mattachine Society, 123–26, 130–31,
    132
Matthews, Connie, 49
Mayer, Martin, 29
McKay, Claude, 36
McWilliams, Carey, 92
media movements, 121–22, 192
Menominees, 115
Meredith, James, 41
Merton, Robert, 181

methedrine, 190
Mexican Americans:
  demographic characteristics, 90
  history of, 93–95
  mobility of, 90
  and other minorities, 77, 265
  prejudice against, 92–93
  protest movements among,
    95–101
Michigan, University of, Survey
    Research Center, Economic
    Behavior Program, 228
middle class, and youth movement,
    169–70, 188–89
midnight hippies, 192–93
millennialism, 63–64
Miller, S. M., 258
Millett, Kate, 154, 156
Mills, C. Wright, 172
minimum wage, 267
minority groups:
  definition of, 249–50
  reasons for prejudice against,
    240–41
minority movements:
  coalitions of, 261–68
  conflict between, 264–68
  conflict with majority, 3–4,
    256–57
  conflict within, 3
  cooptation of, 266
  cultural nationalism in, 265–66
  future of, 255–68
  ideology of, 20, 49–51, 61–64,
    123, 125–26, 131–32, 258–61
  organizations in, 1–3, 53–55
  research methods in studying, 5–6
  and social change, 268
Miss America contest, 140
mobility, social, 90–91, 244–50
Moody, Kim, 258, 263
Morgan, Robin, 144
Morning Star Ranch, 201–2
Mott, Lucretia, 144
Mt. Holyoke, 142
Moynihan, Daniel Patrick, 105, 224

N

National Association for the
    Advancement of Colored
    People, 23–25
National Farm Workers' Association,
    96
National Indian Youth Council,
    116
National Organization for Women,
    133, 148, 149, 153–54
nationalism, cultural, 265-66
Neugarten, B., 175
Neuman, Franz, 247
new left, 172
New Majority, 257–61
New Negro, 22
New York Ciy teachers' strike,
    29–31
Newark, New Jersey, 71–85
Newton, Huey, 46, 51, 52
Niebuhr, H. Richard, 63–64
Nineteenth Amendment, 139
Nixon administration, 257
North Beach, San Francisco, 183
Norton, Sarah, 139

O

Oberlin College, 142
One magazine, 126
O'Neill, William, 142
open enrollment, 264
open marriage, 150–51
organizations, minority:
  instrumental *vs.* expressive, 154
  social base of, 1–2
  structure of, 2–3, 153–55
Owen, Charles, 36

P

Padilla, Elena, 102
Paiutes, 114–15
Parenti, Michael, 232
Parry, Albert, 182
Parsons, Theodore, 93
"passing," 90
patronage, political, 67–70

Peace and Freedom Party, 47
Peterson, Patti, 184
Phillips, Kevin, 247, 257, 258
"pie," size of the (social), 263–64
Pinkney, Alphonse, 93
Piven, Frances, 30
plastic hippies, 191–92
Plessy vs. *Ferguson,* 24
pogroms, anti-black, 20–21
politics (*see also* radical left)
    blacks in, 13, 15, 36–38, 41,
        46–48, 67–86
    Puerto Ricans in, 77, 107–8
Polsky, Ned, 184
poor class, 226–30
Porambo, Ron, 76
Port Huron statement, 176
prejudice, theories of, 240–41
presidential slogans, 257
professional class, 229
Project Talent, 230
protest movements:
    black, 36–37, 41–64
    homosexual, 126
    Mexican-American, 95–101
public housing, 81
Puerto Ricans:
    history of, 101–2
    mobility of, 90
    in politics, 77, 107–8
    power movement among, 105–6
    urbanization of, 103–4

Q
Quaker Emergency Committee, 122
quotas, racial, 14

R
racial minorities, 11–117
racism, 17, 34, 79–80, 233, 262
    ideological justification, 259–60
radical left:
    blacks in, 36–37
    gays in, 133–35
    whites in, 46–48
    women in, 144–47
    youth in, 172–73

radical right:
    as minority group, 240–44
    organizations of, 237–40
    U.S. social structure and, 244–50
Randolph, A. Philip, 36, 37
"rapping," 42–46
Reba Fellowship, 200
religions, new, 205–9
repression-projection theory of
        prejudice, 240
Republic of New Africa, 35
reservations, Indian, 113–15, 116–17
Resnik, Solomon, 81
revolution, possibilities for, in
        United States, 256–57, 268
Rexroth, Kenneth, 184
Richardson, George, 76
riots, 21–22, 27–28
Robinson, Ruby, 145
Rogers, David, 30
Rosen, Moishe, 209
Rossi, Alice, 142
Roszak, Theodore, 171, 217
"rules of the game," 13–14
Rustin, Bayard, 13, 26

S
Sagarin, Edward, 121, 255
scapegoats, 232
schools, *see* education
Schorr, Alvin, 223
Schrag, Peter, 222
Seale, Bobby, 46, 51
segregation, 14–15, 17, 19, 24–25,
        30, 92
Seidman, Bert, 225
"selling out," 266
Seneca Falls meeting, 140, 144
"separate but equal," 24–25
separatism, black, 33–35
sex roles, 145–46, 152–53
sexism, 260
Sexton, Patricia, 103–4
sexual liberation movements:
    of homosexuals, 121–35
    of women, 139–58
Shanker, Albert, 29

Sherrill, Robert, 109
Shibutani, Tamotsu, 90, 241
Shuey, Aubrey, 259
Sierra Leone, 33
"silent generation," 217–18
Sipuel, Ada Louise, 24
Skinner, B. F., 203
Snakepit raid, 131
social change:
    coalition of minorities for, 268
    white working class and, 261–64
    youth and, 210–14
social-class movements:
    of white working class, 221–34
    of radical right, 237–50
social Darwinism, 260
social structure, American, 169–70,
    226–30, 244–50, 261–64
social welfare, U.S. policy toward,
    221–22, 223–26
Society for Human Rights, 122
soul politics, 37–38, 67–86
Standard Family Budget, 227
Stanton, Elizabeth Cady, 139, 144
status, achieved *vs.* ascribed, 245–48
Steinem, Gloria, 154, 155
Steiner, Stan, 116
stigma, contagious, 124
Stone, Lucy, 142
Stonewall riot, 127–28
"straights," 124–26
stratification, ethnic, 89–91
street blacks, 42–46
Student Non-Violent Coordinating
    Committee, 45, 145
students, college:
    black, 267
    protest by, 217–18
Students for a Democratic Society,
    176, 177
substantive conflict, 3–4
suburbs, cities and, 79–83
suffrage, women's, 139
Suttler, Gerald, 232
Sweatt, Hemon Marion, 24
symbolic conflict, 4

T

Tabb, William, 82
taxes, 80–83
Taylor, Clark, 82
Taylor, Paul, 92
teachers' strikes, 29–31
termination, Indian, 113–15
Thom, Mel, 116
Thomas, Carey, 139
Tiger, Lionel, 260
Tijerina, Reies, 100
Tolstoy Farm, 205
Tree, Lloyd A., 231
Troy Female Seminary, 141–42
Turner, Henry M., 34
Turner, Irving, 76
Twin Oaks commune, 203–4

U

Uhr, Carl, 224
underground press, 214
unions, labor, 32, 233, 262, 263
United Farm Workers' Organizing
    Committee, 100
United States:
    class structure in, 169–70, 226–30,
        244–50, 261–64
    future of minority movements in,
        255–68
    revolution in, 256–57, 268
    social welfare policy in, 221–22,
        223–26

V

Vadikan, James, 223
Vander Zanden, James W., 239
variable sum game, 12
Veterans' Benevolent Association,
    122–23
Viera, Rafael, 106
visionaries, hippy, 185–88
Vocations for Social Change,
    210–14, 267
Voting Rights Act of 1965, 27

W

War on Poverty, 115
Warner, William Lloyd, 16

Washington, Booker T., 23, 266
Waskow, Arthur, 21
WASPs, 246
Watts riot, 27
wealthy class, 229–30, 249–50
welfare, *see* social welfare
white leftists, 46–48, 78
white working class:
    life-style of, 222, 226–30
    political consciousness of, 221–22,
      230–34, 263
    and social change, 261–64
Whole Earth Catalog, 199–200
Willard, Emma, 141
Willard Association, 142
Wilson, James Q., 69
Wilson, Woodrow, 68
Wolfe, Alan, 256
women:
    blacks and, 264–65
    demographic characteristics,
      156–57
    education of, 139–40, 141–42
    suffrage for, 139
    working, 140–41, 143–44, 151–52
women's liberation movement:
    future of, 155–58
    history of, 139–47
    in the 19th century, 140–43
    organizational conflict in, 147–53
    radicalism in, 144–47
    today, 143–47
Woodhull, Victoria, 139
work:
    and status, 244–45

women and, 140–41, 143–44,
    151–52
youth and, 164–65
working class, *see* white working
    class
Wright, Richard, 37

X
X, Malcolm, 46

Y
Young Lords, 106–7
youth:
    deviancy in, 167–70
    as minority group, 174
    as social category, 163–65
    status of, 165–66
youth movement:
    communes, 199–205
    the counter culture, 171–78
    future of, 199–218
    the hippie movement, 181–96
    middle class and, 169–70, 188–89
    new religions, 205–9
    popular attitudes toward, 260
    and radical politics, 172–73
    social base of, 169–70, 173–74,
     215–17
    and social change, 210–14

Z
zero sum game, 12
zoning practices, 81